VALENT
D0193053

Published by Pedigree in association with YOURS

Pedigree Books Limited, The Old Rectory, Matford Lane, Exeter, Devon EX2 4PS
books@pedigreegroup.co.uk

YOURS is a monthly magazine for the young at heart. Look out for it in your local newsagent.
YOURS, Bushfield House, Orton Centre, Peterborough PE2 5UW. Tel: 01733 237111

Compiled by Helen Henry, designed by Sharon Reid and David Reid.
Heartfelt thanks to all the readers who contributed to this annual by sending in their letters, tips, stories, recipes and photos. Short stories published in A Year With YOURS book are works of fiction. Any resemblance to actual events or people, living or dead, is entirely coincidental. No responsibility can be accepted for any action arising from information in this annual.

With thanks to all who helped to compile this annual:
Writers: Caroline Chadderton, Bridget Davidson, Hilary Pereira (Brits for all seasons), Maya Isaaks (Beautiful Britain). Sub editors: Mary Ann Fulcher, Christine Curtis. Picture research: Della Smith. Administration: Chris Terrey.

Hello!

Twelve months ago more than 50,000 readers of YOURS magazine opened the pages of a new publication we launched as A Year With YOURS.

This was our first annual, a book that we knew would really last a year.

We were pretty confident that the unique recipe we had prepared for you would delight you and, to our relief, that's how it turned out. Readers who bought their own copy and liked what they saw followed up with orders for friends and family and suddenly we had another success on our hands.

You told us that the nuggets of nostalgia, the charming pictures, the handy tips, the stories and readers' contributions and, of course, the calendar pages combined to leave you wanting more.

We are pleased to oblige, with this second Year With YOURS which will be your companion throughout 2003.

Everyone at YOURS wishes you and yours a wonderful new year, and much pleasure from this book.

Kind regards

Neil

Neil Patrick
Editor-in-chief

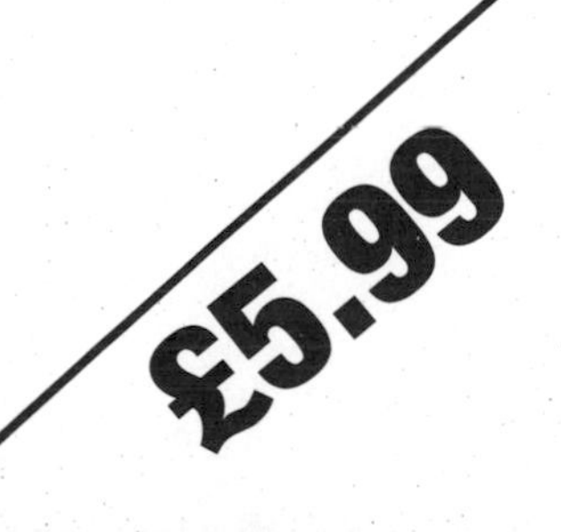

January 2003

High days and holidays...

First-footing (January 1)

Happy New Year to one and all! The clock has struck 12 and, to bring good luck, a tall, dark man bringing symbols of warmth, wealth and food should be welcomed into the house. Ideally the first-footer should be an outsider who carries coal, salt and cake, although this varies regionally.

Twelfth Night (January 5)

The Twelfth Night (January 5) and the Twelfth Day (January 6) after Christmas – called in Scotland Uphalieday, the 'ending of the Holy days' – mark the end of the Christmas season. The celebrations, including the eating of a Twelfth Night cake, were a last fling before the return to work on Plough Monday.

Burns Night (January 25)

PIC: HULTON ARCHIVE

The celebration of the birth of Robert Burns (1759-96) begins with a supper of 'hamely farin', including such delicacies as 'powsowdie' (sheep's head broth) and 'Tinnan toasties' (smoked haddock).

But pride of place goes to the haggis – minced mutton, offal, oatmeal and spices boiled in a sheep's stomach. The haggis is piped in, solemnly addressed and a great many toasts made to it – the 'great chieftain o' the pudden race'.

Wednesday	1	New Year's Day Bank Holiday
Thursday	2	Bank Holiday (Scotland)
Friday	3	
Saturday	4	
Sunday	5	
Monday	6	Epiphany
Tuesday	7	
Wednesday	8	
Thursday	9	
Friday	10	
Saturday	11	
Sunday	12	
Monday	13	
Tuesday	14	
Wednesday	15	
Thursday	16	
Friday	17	
Saturday	18	

SUNDAY	19
MONDAY	20
TUESDAY	21
WEDNESDAY	22
THURSDAY	23
FRIDAY	24
SATURDAY	25
SUNDAY	26
MONDAY	27
TUESDAY	28
WEDNESDAY	29
THURSDAY	30 February YOURS on sale
FRIDAY	31

This month don't forget to...

- Make your New Year resolutions – and try to stick to them!
- Look out for shops in your area that are collecting old Christmas cards for recycling.
- Have an outdoor spring clean! Wash flower pots, seed trays, canes and supports. Clean moss from paths and steps.
- Enjoy Burns Night on January 25. Read a poem from the great Scottish bard, or indulge in a wee dram and a slice or two of haggis.
- Look ahead and plan your summer holiday.
- Look out for Seville oranges to make your marmalade.

Rita Hayworth

PIC: MIRROR

It happened in January...

January 3, 1900: The new royal yacht, Victoria and Albert, capsized as it embarked.

January 8, 1901: Two Manchester retailers were prosecuted for selling beer containing arsenic.

January 27, 1926: John Logie Baird gave the first public demonstration of television to members of the Royal Institution in his workshop in Soho.

January 26, 1953: Rita Hayworth and Prince Aly Khan were divorced after only four years of marriage.

January 2, 1987: Golliwogs were banned from Enid Blyton's books by the publisher.

January 1-5

TEA-TIME TREATS

Jack Frost Bars

Makes 12

- 4 oz/100 g dark chocolate chips
- 6 oz/175 g butter
- 9 oz/250 g dark brown soft cane sugar
- 3 large eggs
- 1 teaspoon vanilla essence
- 6 oz/175 g self-raising flour, sieved
- 4 oz/100 g dried apricots, chopped

Frosting:

- 6 tablespoons icing sugar, sieved
- 2 tablespoons lemon juice
- 6 sugar cubes, crushed

1. Preheat oven to 180°C/350°F/ Gas Mark 4. Grease a 11 x 7½ in/ 28 x 19 cm rectangular tin and line with parchment.
2. Put chocolate chips and butter in a bowl, place over a pan of simmering water and leave until melted. Stir in brown sugar until dissolved.
3. Remove bowl from pan and gradually beat in eggs and vanilla essence. Stir in flour and apricots.
4. Pour into tin and bake for 35 minutes. Remove from oven and leave to cool in tin.
5. For the frosting, stir icing sugar and lemon juice together until smooth. Drizzle over the cake and sprinkle with crushed sugar cubes. Leave to set, remove from tin and cut into 12 pieces.

PIC: TATE & LYLE SUGARS

TIP TIME

To bake deliciously moist cakes, place a small oven-proof dish of water next to it on the baking tray.

Trudy Blacker, Upper Poppleton, York

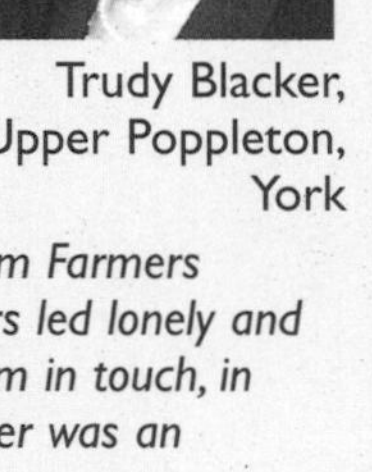

Letter of my life

The letter came nearly 40 years ago when I was living on an isolated farm in Yorkshire with my husband and three children. It was from Farmers Weekly. It understood that many of its readers led lonely and restricted lives and was putting groups of them in touch, in the hope that they would correspond. My letter was an invitation to join a group and I was delighted to accept.

Each group consisted of ten or 12 members, of all ages and circumstances, scattered the length and breadth of Britain. Each member wrote a letter every month, which was sent to an editor who bound them together and posted them on to one writer. She then sent them on to the next on a rota, so that everyone wrote one letter and read ten or more each month. My group was 'Country Scribes'.

As the years passed we became firm friends. We followed the children's progress through education, careers and marriage and later rejoiced in the arrival of grandchildren and great-grandchildren. Inevitably the years took their toll and we gave what comfort we could when our writer friends died or became widows. This year will see the 40th anniversary of the arrival of the letter that brought so much pleasure and interest to my life.

"You must be joking

Q What do vampires sing on New Year's Eve?

A Auld Fang Syne.

HEALTHY LIVING

Exercise – why bother?

● **It helps you to relax.** After exercise, your body produces chemicals called endorphins, which give a sensation of wellbeing.

● **It builds self esteem.** If you exercise, you will feel more confident in your body's abilities, and losing weight and toning muscles will lead to an improved body image.

● **It reduces the chances of developing some conditions.** Exercise has been linked to reduced incidence of high cholesterol levels, heart disease, blood pressure, diabetes, cancer and osteoporosis.

Haworth, West Yorkshire

This hill village, with its cobbled streets and picturesque setting, is known as the home of the famous Brönte sisters, Charlotte, who wrote Jane Eyre, Emily, who wrote Wuthering Heights and Anne, who wrote Agnes Grey. The Parsonage, where the family lived, is now a museum.

However, many visitors may not be so aware of the pioneering Lily Cove, Britain's first female parachutist, who was killed here in 1906 when she became detatched from her parachute. She is buried in the local cemetery and her ghost is said to haunt the area of the town where her body was laid out.

Haworth also has its own steam railway station, and Oakworth Station, along this five-mile stretch of line, featured in the film The Railway Children.

Pause for thought

A Celebration Of Life

We are not old
It is now time for fun.
We've worked our years
And life has now begun.
We've seen changes
Not always for the best,
And our families
Have long since flown the nest.

Our words of wisdom
We've gladly handed down
To a generation
And one yet to be born.
This time is given to satisfy the soul
Not giving half
But gladly giving whole.

We give thanks – for good times
long-since past
And for future happy days
We surely hope will last.
Our prayer is offered
In a world that's sometimes
torn in strife.
It is with thanks
We celebrate our life.

Mrs D S Moss,
Chelmsford,
Essex

I wish I'd said that...

If you resolve to give up smoking, drinking and loving, you don't actually live longer; it just seems longer. – Clement Freud, British writer, broadcaster and politician

Treasured Photo

A chance meeting of old friends is recalled by Bill Burgess of Colchester:
'In 1947 I was posted to 107 MU RAF Kasfareet, Egypt, where I worked as an armourer. The photo of me was taken by a mate on our way to the Great Bitter Lake for a swim. When I first arrived in Egypt we were moored up waiting to go ashore. Another ship docked alongside and I was amazed to see an old boyhood friend standing on the rails. We hadn't seen each other since 1939 when he was evacuated to Canada. We were able to shout across to each other for a few minutes before we went our separate ways – me to Kasfareet, Bob to what was then Palestine. Small world!'

Well, fancy that!
The average amount of time that people spend on travel is 1 hour, 6 minutes, per day, in all societies.
SUEZ
44

January 6-12

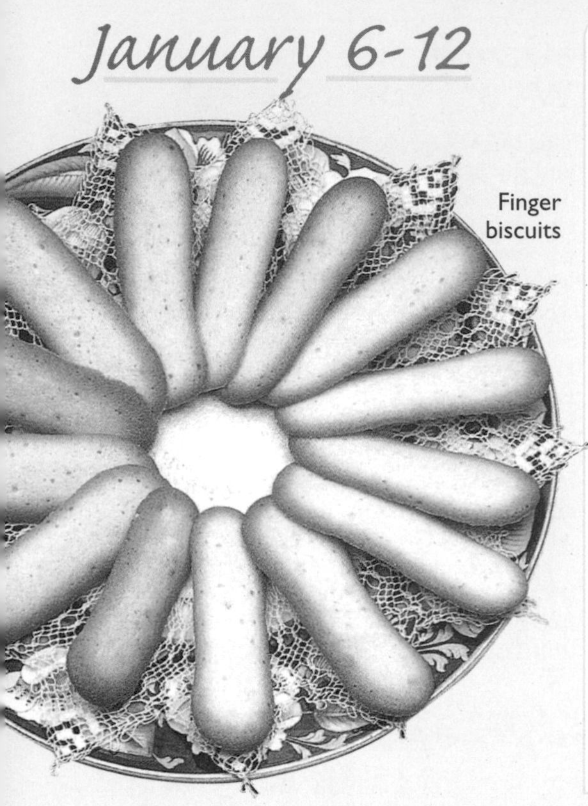

Finger biscuits

TEA-TIME TREATS

Finger biscuits

Makes 25

- 2 oz/50 g icing sugar, sifted
- 2 fl oz/55 ml whipping cream
- 2 oz/50 g plain flour, sifted
- Few drops vanilla essence
- 1 egg white, stiffly whisked

1. Preheat oven to 200°C/400°F/Gas Mark 6. Grease and flour baking sheets. Mix icing sugar and cream together, then stir in flour to make a paste. Fold in vanilla essence and egg white.
2. Place in a piping bag fitted with a ¼ in/5 mm plain nozzle and pipe 3 in/7.5 cm lengths on to baking sheets.
3. Bake in oven for about 12 minutes. Cool on a wire rack.

Well, fancy that!

The phrase 'sleep tight' derives from the middle ages, when mattresses were filled with straw and held up with ropes stretched across a bed frame. Therefore, a tight sleep was a comfortable sleep.

HEALTHY LIVING

Calcium

Most people know diet, particularly calcium, plays an important part in preventing osteoporosis.

Unfortunately, not many foods contain calcium, and substances such as alcohol, salt, caffeine and nicotine can reduce its effectiveness. To boost calcium levels:

- ❑ Eat tinned (or fresh!) salmon on your sandwiches – salmon is an excellent source of calcium.
- ❑ Eat fish on one or two nights a week.
- ❑ Eat low-fat yoghurt as a mid-morning or afternoon snack.
- ❑ A couple of times a day, replace drinks of tea and coffee with a glass of skimmed milk.

Letter of my life

I treasure this little message of love from my wife… 'Darling, I shall be with you all the way. Put out your hand and I will only be a touch away. I love you always. Olive'.

This was the message my wife passed to me when I was about to go for a life-saving operation – a triple bypass and pacemaker – in January 1992.

I went with another patient, Reg, to Southampton General Hospital. He was very frightened so I showed him this note and he later told me that it was a great help to him. We have remained friends ever since.

Ken Manuel, Midsomer Norton, Bath

I WISH I'D SAID THAT...

"One swallow does not make a summer, but it can certainly break a New Year's resolution. – Anon"

Treasured Photo

This beautiful photo was sent in by Mr N H Swanborough of Bristol:

'The baby in front on the right is my Uncle Ashley. He is on my grandmother's lap.

Seated on the left is my great-grandmother, with my great-great-grandmother standing on the right. The lady wearing the impressive headdress is my great-great-great-grandmother. All five generations are captured in one photograph.'

Woman in butcher's shop: "I want four pork chops, please, and make them lean."

"Certainly madam, which way?"

Pause for thought

Mrs V Vine from Kemsing, Kent, sent in a miscellany of items to ponder:

- Laughter is the sun that drives winter from the human face.
- You don't have to know how to sing; it's feeling as though you want to that makes the day successful.
- You may be only one person in the world, but you may also be the world to one person.
- Have a lovely day, and know that someone has thought about you today.

TIP TIME

Press your nails into soap before tackling dirty jobs. The dirt will rinse off easily when you wash your hands.

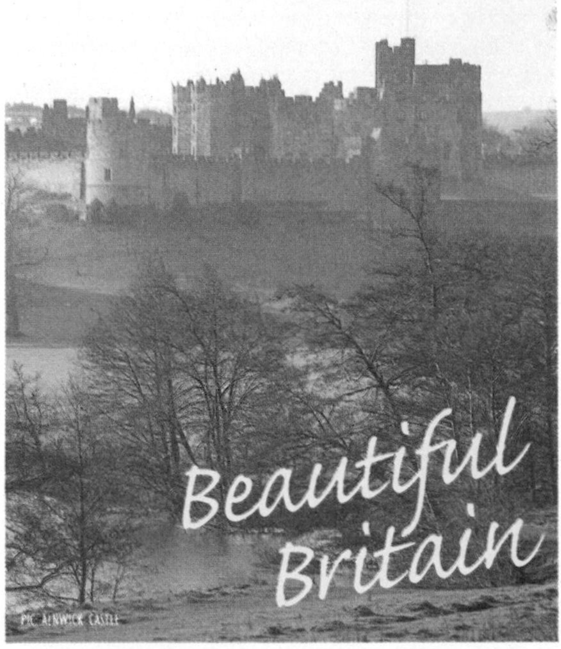

Alnwick Castle, Northumberland

Located to the north of a market town with narrow, cobbled streets and an old-fashioned market square, this magnificent castle is the ancestral home of the Duke of Northumberland and is set in beautiful gardens designed by Capability Brown.

The castle also leads a double life – as a film and TV star. Possibly its most famous recent role is that of Hogwarts School of Witchcraft and Wizardry in the film version of Harry Potter and the Philosopher's Stone. Among its many other credits are the films Elizabeth and Robin Hood, Prince of Thieves and the TV programmes, Blackadder starring Rowan Atkinson, Treasure Hunt with Anneka Rice and Highway with Harry Secombe.

The castle dates back to the 11th century and houses collections of paintings, including works by Titian and Van Dyck, china and furniture, along with some curiosities such as a hairnet used by Mary, Queen of Scots – made from her own hair!

January 13-19

I WISH I'D SAID THAT...

"The English winter – ending in July, to recommence in August.
– Lord Byron, English poet"

PERFECT PUDDINGS

Coconut Bakewell Tart

Serves 6-8

- 9 oz/250 g shortcrust pastry
- 8 oz/225 g frozen raspberries
- 3 oz/75 g butter
- 1 oz/25 g creamed coconut, grated
- 1½ oz/40 g desiccated coconut
- 4 oz/100 g caster sugar
- ¼-½ teaspoon almond essence
- 2 medium eggs, beaten
- 4 oz/100 g self-raising flour, sifted
- 1 oz/25 g flaked almonds
- Icing sugar for dredging

1 Preheat oven to 220°C/425°F/Gas Mark 7. Line and grease an 18 in/20 cm deep-sided sandwich tin.
2 Roll out pastry and line base and sides of tin.
3 Sprinkle over raspberries. Cream butter, creamed and desiccated coconut, and caster sugar until pale and fluffy. Stir in almond essence. Beat in eggs slowly. (If mixture begins to curdle, add a little of the measured-out flour.) When all the eggs have been added, fold in flour.
5 Top raspberries with sponge mixture. Sprinkle over flaked almonds.
6 Reduce heat to 200°C/400°F/Gas Mark 6 and bake for 40 minutes until well risen. Dust over icing sugar.

PIC: TATE & LYLE SUGARS

Letter of my life

Mrs V Wragg, Matlock, Derbyshire

The letter that changed my life was not for me, nor about me, but I will never forget it, or the day – 18th January, 1993.

My husband was suffering from indigestion so his doctor sent him for an endoscopy to see whether he had an ulcer. I went with him to the hospital and left him for a couple of hours, then returned to collect him. 'Yes', said the nurse, 'he's got a large ulcer and here is a letter to give to his doctor'.

When we got home I decided to go to the GP's surgery there and then because my husband asked if I would ask the doctor to prescribe some sleeping tablets. I handed the letter to the receptionist and asked if I could see our doctor. Unfortunately he wasn't in and I was asked to wait until the end of surgery when I could see another doctor. After about an hour I saw the remaining doctor open the letter. He read it and beckoned me to follow him to his office. As we walked I explained that I only wanted a prescription, but as we entered his office, without any preliminaries and very matter of factly he said, 'He's got cancer'.

I was still standing and never, during the next few minutes, was I asked to sit. The feelings I vividly remember are my legs turning to jelly and my heart beginning to thump, while the only movement I made was to clamp my hand across my mouth (is this an involuntary movement to prevent screaming I wonder?).

Walking out, going to the chemist and walking back home was the worst journey of my life. I had to go along with the pretence of an ulcer and smile when my husband said, 'I'm pleased it was nothing more serious'. I carried the secret alone for two weeks until he went back to see the consultant, who told him the truth. He died on 21st March, 1993, aged 67 years.

Well, fancy that!
The width of your arm span is roughly the same length as your height.

HEALTHY LIVING

Fat busting!

- ❑ Spread low-fat mayonnaise on your sandwich instead of butter.
- ❑ Avoid croissants or muffins at breakfast. Go for wholemeal toast instead.
- ❑ Choose low-fat dairy food.
- ❑ Select lean cuts of meat and grill rather than fry. Remove skin from chicken.
- ❑ Replace meat with fish a couple of times a week.

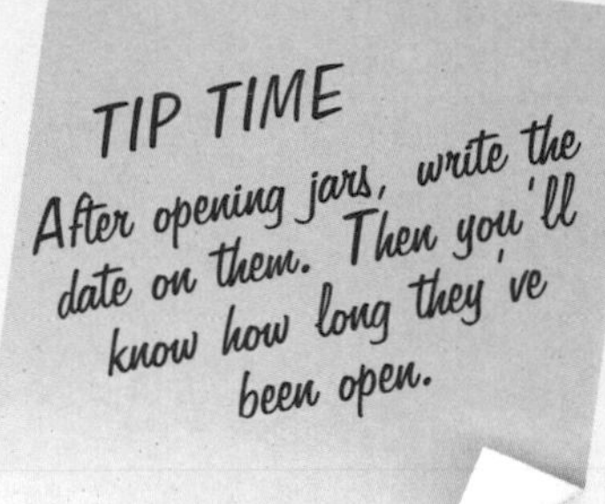

Brixham, South Devon

A pretty town on what is known as the English Riviera, Brixham was the country's busiest fishing port in the 19th century, and fishing is still thriving there today.

In the 17th and 18th centuries, Brixham was also renowned for smuggling, which was more profitable than fishing, albeit risky – if the smugglers were caught they were hanged.

Brixham is full of little streets and pretty cottages, and one particularly interesting building is the Coffin House. This was said, so the story goes, to have been built by a young man whose girlfriend's father told him he would rather see his daughter in a coffin than married to him.

Her suitor built a house in the shape of a coffin, impressing the girl's father so much that he gave his consent to the marriage after all. These days, the coffin house does a brisk trade as an antique clock shop.

Pause for thought

Waiting

I stood at the door of time
last night
And watched you stride
purposefully
Across the stepping stones of love
You placed to stay with me.
Excitement, elation filled my heart;
Too long with hope I'd waited.
Our arms outstretched,
our fingers brushed
But you'd gone, dear one, belated.
As I stand at the door of time
this night
I'll not turn the key for sure.
Your kindness, love, sincerity,
Bide with me evermore.

Margaret Vass, Waterlooville

Treasured Photo

Mrs B W Thomson of Bebington, Wirral, writes:

'I enclose a photo taken in the early 1970s by my late husband, Frank, when he opened a hardware shop on the outskirts of Birkenhead. His family firm of corn merchants, based in Liverpool, had closed down and it had been a worrying time.

The photograph shows Frank's sister in the shop. I wonder how we ever coped with stocktaking as, besides the items pictured, we travelled regularly to The Potteries for china and glass and attended Trade Fairs in Blackpool and Harrogate.

We also sold pet food, Do-It-Yourself items, garden tools, plants and fertilisers and much more. Yet after retirement Frank said those busy days in the shop were the happiest of his life.'

"You must be joking"

A householder rang up his local police station to report that a large hole had appeared in the road opposite his house.

The police are now looking into it.

January 20-26

Well, fancy that!
The Bible is the world's best-selling book.

Letter of my life

In early 1943 I was staying with my sister, who was in the WAAFs, stationed at Boscombe Down. One day she asked me if I'd like to make up a foursome with herself, her airman friend and another young airman. I said yes – I was just 15 at the time, so it was quite a new experience.

The young airman, just 20, came along as planned but it didn't turn out to be the occasion I'd hoped! He was very shy and only spoke a couple of times during the whole time we were together. I didn't take to him at all, and except for a freak accident I would never have seen him again. But fate stepped in.

The following morning I was in the NAAFI when I heard an ambulance siren. A young WAAF told me one of the airmen had been injured while working with a gun… 'Quite serious,' she said. To my horror it was the shy, young airman I'd met the previous day. He was taken to hospital – the tops of the fingers on his right hand having been severed completely.

The following week, feeling ashamed at my judgement of him, I wrote saying how sorry I was, and that I'd write again the following week – even though I knew he couldn't reply until his hand had healed. After about three months the longed-for reply came. He thanked me for my letters and asked if he could come to see me on his way home to Devon on sick leave. That was the beginning of our romance.

I didn't see him very often but grew to love him and, yes, he did speak more over the following months, although he was still shy.

We were married in 1946 and had a happy life together. We were together for 54 years and he was a great husband, living for his family and his work. Sadly he died in April 2000 so I am now alone, but I have some wonderful memories, especially of that first meeting. It just shows how wrong one can be… and just what a letter can do!

Sylvia Jones, Knowle, Bristol

TEA-TIME TREATS

Auntie Peggie's Boiled Fruit Cake

- 8 oz/225 g margarine
- 1 cup brown sugar
- 1 cup water
- 1 cup sultanas
- 1 cup currants
- 1 small teaspoon bicarbonate of soda
- 1 large egg, well beaten
- 2 cups self-raising flour

1. Put all ingredients, except eggs and flour, in a saucepan. Bring to boil. Simmer for 15 minutes. Cool completely.
2. Preheat oven to 170°C/325°F/Gas Mark 3 and grease a loaf tin. Add eggs and flour to fruit mixture, stirring to combine.
3. Spoon into prepared tin and bake in centre of the oven for 1½ hours (check after 1¼ hours).

"You must be joking"

The phone rang on the hospital ward Sister's desk.

"Excuse me, but could you tell me how Mr Jackson is getting on?"

"He's making excellent progress," Sister replied. "In fact, he's being discharged on Friday. May I inquire who's asking?"

"This is Mr Jackson," said the voice. "Nobody tells me a damn thing in here!"

Jack Lacy, Burnley Lancashire

HEALTHY LIVING

Fill up on fibre

A diet rich in fibre is thought to reduce the risk of developing bowel cancer. It can also help to reduce the incidence of other bowel disorders such as constipation and irritable bowel syndrome. Here's how to boost your fibre intake:

- ❑ Eat plenty of fresh fruit and vegetables.
- ❑ Eat potatoes baked in their jackets.
- ❑ Baked beans are an excellent source of fibre.

Pause for thought

If at 65 you are still able to do all the things you did at 25, you must have been a very boring 25-year-old!

Ralph Sheffield,
Weston-super-Mare

I WISH I'D SAID THAT...

A comfortable house is a great source of happiness. – Frank Lloyd Wright, architect

TIP TIME

After it's cooled, use the water you've boiled an egg in to water your plants — it's full of nutrients.

TREASURED PHOTO

When her mother died, Mrs B Elwood of Bromley, Kent, found this old photo:

'My mother is on the left, aged nine, with her sisters Alice ,13, and Rose, 7½. The photo was taken when they were in a Home in Ongar, Essex. Unfortunately, their father died early so their mother had to go out to work. Eventually when they left the home they were put into service, which often happened in those days. What fascinates me about the picture is the clothes – and also that my mother and Aunt Rose looked like twins, always being mistaken for each other. Now the same thing happens to my sister and me!'

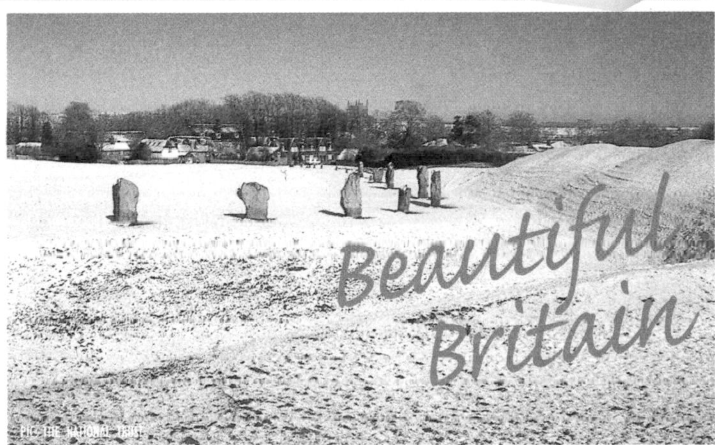

PIC: THE NATIONAL TRUST

AVEBURY, WILTSHIRE

The picturesque village of Avebury is located in an area of ancient mystery, ceremonial sites and burial chambers, and is surrounded by the largest prehistoric stone circle in the world.

Mysteriously, given that the stones are thought to date from around 2600BC, a medieval skeleton was found underneath one of them. The skeleton is thought to be that of a medieval travelling barber-surgeon who suffered an untimely end when the stone accidentally toppled on him. To mark his passing, the stone is now called the Barber Surgeon Stone.

During the middle ages, people were afraid of paganism and many of the stones were buried. In fact, when the village was growing in the 17th and 18th centuries, some of the stones were broken up and used as building materials.

In 1934, Alexander Keiller (of Dundee marmalade fame) was so shocked at the decimation of the site that he bought the Avebury circle, together with most of the village and some of the surrounding sites, so that they could be restored.

January 27-February 2

Lerwick, Shetland Islands, Scotland

Lerwick is the main point of entry into the Shetland Islands and, until the 15th century, it was part of Scandinavia.

Famous for its wildlife, such as puffins, whales, and of course the tiny Shetland ponies, there's a lot to see here. In mid-summer, known as the 'simmer dim', there is virtually no darkness at night and the days stretch on and on.

In the heart of every winter, on the last Tuesday in January, this peaceful spot is transformed when the Up-Helly-Aa, Britain's biggest fire festival, takes place here.

Up to 1,000 torch-carrying paraders (in squads known as guizers), dress up as Vikings, footballers – or anything else they want, even vegetables! – and drag a huge Viking galley to a burning-ground, whereupon they hurl their flames into the boat which goes up in a massive blaze. The revelry continues through the night with the 40 or more guizer squads visiting local halls and putting on wild sketches for the local people.

Q Why is a ship called a 'she'?
A Because she shows her topsides, hides her bottom and when coming into port, always heads for the buoys.

Well, fancy that!
The can opener was invented in 1858... 48 years after cans were introduced. Before then, they were opened with a hammer and chisel.

TIP TIME
Keep a lump of charcoal in a tool box to prevent tools from rusting.

Healthy living

Stub it out...
Only three out of every 100 smokers who attempt to stop smoking by going 'cold turkey' succeed. So if you've tried – and failed – here are a few tips.

- ❑ Book restaurant tables in advance and always ask for a non-smoking table.
- ❑ Leave your cigarettes at home when you go out.
- ❑ Set achievable targets – for example, 'This week, I will cut out the cigarette I have in the morning'.
- ❑ Avoid situations you associate with smoking – perhaps it's a cup of coffee or a night out with friends who smoke.
- ❑ Speak to your GP about nicotine replacement therapy (such as patches). Good luck!

TREASURED PHOTO

The policeman pictured was John Regan, father of YOURS reader Christine Regan: 'As an ex-Irish Guardsman he always carried himself proud and tall. The photo was taken in 1950, the year I was born. It shows the King and Queen outside the Council House in York. Look at Princess Margaret's shoes! She was in fashion with her platforms long before the Spice Girls!'

Letter of my life

Katie Percy, Southampton

'Dear Sir, We are pleased to offer you and your wife £10 assisted passages to Australia, the children to travel free, subject to you passing the medical examinations, which you will arrange yourselves…'

Tears of joy filled my eyes. It was a bleak winter's day in 1954, but it seemed as though a beacon of hope had suddenly illuminated the shabby room.

My unemployed husband was still in bed. The older children were at school and my little girl was asleep in her pram. The house was cold, we had no money for coal and there was very little food in the pantry. We had no money for the fare and no money for clothes. But I wanted to jump for joy! At last, my three years of letter-writing to Australia House, Strand, London, had paid off!

It was a hard struggle preparing for the trip – the biggest step of our lives! And we sailed on 14th June, 1954 for Sydney.

PS. We returned in 1971… but that's another story!

I WISH I'D SAID THAT...

Medicinal discovery,
It moves in mighty leaps,
It leapt straight past the common cold
And gave it us for keeps.

– Pam Ayres, English poet

Pause for thought

City Houses

All the little houses fit together neatly
Like a giant jigsaw, finished now completely,
A randomness of sizes and lines that interplay,
A sympathy of colours and roofs of slate grey.

I think of every person, yet concealed inside
These small, earthly dwellings where humans like to hide,
Busy with their lifetimes, filled with hopes and fears,
Seeking something lovely to crown their mortal years.

In these city houses where each person wakes and sleeps
We scarcely notice time pass, so quietly it creeps;
And nearby is another door, it needs a different key,
It leads to a greater City, beyond what we can see.

Enid Pearson, Boston, Lincolnshire

TEA-TIME TREATS

Oaty Bars

Makes 15

- 4 oz/100 g butter
- 4 oz/100 g brown sugar
- 1 egg yolk
- 2 oz/50 g plain flour
- 2 oz/50 g porridge oats

Topping

- 3 oz/75 g plain chocolate
- 1 oz/25 g butter
- Chopped walnuts

1 Grease a Swiss roll tin. Preheat oven to 190°C/375°F/Gas Mark 5.

2 Beat butter, sugar and egg yolk until smooth. Add flour and oats. Press mixture into tin and bake for 15-20 minutes. Cool.

3 Melt butter and chocolate and spread over mixture in the tin. Cover with chopped walnuts. Cut into bars while warm but leave in the tin until completely cold.

DO YOU REMEMBER...

PIC: HULTON ARCHIVE

...the Teasmade?

WHAT luxury it was to wake up to the sound of the teapot filling with water? All you had to do was wait until the tea brewed, sit up, extend a sleepy hand and pour out!

The first automatic tea-making machine was patented in 1902 by gunsmith Frank Clarke – called An Apparatus Whereby a Cup of Tea or Coffee is Automatically Made! The first Goblin Teasmade sold in 1937 for £5 15s 6d.

But their days may be numbered. From summer 2003, they are threatened by new EC safety regulations banning hot water by the bedside.

The supporters' site www.teasmade.com is a source for those needing repairs.

...good manners?

Your Guide to Omnibus and Train Manners, extract from Correct Conduct c 1930

- Do not push when entering a public vehicle; take your turn.
- Do not monopolise more than your allotted space when the vehicle is full. It is not unusual for some people to keep attaché cases by their side, even when others are standing.
- Do not say 'goodbye' to your friends on the pavement while an uncomplaining conductor is waiting to start the bus or tram.
- Talking loudly in public vehicles is not a sign of aristocracy; it is a nuisance to people who want to read.
- A woman with a baby and a number of parcels is an object for pity. Make the journey as easy as possible for her. Give her a hand with the parcels.
- Personal cleanliness is of prime importance when in the near vicinity of other passengers. Do not dislodge foreign matter from the nails with your railway ticket.

Brits for all seasons

RELUCTANT RESOLUTIONS

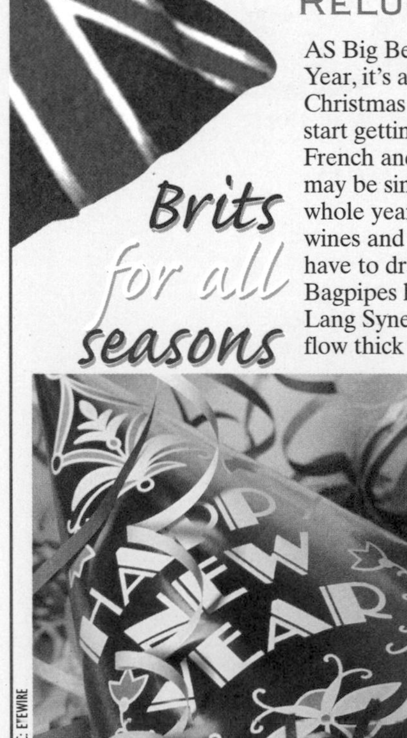

PIC: E'TEWIRE

AS Big Ben chimes in another New Year, it's a signal that the best of Christmas is over and we had better start getting back to normal. For the French and Italians, New Year's Eve may be simply the culmination of a whole year's indulgence in fine wines and rich food, but we Brits have to draw the line somewhere. Bagpipes have hardly finished 'Auld Lang Syne' before the resolutions flow thick and fast.

New Year was first observed in ancient Babylon about 4,000 years ago, but in those days it was celebrated with the first new moon after the spring equinox. And instead of vowing to lose weight, the Babylonians were more likely to resolve to return borrowed farm equipment to a neighbour. The tradition of making those New Year resolutions began in ancient times when, in order to have a 'clean slate' on which to start the year, people cleared all their borrowings.

These days, the scope for resolutions know no bounds! Still, giving up little pleasures does mean we can indulge in one of our favourite national pastimes: Having a good grumble.

Whether we admit it or not, for many of us the passing of time brings a propensity to make unfavourable comparisons between modern times and life 'in our day'. Politicians seem to be getting younger, children have more material things than ever, youngsters have too much freedom – and yet didn't we bite our tongues when our own parents would go on about these same things? Didn't we resolve, in our youth, never to become like them? Ah well, so much changes and yet remains the same. Roll on next New Year when we can do it all again.

Winter cryptic

Try our tricky crossword

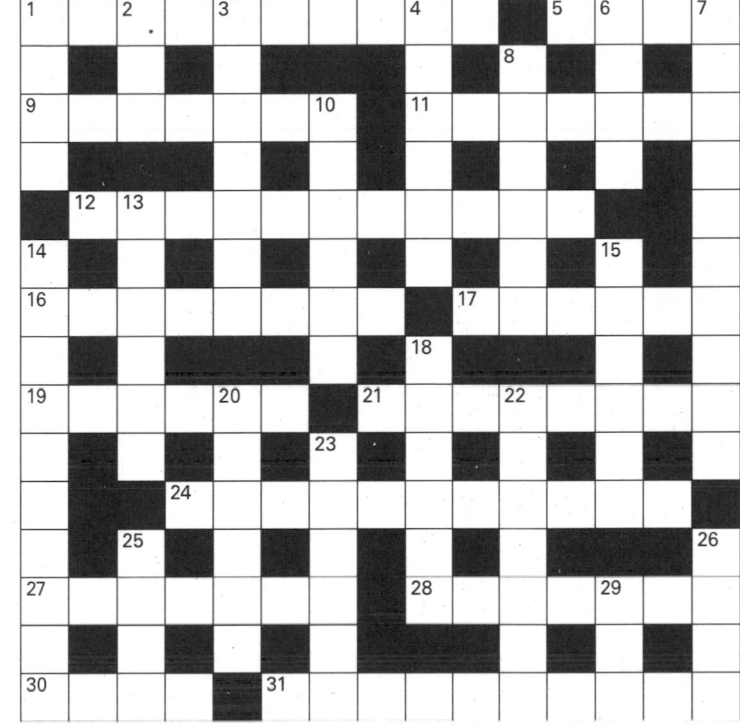

ACROSS

1 'Now is the winter of our ___' (Shakespeare) (10)
5 & 30 Across Shows one variety of winter wear (4-4)
9 Bungled ice trick loses one the game (7)
11 Holding back ice, an older relative from another country (7)
12 Passing the winter thus would get the robin in a mess (11)
16 Bad weather for artist before winter (8)
17 Begin journey during onset of frost (3,3)
19 Hail, for example, might make us late (6)
21 It's close, perhaps, in the middle of December (8)
24 Plant a seasonal vegetable? (11)
27 Snow-covered mountain is always 17 Across (7)
28 Not much use for wintertime, this device? (7)
30 See 5 Across
31 Inexpensive winter sports equipment for miserly type (10)

DOWN

1 After short winter month, king gets pack of cards (4)
2 Risking a bit to travel in winter (3)
3 Royalist emblem – it's fallen by winter (3-4)
4 Strange things getting longer in winter (6)
6 Fix on Montana ski school, finally (4)
7 Tender wife arranged seasonal food for stock (10)
8 Interpret a winter poem? (6)
10 Feel effects of cold during skating lesson (6)
13 In Arctic, I clear frozen spike (6)
14 Unfriendly manner that's experienced in winter (10)
15 Observe water's thawed? (6)
18 Gathers there are frosts coming round first of December (6)
20 Winter break for weaver (6)
22 After winters, they come in leaps and bounds (7)
23 Frost – it chills somewhat, without one of these on (6)
25 Temperature producing frozen contents, perhaps (4)
26 So sad because one's freezing? (4)
29 Girl appearing in après-ski dance (3)

Solution on Page 159

Word wise

How many dictionary words of FOUR or more letters can you make from the nine letters provided? More than 30 earns you a pat on the back. More than 40 deserves a medal.

Have you spotted the nine-letter title of a 1950s No.1 hit by the pictured singer that can be made from all the letters?

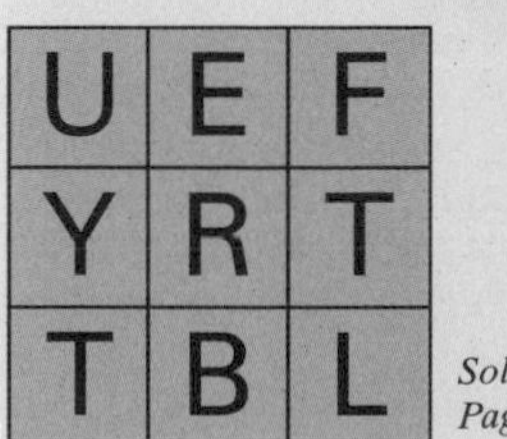

U	E	F
Y	R	T
T	B	L

Solution on Page 159

SAYING GOODBYE

By June Holland

The memories come flooding back as Tessa faces up to parting from the one man who means the world to her

Tessa walked with difficulty across the thick, soft sandy beach, leaning her weight against the wind. She thrust her hands into the pockets of her inadequate jacket, glancing at the man beside her. The man who meant everything in the world to her.

Looking down at her leather boots, already bearing salt marks, she wondered why she hadn't had the sense to wear Wellies? For someone who'd lived for so long by the sea, it seemed she still had a lot to learn.

It was a pity that this last visit together to what had always been their favourite haunt had to be in winter. She wanted to hold the memories of all the good times they'd enjoyed for so many summers and not remember it as the scene of their parting.

The pair had remained silent as speech would have been impossible above the roar of the waves and the gusting wind. Momentarily the wind dropped and he quickly took advantage of this.

"Tessa?" He freed one hand from a deep pocket and linked her arm, "let's try not to be sad. We knew this day was coming..."

As the wind began to gather strength, she felt the tears spring to her eyes. She quickly blinked them away, letting them fall on to her cheeks. He looked concerned. She dashed a hand across her face impatiently. "It's the wind," she said, as a gust snatched her words away.

"What?" he shouted.

"The wind! It's making my eyes stream!"

He nodded and pulled his collar up to shield his neck. The sand was being whipped up like a desert storm, stinging their faces like pinpricks. As one, they turned their backs to the wind and changed their direction of walking. They had always been completely in tune with each other.

Looking at his craggy profile, she realised how was going to miss him, how much she had taken for granted

It was after meeting Sarah that he'd changed. Or perhaps, not changed but come to realise that his life was incomplete. No longer could Tessa be everything to him as she once had. In the early days, finding out about Sarah had come as a shock, a body blow. Of course there were bitter arguments, tears and long periods of not speaking to each other. And then, after the anger, just sadness.

In the end, because of her obvious distress, he didn't leave her and for a while, everything seemed fine to Tessa. But she was only fooling herself. He never mentioned Sarah, but she knew he was thinking about her.

There were also the occasions when he went out for long walks, taking not only the dog but also his mobile phone. The long weekends working away... or supposedly working away. It would have been so easy to have checked up on him, but didn't want to face what was so obvious.

She had buried her head in the sand, pretending that nothing was wrong. Then came the day when she had asked herself why she was holding on to him at any cost. Surely if she loved him so much she should let him go.

She felt him tugging at her sleeve, as he indicated a sheltered cove. She followed him and they sat on a dry, flat rock out of the worst of the wind. Looking at his craggy profile, she realised how she was going to miss him, how much she had taken for granted. But it was time to do the right thing. For too long, she'd behaved badly, selfishly.

"I'm sorry I've been so beastly to you over the last few months."

He turned and smiled at her sadly. "Please don't say that. You have nothing to be sorry for..."

"Of course I have. But I am sorry. I handled it all wrong."

"Tessa, I just didn't want you to be hurt."

"But you were hurting weren't you? Silently hurting. I realise that now and I just want you to be happy."

There were tears in his eyes as he grasped her hand.

"That means an awful lot to me, coming from you. You know, Tess, one day, you'll meet somebody yourself and all of this will make more sense."

She looked at him sharply. In fact, there was a certain person. Vague and shadowy at the moment, but possibly...

"There is somebody actually. Well, somebody I think I could like, given time." The relief on his face was obvious as anxiety melted away, leaving in its place a broad smile.

"Really? You've never mentioned anything before."

"He hasn't asked me out yet or anything. It's still very much in its infancy."

"But he will, I'm sure he will. Oh, Tess, I would feel so much better if I knew that you weren't going to be on your own. Perhaps I wouldn't feel so guilty."

"Guilt doesn't come into it. You must promise me not to feel guilty."

They began walking slowly up the beach. Since he'd made arrangements to move in with Sarah, he had left everything in order for Tessa. The house was to be hers and he had gone to the solicitor's office, transferring it into her name. She had packed his things for him, keeping a few special mementos for herself. All that remained now was for him to drive her home before setting off to begin his new life.

They reached the car and stood for a few moments leaning against it. Reluctance to leave was almost tangible.

"If there's anything I've forgotten to do or if you can't manage... you will let me know, won't you?"

"There's nothing you've forgotten and I will manage but yes, I will let you know."

"Promise?"

"Yes! Now stop worrying, you've got a really long journey ahead of you. How long will it take you to get to Aberdeen?" He threw his eyes up to the sky.

"For ever! No, I'll do it over a couple of days., then sleep for another couple!"

Tessa took a deep breath."I don't want to say 'goodbye' at home."

"No, I understand that. Shall we... shall we do it now then?"

She fell into his strong arms fighting back tears and they clung to each other. Finally, she found the strength to say what she needed to say.

"You've always been my best friend you know, as well as being the best father any girl could have. I love you very much, I want you to be really happy. And you'd better come back one day soon."

He stood back from her, holding her by the shoulders.

"Try keeping me away."

"And, bring Sarah, please."

"I will." He nodded, holding her tightly in his arms.

"Take care, Dad."

February 2003

High days and holidays...

Hurling the Silver Ball (February 3)

On the first Monday after February 3, known as Feast Monday, St Ives in Cornwall holds its annual Hurling the Silver Ball contest for local children. The Mayor throws the silver-coated cork ball to them at 10.30 am, and sets the bizarre game in motion. Part pass-the-parcel and part scrummage, the child left holding it at noon is given a crown piece.

St Valentine's Eve (February 13)

PIC: HULTON ARCHIVE

Legend has it that to catch a glimpse of your future lover on Valentine's Eve, 'take a hard-boiled egg, take out the yolk, fill the cavity with salt and eat the delicacy in silence before going to sleep, taking no water during the night. Do not forget to rid your mouth of the resultant Satan's Breath before greeting your Valentine the following morning'. Not a practice to be recommended – why not try Friends of YOURS (every month in YOURS magazine) for a penpal instead!

St David's Eve (February 28)

In Wales, this is one of the notable nights for the Cwn Annwn, when the hounds of Annwn (the underworld) take to the skies. Howling and racing across the heavens in dog form, they portend death for anyone unfortunate enough to hear them.

Saturday	1
Sunday	2
Monday	3
Tuesday	4
Wednesday	5
Thursday	6
Friday	7 Cheltenham Folk Festival
Saturday	8 Cheltenham Folk Festival
Sunday	9 Cheltenham Folk Festival
Monday	10
Tuesday	11
Wednesday	12
Thursday	13
Friday	14 St Valentine's Day
Saturday	15
Sunday	16
Monday	17 Chinese New Year
Tuesday	18

WEDNESDAY	19
THURSDAY	20
FRIDAY	21
SATURDAY	22
SUNDAY	23
MONDAY	24
TUESDAY	25
WEDNESDAY	26
THURSDAY	27
FRIDAY	28 March YOURS on sale

This month don't forget to...

- Take advantage of the occasional sunny day. Walk to the shops and leave the car in the garage.
- Brighten someone's day – write them a letter.

- Keep up your intake of Vitamin C to ward off those winter sniffles.
- Tidy the garden. This includes pruning, cutting back overgrown shrubs and checking stakes and ties – but gently does it!
- Spend some time relaxing and listening to your favourite romantic music on St Valentine's Day.
- Stock up on dusters, washing powder and polish for the great spring-cleaning push!

PIC: MIRROR

Tom Jones with his Rolls-Royce cars

It happened in February...

February 4, 1911: Rolls-Royce adopted the Spirit of Ecstasy statuette.

February 5, 1923: The BBC time pips were first broadcast.

February 1, 1953: Twentieth Century Fox announced that all its films would be made in Cinemascope.

February 12, 1975: Workmen uncovered a perfectly preserved rose that had been cemented into a wall at Romsey Abbey, Hampshire in 1120.

February 3-9

Letter of my life

K Mitchell, Southwick, Sussex

'The letter that changed my life was from a radio ham.

I was engaged at the time. My husband-to-be was a radio operator in the RAF, flying Lancasters with Five Group Bomber Command. In December 1943 he was on a raid over Trier and was shot down by a German night fighter and taken prisoner. However, his mother was merely notified that he was missing, and that was all we heard of him. Christmas that year was a very unhappy time for me and his family.

But in February 1944 I had a letter from his mother to tell me the good news. She had heard from a radio ham who had been listening to a German broadcast that announced the names of men who had been taken as prisoners of war – and my husband-to-be's name was among them. That letter changed my life. Shortly afterwards we had official notification that he was a POW.

We were married as soon as the war ended.

Well, fancy that!

What is the only sport ever to have been played on the moon? Answer: Golf. On February 6, 1971, astronaut Alan Shephard hit a golf ball. Zero gravity ensured he won the record for achieving the world's longest ever golf drive!

Pause for thought

'This prayer has helped me over the years,' writes Margaret Dinsdale of Newcastle upon Tyne. 'I keep it in my purse, and whenever I'm feeling sad, I read it and think about the words.'

Don't dwell upon the past (it's done),
Nor worry what might be;
The present moment is the one
In which to live and be.
What's gone cannot be altered,
The future we don't know;
So make the most of every day
In which to live and grow.

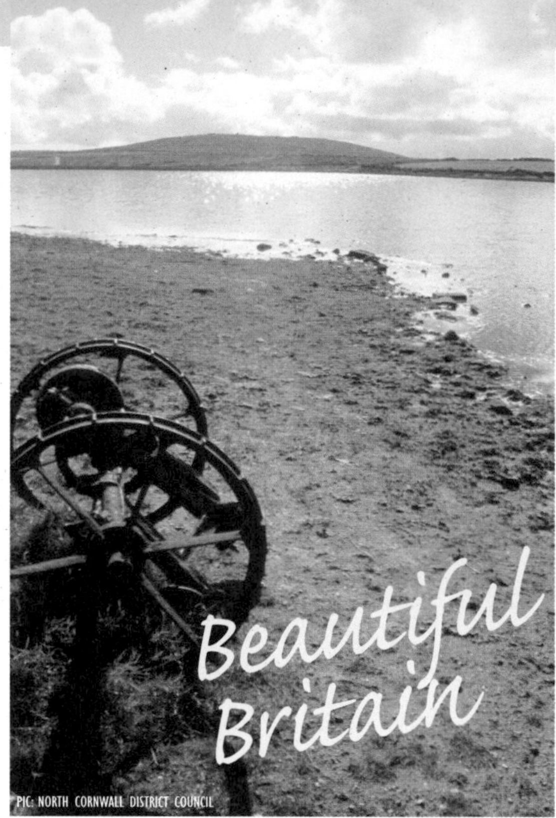

PIC: NORTH CORNWALL DISTRICT COUNCIL

Bodmin Moor, Cornwall

Bodmin Moor is a place of deep legend and, in prehistoric times, it was the most heavily populated part of Cornwall, as can be seen from evidence of hut circles, burial grounds and sacred sites.

It is thought that Dozmary Pool, rumoured to be bottomless, is where the dying King Arthur instructed Sir Bedivere to throw his mighty sword, Excalibur.

Bodmin Moor has its fair share of ghost stories too and probably the most famous is that of Charlotte Dymonds, who was murdered by her lover. He was hanged at Bodmin Gaol for the crime and on the anniversary of her death Charlotte is said to have been seen walking in the vicinity dressed in a gown and a silk bonnet.

The Beast of Bodmin Moor is a puzzle – there have been many sightings in recent years of a big cat on the moor, and there is even some video footage, leading many local people to believe that there is a large animal – or possibly several – living there. A teenage boy found a large-fanged skull on the moor and the Natural History Museum proved it to be that of a large cat. Official investigations have proved inconclusive, so the mystery remains.

I WISH I'D SAID THAT...

There are seven ways to warm your feet in February. Dipping them in the Caribbean is one. If you can afford that, forget the other six.
–The Kiplinger Magazine, quoted in Reader's Digest

TREASURED PHOTO

Ex-Bombardier D A Young of Brighton, on the right of this photo taken outside his barracks, has vivid memories of 1952: 'I was doing my National Service with the Royal Artillery in Germany. We were out in a Jeep when, through the earphones, I heard a voice announcing 'The King is dead'. I had picked up a news broadcast from London! I radioed in to Control and we were all called back to base, where I was put on a charge by the Battery Sergeant Major for breaking in on the radio. I was cleared when it was realised the news was true. We were still in Germany for the Coronation in 1953 – plenty of spit and polish parades then – so we actually served two monarchs.

TEA-TIME TREATS

Almond Shortbread

Makes 16

- 9 oz/250 g unsalted butter
- 4½ oz/125 g caster sugar
- 4 oz/100 g ground almonds
- 12 oz/350 g plain flour

To dust:

- 1 teaspoon ground cinnamon
- 2 tablespoons icing sugar

1. Beat butter until soft and then gradually beat in caster sugar.
2. Sieve in the ground almonds and flour. Stir well, then work together to form a smooth dough.
3. Wrap in greaseproof paper and chill for 30 minutes.
4. Preheat oven to 170°C/325°F/Gas Mark 3. Grease an 11 x 7½ in/28 x 19 cm shallow rectangular tin and press in the shortbread dough evenly. Prick all over with a fork and mark into 16 triangles.
5. Bake for 45 minutes. Re-mark triangles and cool in the tin. Cut when cold and dust with icing sugar and cinnamon.

PIC: TATE & LYLE SUGARS

"You must be joking"

A boy took his dog with him to see Gone With the Wind. The usherette was supposed to turf out pets but took pity on this pup. Later she told the boy: "I was surprised to see your dog enjoying the film."

"So was I," said the boy. "He didn't enjoy the book one bit."

TIP TIME

To prevent bacon from 'spitting' when you fry it, dust it with flour first.

HEALTHY LIVING

Salt sense

Lowering the amount of salt in your diet can help to lower blood pressure.

- ❑ Microwave or steam vegetables – you're less likely to need salt for lost flavour.
- ❑ Avoid processed meat.
- ❑ Break the habit of salting food on your plate without tasting first.
- ❑ Use herbs or lemon juice to season food.

February 10-16

Pause for thought

Philip Swallow, from Newcastle upon Tyne, sent in this inspirational poem:

Voices

The weakling says 'I'm beaten' but the fighter says 'Not I'
The shirker says 'It can't be done', the worker says 'I'll try'.
The laggard says he's weary and must give up the race
The plodder says 'Keep going at a good and steady pace'.
The pessimist, when clouds appear, predicts a rainy day
The optimist declares he sees gold streaks in the grey.
The grumbler says he's sick of life, of work and dull routine,
The poet says 'The stars still shine, birds sing, the grass is green'.
The cynic says this crazy world is rushing to its doom;
The dreamer cries 'I see the peaks of glory shining through the gloom'.
The doubter asks 'Where now is God, what sign do we perceive?'
And someone at a cross is kneeling, saying…'I believe'.

I WISH I'D SAID THAT...

Love is not looking into each other's eyes, but looking together in the same direction. – Antoine de Saint-Exupéry, French author

"You must be joking"

Q How many politicians does it take to change a light bulb?
A Four, one to change it and three to deny it.

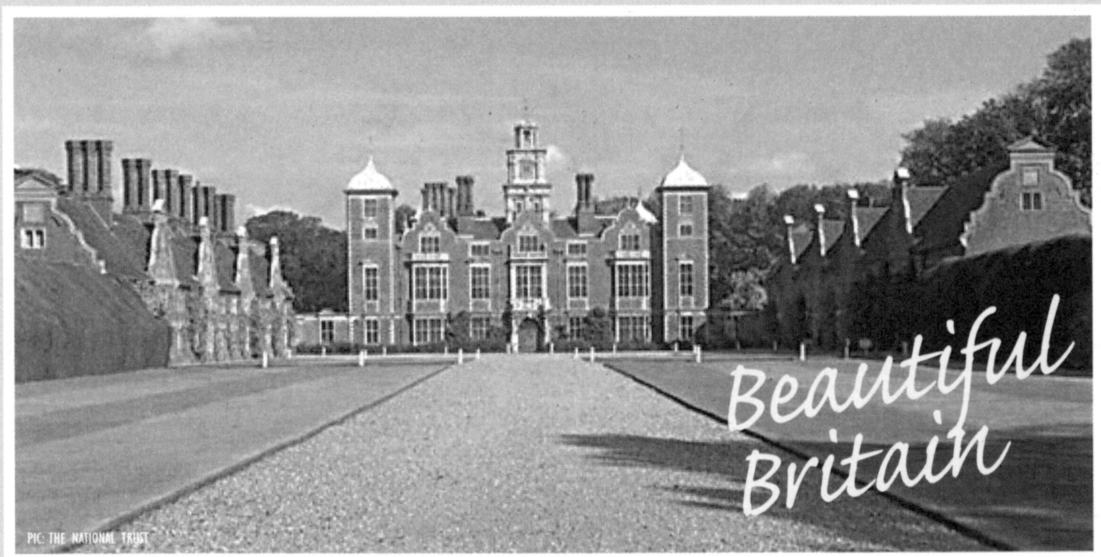

PIC: THE NATIONAL TRUST

Blickling Hall, Norfolk

Not only is this the site where the family of Anne Boleyn (wife of Henry VIII) lived, but there's a 45ft pyramid in the garden – and what's more, it's a pyramid with a story to tell.

Blickling Hall is a red brick mansion set in extensive grounds with gardens, woods and a lake. The 45ft grey stone pyramid is based on a tomb in Rome and was commissioned by Lady Caroline Suffield in the 1790s to house the remains of her father John Hobart, the second Earl of Buckinghamshire and his two wives, Mary Anne and Caroline. According to Horace Walpole, the earl suffered from gout and dipped the affected foot in cold water, so killing himself!

For those who like a ghost story, it is said that Thomas Boleyn, who lived on this site and whose daughter Anne was executed by King Henry VIII in 1536, drives a coach drawn by four headless horses over a circuit of 12 bridges, with his head under his arm, around the anniversary of her death.

TIP TIME

Keep your freezer full. It'll stay colder for longer if there's a power cut.

Well, fancy that!

Did you know that our eyes always stay the same size from birth?

TREASURED PHOTO

In 1940 Shirley Soulsby, from Ryton, Tyne and Wear, was pictured as a three-year-old with her mother, grandmother and great-grandmother.

In her letter Shirley remarked how smart everyone looked.

HEALTHY LIVING

Look after your eyes

- ❑ Good lighting is vital at any age, but the eyes of a 40-year-old need twice as much illumination as that of a 20-year-old. At 60, you need three times as much.
- ❑ Soothe tired eyes with cool damp teabags or slices of cucumber. Leave for ten minutes.
- ❑ Protective nutrients include vitamin C, beta-carotene, vitamins B2, A and E, zinc and selenium
- ❑ Have an eye check every two years. This will pick up on more serious conditions such as cataracts or glaucoma.

Letter of my life

Mrs S Jarvis, Cwmbran, Gwent

In 1995 our local radio station ran a competition. Listeners were asked to write in nominating their Valentine. Winning letters would be mentioned on the programme, the writer's request would be played – and there was a bottle of bubbly, too! I wrote in, nominating my husband who had supported me so lovingly after I was diagnosed with cancer in 1990.

One day we were listening to the radio and we heard my letter being read out! I had won an all-expenses-paid trip to Paris! It was even more special because I had just got the all-clear from the hospital I'd been attending for so long.

It was wonderful, the very best weekend we had ever spent, and on returning home we booked for the autumn of 1996. Sadly, we didn't make the second trip as my darling husband passed away very suddenly the week before Christmas 1995.

So the best holiday was the last holiday... and I have wonderful memories of our trip to Paris.

PERFECT PUDDINGS

Steamed Orange Sponge with Hot Orange Sauce

Serves: 4-6

For the sponge:

- 4 oz/100 g unsalted butter
- 5 oz/150 g caster sugar
- 2 eggs
- 1 egg yolk
- Finely grated zest of 1 orange
- 7 oz/200 g self-raising flour
- Juice of 2-3 oranges, boiled to reduce by ⅔, then cooled

For the sauce:

- 1 pt/570 ml fresh orange juice
- 1-2 oz/25-50 g caster sugar
- 1 teaspoon cornflour
- 1 tablespoon cold water

1. Cream butter and sugar together. Mix eggs and egg yolk together and beat into butter and sugar mix. Add orange zest and fold in the flour. Add cold orange juice.
2. Line a 1½ pt/900 ml mould with butter and flour. Spoon in sponge mix to fill three quarters of the mould and cover with buttered paper. Steam for 1¼-1½ hours.
3. Make orange sauce. Boil orange juice until reduced by half, then add sugar to taste. Mix cornflour with water, then whisk a few drops at a time into the simmering juice until a good coating consistency. Allow to cook for 3 to 4 minutes.
4. Turn out the pudding and serve with the hot orange sauce.

February 17-23

Letter of my life

Dad had done the football pools for 20 years without winning a penny. One Saturday afternoon in 1959 he sat by the wireless checking his coupon. Suddenly he seemed very excited – he had eight score draws!

The whole family hurried in the dark up to the phone box where Dad rang Vernons Pools to stake his claim. We couldn't believe this was happening to us; Mam and Dad had married young, had four children, and we lived in a council house in Bradford. Our parents had struggled and worked hard to give us everything they'd never had.

It was some time later that we had confirmation of our win. One lunchtime I went home from school as usual and was surprised to find Dad in the kitchen talking to Mam – he was usually at work until 5pm. As I walked in he grabbed me by the hands and danced around the room with me, shouting, 'We've won, we've won!' That morning a representative of Vernons Pools had visited him at his work and handed him the letter confirming the amount. Dad had won £20,484 – a quarter share of that week's jackpot and an absolute fortune in those days.

Of course, our lives changed. Mam and Dad bought their own home; they learned to drive and bought a new car each, and our lives changed in so many ways. It wasn't exactly the letter that changed our lives, but it confirmed Dad's pools win, which certainly changed our lives for ever.

Kay Spurr, Bude, Cornwall

TEA-TIME TREATS

Healthy Fruit Loaf

Nora Varty from Ferryhill in County Durham sent in this recipe to go with a cup of tea.

- 1 cup All Bran
- 1 cup mixed fruit
- 1 cup plain flour
- 1 cup milk
- ½ cup sugar

1. Soak all the ingredients, except the flour, in the milk overnight.
2. The following morning, heat oven to 180°C/350°F/Gas Mark 4 and grease a loaf tin.
3. Add flour and mix well. Bake in middle of oven for 1½ hours approximately.

Pause for thought

Innocence

Whispers in the playground, giggles behind a hand,
Being all of six years old, isn't life just grand?

Handstands up against the wall, games of hopscotch too,
The innocence of childhood should be bottled, and kept in view.

Hazel Ratcliffe, Chorley, Lancashire

TIP TIME

Use kitty litter to soak up oil from your garage or drive.

Well, fancy that!

Sir Walter Raleigh raised money for his trip to America by making a bet with Queen Elizabeth I that he could weigh smoke. He did this by placing two identical cigars on opposite sides of the scales. He lit one, taking care not to lose any of the ash. Raleigh claimed that the difference in weight after the lit cigar had burnt out was the smoke.

I WISH I'D SAID THAT...

You can't be at a loss for words while courting. Women will always give you two for one. – Elizabeth Inchbald, English playwright and author

PIC: THE HIGHLANDS OF SCOTLAND TOURIST BOARD

Kingussie, Cairngorms, Scotland

This is Monarch of the Glen country, where the popular BBC series is filmed, and it's whisky country, too, thanks to the pure mountain water here – an essential ingredient in this important local industry.

Kingussie is the location of the Ruthven Barracks, built in 1721 on the site of a 13th century castle and designed to house 120 soldiers. These Government barracks were captured by Bonnie Prince Charlie's Highlanders in the Jacobite Rising and, after the Battle of Culloden in 1746 where the prince was defeated, 3000 Jacobites gathered here, intending to fight on. But instead they received a farewell message from him, saying that each man should save himself as best he could. Following this, the Government suppressed the Jacobite uprising, once and for all.

There's a ghostly tale dating back to the original castle, which was occupied by the 'Wolf of Badenoch', the son of Robert II, in the 14th century. It is said that one dark evening in 1394, a visitor clothed in black arrived at Ruthven Castle and challenged the Wolf of Badenoch to a game of chess. By the morning, nobody in the castle was left alive – but then, such is the danger of playing chess with the Devil.

Treasured Photo

This picture reminds Mrs Hazel Biggs from Hadleigh, Suffolk, of her years as a Service wife:

'It was taken in the married quarters where we lived. I had just joined my husband who was in the RAF Regiment in Shallufa, Egypt. My two children were with us and the bus that ferried them to school had an armed escort. Because of the unrest in Egypt we couldn't go shopping so I made the dress myself. But look at the belt! It was all the rage and certainly made my waist smaller.'

"You must be joking"

A ham salad roll sidles up to the bar and says: "A pint of lager, please." To which the barman replies: "Sorry, sir, we don't serve food."

Healthy living

Check it out

Daily breakthroughs in medical research are now commonplace. Many complaints that were once thought to be incurable only a few years ago can now be relieved or even cured. It's important for your wellbeing to visit your GP for a medical check-up at least once a year. Don't let fear of what may be discovered deter you – the sooner a suspected medical problem is investigated, the more likely it is to be successfully treated.

February 24-March 2

I WISH I'D SAID THAT...

"A man in love is incomplete until he's married. Then he's finished.
– Zsa Zsa Gabor, Hungarian-born film actress"

TREASURED PHOTO

This photograph from the 1920s shows Irene Collings of Sherborne, Dorset.

'I am the youngest shown here – not a bit spoiled! Next to me are my twin brothers Cyril (now in Australia) and Roy (deceased). Brother Ronald was killed in World War II and I have visited his grave in a war cemetery in Italy. At the top of the line is brother Clifford who lives in Devon. At that time, when babies were born it was a custom to inform relatives. I can remember 'baby arrived safely – complete with tassel' for a boy!'

Well, fancy that!

In China, when people look to the sky at night they see much more than stars! In this country we talk of the man in the moon but in China they don't see him – instead they see a toad!

TIP TIME

For fat-free gravy, add a few ice cubes to warm meat juices. The fat will solidify around the ice cubes and can easily be removed.

BLENHEIM PALACE, OXFORDSHIRE

Blenheim Palace is one of the largest in Europe. The manor that stood here was a gift in 1704 from Queen Anne to the Duke of Marlborough, John Churchill – an ancestor of Winston Churchill – following his role in defeating Louis XIV of France.

There had been an earlier palace on this site, built by Henry I, which was where Mary Tudor imprisoned Elizabeth for nearly a year, and which fell into ruins following its destruction during the Civil War. When the new Blenheim Palace was built, the architect wanted to keep the ruins of the old palace as part of the landscape, but the Duchess of Marlborough insisted that it was destroyed.

There is an old custom, kept up every year at Blenheim on the anniversary of the victory over the French, where the duke presents a blue silk banner to the monarch at Windsor, as rent for the property.

Winston Churchill, grandson of the seventh Duke of Marlborough, was born at Blenheim Palace in 1874 and spent many holidays here during his childhood. He also honeymooned here, and, when he died in 1965, he was buried in the churchyard in the grounds, within sight of the palace. In the room where he was born, you can now see Churchill's slippers, and a lock of his hair.

TEA-TIME TREATS

Monster Peanut Cookies

Makes 10

- 4 oz/100 g butter, softened
- 5 oz/150 g caster sugar
- 1 medium egg, beaten
- Few drops vanilla essence
- 7 oz/200 g plain flour
- ¼ teaspoon bicarbonate of soda
- 4 oz/100 g plain chocolate chips
- 2 oz/50 g unsalted peanuts (shelled weight)

1 Grease 3 baking sheets. Preheat oven to 190°C/375°C/Gas Mark 5.
2 Beat together softened butter and caster sugar until creamy. Beat in egg and vanilla, then sieve in flour and bicarbonate.
3 Stir well, adding chocolate chips and peanuts.
4 Divide into ten equal amounts and roll into balls. Divide between baking sheets, well spaced apart. Press down lightly with a fork. Bake for 20 minutes until light golden.
5 Allow to cool, then lift on to wire rack. When cold, store in tin.

PIC: TATE & LYLE SUGARS

HEALTHY LIVING

Budget conscious

❑ Make bread, rice, pasta or potatoes the central part of your meal.
❑ Use beans and lentils instead of meat in casseroles and stews. You'll cut down on fat too.
❑ Make filling soups from vegetables and left-overs. Add lentils, pulses and potatoes to bulk it out, and use herbs to add flavour.

Letter of my life

In February 2001 I received a letter that turned my whole life upside down. You see, all my life I'd been told my father had died in the war and then, after years of asking, my mother told me his name. I then wrote many letters to war departments, Royal British Legion and Family Records Centres. Then, in the Saturday Daily Mail I found a missing persons feature, so I wrote to a lovely lady who was also looking for her father. She wrote back, suggesting a few addresses to write to. One week later I had a phone call from the matron of a care home in Blackpool. I'd found my dad! I was 57 years old and I can't describe to you that meeting. Everyone was in tears – Dad, me, the staff. Dad and I are together in the picture.

I only had my lovely dad for ten months, as he died after suffering a stroke. But I am grateful that at least I got to know him and, as he said to me the week before he died: "I'm at peace now; the jigsaw is complete."

Mrs J Jones, Prestatyn, Denbighshire

Pause for thought

I Remember

I remember, I remember
As sharp as yesterday.
The village dance,
His uniform
The slim and handsome,
dark-eyed boy.

The solemn vows,
Exchange of rings,
Our future beckoning,
full of home.

The babies, young,
The children, grown,
The joys, the pains,
the rush of years.

Then soon, too soon!
The golden watch
A token thanks for
years of toil.

And then the peace
Of slower pace.
Time for ourselves – the
golden years.

A woodland walk,
A game of bowls,
And dancing – far more
stately now!

And held within
Forever young,
The two who met and
danced and loved.

Do I remember? Years
have passed
But yes, indeed I do.
Though you are gone
And I am old
The memory of our love
sustains me still.

Hazel Newton, St Ives, Cambridgeshire

Do you remember...

...Women's Land Army songs?

DURING the War, many town girls were eager for a taste of country life, lured by jolly posters advertising a healthy, rustic, yet patriotic life. They arrived bright-eyed with anticipation, only to find their new life was tough and poorly paid. While working in the fields, singing often proved a welcome distraction. Here are a few examples:

When this silly war is over
Oh how happy I shall be
When I get my civvy clothes on
No more Land Army for me.
No more digging up potatoes
No more threshing out the corn
We will make that bossy foreman
Regret the day that he was born.

....

If you wanna go to heaven when you die
You must wear a green pullover and a tie,
You must wear a khaki bonnet
With WLA on it
If you wanna go to heaven when you die.

....

Back to the land, we must all lend a hand
To the farms and the fields we must go.
There's a job to be done,
Though we can't fire a gun
We can still do our bit with the hoe.
When your muscles are strong
You will soon get along
And you'll think that the country life's grand;
We're all needed now,
We must speed with the plough,
So come with us – back to the Land.

Brits for all seasons

Love is... something simple

ROMANCE is in the air for those of us who have someone to share it with. And even for those who have lost a loved one, Valentine's Day is a time for reflection and happy memories.

Valentine's Day has been celebrated for hundreds of years, and the tradition dates back to the beginning of the first century AD.

Although the history surrounding this day is shrouded in mystery, it's thought to be associated with the execution of a Christian martyr.

One version of the legend is that Valentine was a Christian Roman who was martyred for refusing to renounce his faith, and was beheaded on February 14 in the year 269. Before he died, he apparently left a love note for the jailer's daughter, and signed it simply 'Your Valentine'. This tragic, romantic tale has led to the custom of sending Valentine cards to loved ones. The tradition has carried on ever since: The Royal Mail, which handles around 81 million items of mail per day, reports that in 2001 around 11.2 million Valentine cards were delivered.

The commercial world has turned Valentine's Day into a competition leaving many men feeling inadequate if all they give is a bunch of flowers and a card. But we old romantics know that less is more. A certain smile, a slow dance says more to a golden oldie than a showy bouquet and dinner at a posh restaurant ever could.

And forget the Champagne on ice: For us British women of some years, love is a good cup of tea made by a man who warms the pot and serves it in a bone china cup and saucer. Who needs a tall, dark, handsome stranger bearing gifts? But then again…

PIC: E'EWIRE

A LIFETIME'S SEARCH

By Frank White

I CAN'T explain this quirk in my personality. Perhaps it was something I read or something that was once said to me. I've really no idea. But surely, that initial stirring of the senses must have happened in my childhood, as I've been plagued with this all my life.

It concerns, believe it or not, walnut trees. For as long as I can remember, I've had this peculiar fascination with them – or rather, with the idea of them, for the truth is that for most of my life I never saw one.

While I was a lad, these objects of wonder were simply photographs in books, as remote from my life as those other tales I read about – Treasure Island, and daring adventures up the Orinoco.

I lived in the inner suburbs of Manchester, where walnut trees were more rare than man-eating tigers. Every summer, I kitted myself out for a safari with tree spotter's book, bottle of orange pop and sandwiches, and penetrated deep into the city's parks.

Oak, ash, sycamore and lime abounded. But a solitary walnut hunter went home sadly disappointed, having gained nothing more than the tuppence returnable on the empty pop bottle.

Later, travel at the expense of the Royal Navy, as far afield as the International Date Line and beyond, presented sights of olive, cedar, eucalyptus (with koala bears), date palm, oil palm, sago palm and coconut palm – all satisfying in their own way, but definitely not a cause of exultation for me.

By the time my 35th year had begun to reap the harvest of my hair, I was living in Bradford and preoccupied with earning a living. But the dream that, one day, I might spot my heart's desire, lingered on. It lurked at the back of my mind, with those other hopes – that one might be useful in life and one's children might grow up healthy and happy – which keeps you slogging away at your desk year after year.

What I didn't know about walnut trees was nobody's business. Its botanical name is Juglans Regia, usually translated as Royal Nuts of Jupiter. I knew its fruit yielded an oil rich in Omega 3 fatty acids. An infusion of walnut leaves is used as an aid to digestion and as a gargle for mouth infections.

I knew all this and more, but I had to reach the age of 59 before my lifelong ambition to see a walnut tree was fulfilled. Over the years, I had asked the question more times than I could count, and finally, in 1986, someone answered, 'Yes, I know where you can find one!'

I drove to Cawthorn, near Barnsley, and at last, after the leaf-fall of autumn, found not one, but a small family of five trees. They stood at the side of the road, intimately holding hands, joined together in a twisted little dance. Twilight had begun to fall. The trees were silhouetted against a sky resplendent with shepherd's delight and I have to confess that I felt tears in my eyes.

Such long-sought satisfactions do, thank God, sometimes occur in the autumn of one's years. But there was more to come.

Six years later, we decided to build a home in Lincolnshire and began to search for suitable plots. At Marshchapel, the diocese of Lincoln was selling off part of its redundant vicarage garden and we drove out to take a look at it.

The first thing I noticed, there, in the corner of the plot, was the glorious canopy of a magnificent walnut tree. Transfixed, I remarked to my wife that we had come upon a moment of great significance. Surely, this was a matter of destiny? This plot, with its walnut tree, had been planned for me, waiting for me, since the day I was born. June was too kind a wife to want to disabuse me of such nonsense, so the plot was bought and the house was built.

That was nine years ago. We're too far north for the fruit to ripen properly, although we always have pickled walnuts by Christmas.

However,the point of my story is this…

The garden soil here is exceedingly fertile. Seeds dropped in autumn burst through in spring like eager litters clustering around their mothers. We have a resident squirrel, whom we see darting along branches or tight-rope walking along the top of the fence. As a result of his energies and his expert, if accidental, propagating skills, the entire garden is chaotic with walnut seedlings, walnut saplings and adolescent walnut trees.

We just can't move for them. After a lifetime of searching for a walnut tree I now have so many I don't know what to do with them.

Obviously, there's a life's lesson here. But I'm not quite certain what it is!

March 2003

HIGH DAYS AND HOLIDAYS...

Shrove Tuesday (March 4)
The Tuesday 41 days before Easter is the eve of the Lenten fast. On this day, in medieval and earlier times, Christians made their compulsory pre-Lent confessions, or 'shrifs', hence 'Shrove' Tuesday – and seized the last opportunity to eat the meat, eggs, butter and other luxury foods prohibited during the coming season of privation. Thus fried rashers ('collops') of meat were the traditional dish on the previous Collop Monday and on Tuesday, all eggs, butter and fat remaining in the house were made into pancakes.

PICS:HULTON ARCHIVE

The pancake race at Winster, near Matlock in Derbyshire, is open to anyone who brings their own pan and pancake.

Shrovetide sports
Shrovetide football is a mixture of soccer, rugby and hurling and there are around 50 traditional sites for the game, although only a few survive. These include Sedgefield in County Durham, Alnwick, Northumberland, Ashbourne in Derbyshire and St Columb Major in Cornwall.

Mothering Sunday (March 30)
Mid-Lent Sunday, the fourth Sunday in Lent, is Mothering Sunday. Originally the matron referred to was the Mother Church and today was when everyone tried to return to their home-town church.

SATURDAY	1	St David's Day
SUNDAY	2	
MONDAY	3	
TUESDAY	4	Shrove Tuesday (Lent begins)
WEDNESDAY	5	
THURSDAY	6	Crufts Dog Show, NEC
FRIDAY	7	Crufts Dog Show, NEC
SATURDAY	8	Crufts Dog Show, NEC
SUNDAY	9	Crufts Dog Show, NEC
MONDAY	10	
TUESDAY	11	YOURS Spring Special on sale
WEDNESDAY	12	
THURSDAY	13	
FRIDAY	14	
SATURDAY	15	
SUNDAY	16	
MONDAY	17	St Patrick's Day
TUESDAY	18	

WEDNESDAY	19
THURSDAY	20
FRIDAY	21
SATURDAY	22
SUNDAY	23
MONDAY	24
TUESDAY	25
WEDNESDAY	26
THURSDAY	27
FRIDAY	28 April YOURS on sale
SATURDAY	29
SUNDAY	30 Mothering Sunday British Summer Time begins, clocks go forward
MONDAY	31

This month don't forget to...

- ☐ Wear a daffodil (or a leek!) in your buttonhole on St David's Day.
- ☐ Buy lemons for your pancakes on Shrove Tuesday.
- ☐ Look out for Lenten lunches in your area.
- ☐ Clear the lawn of moss and feed with nitrogen.
- ☐ Have your shamrocks to hand for St Patrick's Day.
- ☐ Relax on Mothering Sunday – let somebody else do the washing up! Don't forget to put the clocks forward one hour before you go to bed on the Saturday night.

Debutantes

PIC: HULTON ARCHIVE

It happened in March...

March 18, 1904: In a Royal Command Performance of John Bull's Other Island by George Bernard Shaw, King Edward VII laughed so much he broke his chair.

March 29, 1929: Metal strips were put into banknotes for the first time to protect against forgery.

March 24, 1950: The Boat Race was called off when the Oxford team boat sank.

March 18, 1958: The last presentation of debutantes took place.

March 3-9

I WISH I'D SAID THAT...

"Consider the postage stamp; its usefulness consists in the ability to stick to one thing till it gets there."
– John Billings, American humorist

FIELDS OF HOPE, OVER BRITAIN

The bright, cheerful sight of daffodils in bloom is a sign that winter is over and spring is on its way. The yellow splash of a simple daffodil is a symbol of hope and optimism.

But did you know many of the daffodils you see are planted with a charitable purpose? All over Britain, Marie Curie Fields of Hope (daffodils that have been sponsored to support people with cancer) burst into bloom at this time of year. From a tiny corner of a playground to a whole swathe of a public park, a Field of Hope can be any size, any shape, any place, raising both spirits and funds at the same time.

Probably the most spectacular display is in Sefton Park, Liverpool, where a sea of daffodils represent the improved quality of life on offer to those in a hospice or having cancer care.

HEALTHY LIVING

An all-round exercise programme

- Aerobic exercise – helps deliver oxygen to the muscles. It's important for maintaining a healthy heart and is good for weight loss.
- Building strength in your muscles minimises the likelihood of injuries. It can also improve stability, reducing the chance of falls. Building supporting muscle around the joints and back helps to keep you upright and mobile.
- Stretching keeps muscles and joints flexible and supple.

Letter of my life

The letters was dated 1981. It came from Australia and changed my life completely.

When I was 11 a family came to live next door to us in Nottingham. The eldest son, Vic, was five years older than me and I worshipped him. In the late 1960s he emigrated, with his young family, to Australia.

Over the years our mothers kept in touch. I went to stay with my mother for Christmas 1980 and was upset to learn Vic's marriage had ended. I felt an urge to write to him, as I had been on my own for a number of years and had gone through the same experience. His mother forwarded my letter on to him.

In his first letter to me, he told me he had been 'head over heels in love with me'. I later learned he had loved me for eight years but, as we were both shy, he had let me marry someone else. In his letter of February 1981 he asked me to consider going out to Australia for a visit. I went and we got engaged. I returned in May and married him.

I never wanted to emigrate but I enjoyed it out there. We finally, came back to England in 1992.

Mrs S Holland, Derby

Well, fancy that!

A would-be bank robber had been casing a bank in Boston, USA, waiting for just the right time to hold it up. He queued in line and when he reached the window he told the cashier, 'This is a hold up, hand over the money!' Much to his dismay, the five customers behind him were armed FBI agents trying to cash their cheques while on their lunch breaks. What the hapless robber had failed to notice as he 'cased the job' was the FBI Field Office next door.

Pause for thought

'I thought you might like my latest monologue, which I recited at a pensioners' club', writes Kathy Reeve, from Hemel Hempstead in Hertfordshire. 'Everyone liked it and thought how true it was':

Things Aren't Quite the Same

Everything is farther away than it used to be. It is twice as far to the corner, and I've noticed they've added a hill. I have given up running for the bus. It leaves faster than it used to.

It seems to me they are making steps steeper than in the old days. And have you noticed the smaller print they use in the newspaper and telephone directories? There is no sense in asking anyone to read aloud – everyone speaks in such a low voice, I can hardly hear them.

The material in dresses is getting so skimpy, especially around the waist and hips. Even people are much younger than they used to be when I was their age. But people my own age are so much younger than I am.

I saw an old friend the other day. She didn't recognise me. I got thinking about her while I was combing my hair this morning and, in doing so, I glanced at my reflection in the mirror and – would you believe it – they don't make mirrors as clear as they used to. Oh, well…

TREASURED PHOTO

Edna Burley (née Nicholas) treasures a pressed flower from 1948. It came from a bouquet given to her by her mum when Edna played soprano lead, Yum Yum, in The Mikado in Chard, Somerset. Edna sent us this photo of herself in the costume she wore, and wrote:
'I sold 100 tickets for the show, including two to my boss who so enjoyed it that he bought tickets for another night.'

TIP TIME

When pruning thorny bushes, use barbecue tongs to hold back the branches.

"You must be joking"

A vicar thought that a spot of advertising for his church would do no harm. So he put up a large poster that read, 'If you are tired of sin, please step inside'.

The next day, he saw scribbled underneath it, 'But if not, telephone St John's Wood 567898.'

PERFECT PUDDINGS

Almondy Tart

- 8 oz/225 g shortcrust pastry
- 4 oz/100 g butter
- 4 oz/125 g caster sugar
- 3 eggs
- 4 oz/100 g ground almonds
- 3 tablespoons raspberry jam
- 2 oz/50 g icing sugar, sifted
- 1-2 teaspoons water
- 1 oz/25 g flaked almonds

1 Roll out pastry on a floured surface and use to line a 9 in/23 cm flan ring placed on a baking sheet. Bake blind in a preheated oven, 200°C/400°F/Gas Mark 6 for 20 minutes. Remove paper and beans after 15 minutes.

2 Beat butter and caster sugar together until light and fluffy. Add and beat in eggs one at a time. Mix in ground almonds.

3 Spread jam over flan base and cover with the almond mixture. Bake in a preheated oven 180°C/350°F/Gas Mark 4 for 30-35 minutes.

4 Mix icing sugar and water to make a thin pouring consistency and spread over tart while still hot. Sprinkle with almonds and return to oven for 5 minutes. Serve warm or cold.

March 10-16

I WISH I'D SAID THAT...

"Every man's life is a fairy tale written by God's fingers.
– Hans Christian Andersen, Danish author"

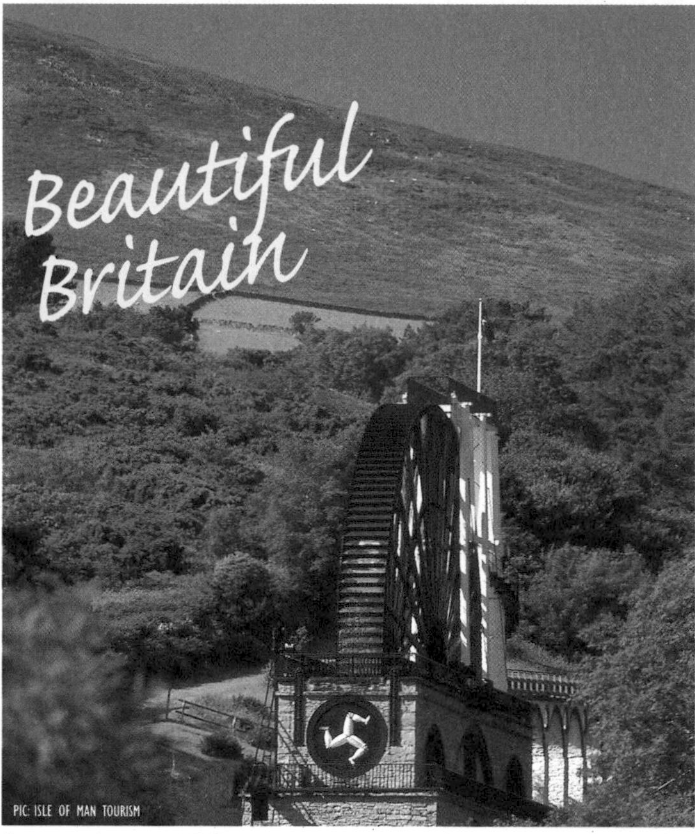

PIC: ISLE OF MAN TOURISM

ISLE OF MAN

Located in the middle of the Irish Sea, the Isle of Man is, quite literally in some ways, a world of its own. Although part of the British Isles, it is actually a self-governing Crown dependency with its own parliament, known as Tynwald, laws, traditions and culture. People born here are entitled to both Manx and British passports.

The Isle of Man is famous for its cats with no tails – the only tail-less breed in the world – and it is thought they were first bred around 300 years ago. There is, however, a legend that refers to an earlier time: That during the Great Flood, a pair of cats rushed into Noah's Ark at the last moment just as the door was closing, and their tails were caught in the door and cut off!

The popular TT (Tourist Trophy) motorbike races also take place here each year and attract a huge number of visitors, but the island also has lots of other things to see, including castles, museums, steam and electric railways – and the massive Laxey water wheel, which, when it was built in the mid-19th century, was the largest in Europe.

TIP TIME

Pop your toothbrushes in the dishwasher with the rest of the dishes once a month. The hot water will sterilise them.

TEA-TIME TREATS

Hazelnut shorties

Makes about 18

- 2 oz/50 g butter
- 1 oz/25 g caster sugar
- 2 oz/50 g plain flour
- 1 oz/25 g ground hazelnuts
- 1 oz/25 g plain cooking chocolate

1. Cream butter with caster sugar until light and soft. Stir in flour, ground hazelnuts and cooking chocolate, grated.
2. Lightly knead. Carefully roll out on floured surface. Cut out as 2 in/5 cm round biscuits.
3. Place on an ungreased baking sheet and bake at 170°C/ 325°F/Gas Mark 3 for about 12 minutes.
4. Transfer to a wire rack to cool. Decorate with whole toasted hazelnuts fixed with a dot of melted chocolate.

HEALTHY LIVING

Food wise

As we age, we're more susceptible to food poisoning. Avoid becoming a victim by following these tips:

- ❑ Avoid raw eggs – often used in home-made mayonnaise or mousses.
- ❑ Don't ignore the best-before or sell-by dates on packaging.
- ❑ Take care with 'cook-chill' foods, such as ready-cooked chickens, pork pies and processed meats. They can be a breeding ground for bacteria.
- ❑ Use separate chopping boards and utensils to prepare chicken.
- ❑ Don't keep cooked food for longer than two days.

Pause for thought

Thank You Lord

Another day draws to its end.
To the Lord my prayers I send.
I thank Him for giving me today,
For guiding me along life's way.

I pray the night be quiet and calm,
For Him to keep me free from harm.
That the day to come will bring peace.
For all worldly ills to cease.

When day breaks fresh and new,
I thank Him for the morning dew.
Welcome its newness like a bird,
I thank the Lord, my prayers He heard.

Josie Rawson, Selston, Nottinghamshire

TREASURED PHOTO

The wedding shown in this picture took place on March 16, 1929: Vera Ruper of Southend-on-sea, Essex, who is pictured with her husband has been married for 73 years. She writes, 'I don't know if this is a record. My husband says it's a life sentence!'

"You must be joking"

"Doctor, doctor I'm having trouble with my diet."

"What have you been eating?"

"Snooker balls. I have three reds for breakfast, a brown, a yellow and a blue for lunch and the black and the pink for supper."

"Aha – the problem is you're not eating enough greens."

Well, fancy that!

Strange laws...

- *In Hawaii, it's illegal to laugh after 10pm.*
- *On the island of Jersey, it's illegal for a man to knit during the fishing season.*
- *In the Amercan state of Michigan, it's illegal to tie an alligator to a fire hydrant.*
- *A British law passed in 1845 stated that it was illegal to commit suicide. The punishment: Offenders would be hanged!*
- *In Athens, a driver's licence can be revoked if he is considered 'poorly dressed' or 'unbathed'.*
- *An old statute in Kentucky states that men who push their wives out of bed for inflicting their cold toes on them can be fined or jailed for a week.*

Letter of my life

The letter that changed my life was from my employer approving my application for early retirement, which materialised in 1984 at the age of 55. The picture of tyranny and oppression presented in George Orwell's novel, '1984' was very far from reality in my case. 1984 liberated me from an externally imposed timetable of demands on my time and energy, and provided me with the freedom to do more or less what I liked, when I liked, where I liked, and so on. I'm not sure most retired people would agree with me. Retirement? Superb!

Gordon Malt, Lowestoft, Suffolk

March 17-23

Well, fancy that!
Fishing is the biggest participant sport in the world.

Treasured Photo

Here's a grand baby carriage, photographed in the Queen's Coronation Year. Mrs Banks, Ynysybwl, Cardiff, explains:
'When my husband obtained a post overseas we had to take some household effects with us by sea. These included the (large) Silver Cross pram. It caused quite a sensation. We eventually gave it to a Nigerian father of six!'

Tea-time treats

Apple and Ginger Eccles Cakes

Makes 12

- ½ oz/10 g butter
- 2 oz/50 g raisins
- 1 small apple, peeled, cored and grated
- ½ teaspoon ground ginger
- 1 oz/25 g Demerara sugar
- 13 oz/375 g puff pastry
- Milk and caster sugar, to glaze

1 Preheat oven to 220°C/425°F/Gas Mark 7. Melt butter in a saucepan over a low heat. Stir in raisins, grated apple, ground ginger and Demerara sugar until combined.
2 Roll out pastry on a lightly floured surface, ¼ in/5 mm thick and cut out 12 3½ in/8 cm rounds. Spoon a heaped teaspoonful of the apple mixture in the centre of each.
3 Dampen pastry edges with water and draw up round the filling to enclose. Press edges together firmly, turn cake over and pat out until ½ in/1 cm thick. Place on a baking sheet and make three cuts in each.
4 Brush tops of eccles cakes with milk and dust with caster sugar. Bake for 10-12 minutes.

"You must be joking"

A young man was asked by his housemaster at school if he was troubled by naughty thoughts. "Oh no, I enjoy them enormously," he replied

I wish I'd said that...

"And in green underwood and cover blossom by blossom the spring begins."
– Algernon Charles Swinburne, English poet

Healthy living

Fingernails are a guide to your health

- ❑ Grooves – Fine grooves running across your nails may indicate you suffered an illness a few months before.
- ❑ Misshapen nails, especially ones growing upwards, away from the nail bed – often a sign of anaemia.
- ❑ White flecks – this is not a sign of vitamin deficiency, but an indication your nails have received a slight knock.
- ❑ Blue nails – this could be a sign you are cold, or there is a shortage of oxygen in your blood. It's worth checking with your GP.

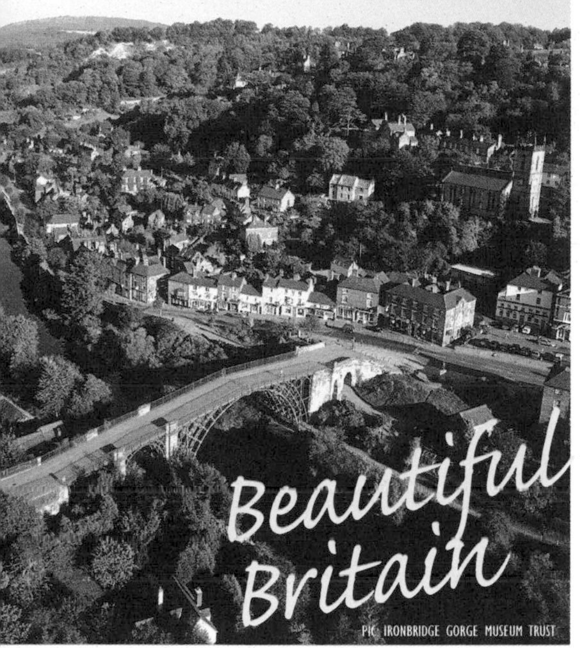

PIC IRONBRIDGE GORGE MUSEUM TRUST

Ironbridge Gorge, Shropshire

A key area during the Industrial Revolution, Ironbridge is named after the bridge that was built across the gorge in 1779 – the first cast-iron bridge in the world. The gorge itself is beautiful – a deep valley rich with seams of coal, clay, iron ore and limestone. This mineral wealth, combined with the River Severn that could be harnessed for both power and transport, meant that Ironbridge was the birthplace of many important industrial developments during the 18th and 19th centuries.

It was here in 1709 the technique of smelting iron ore with coke was pioneered by Abraham Darby, making the production of iron wheels, iron rails – and later the iron bridge – possible.

As other areas, such as Birmingham and Manchester, developed their iron-producing skills, Ironbridge became a centre known for its china and decorative tiles and the 19th century workshops of the Coalport Porcelain Company, now house the Coalport China Museum.

Letter of my life

In 1941 I met a lad who lived in my home town. He was a corporal in the RAF and after about eight months I took Frank home, to meet my mother. On our last date we went to the pictures. He walked me home and, as he kissed me goodnight, told me he was being posted overseas and was leaving the next day.

Later on I joined the WAAF. One day I went to collect my mail. There was a parcel from Reg. In it was a lovely butterfly brooch, a watch and a ring. He asked me to wear the ring as an engagement ring. There was a big 'but'… we would have to get married in a Catholic church.

When I went home I told Mum that I was unofficially engaged to Frank. She said there was no way I was going to marry him – he was a Catholic, his family lived next to a pub – and that was her last word. If I married Frank I would never set foot over her doorstep again. I knew it was Frank or my family. Two weeks later I wrote the saddest letter of my life to Frank, telling him I had changed my mind. I couldn't bear to tell him the truth.

Frank wrote, begging me to re-consider. Attached to his letter was one from the War Office, stating I was not to reply as all letters were being opened and censored.

Much later I met someone else and told him about Frank, but he said we were meant for each other and so we were married in February 1946. Frank later married.

My husband was a wonderful man and we had more than 24 years together. We had two children. I've heard Frank has since died. My biggest regret is I didn't have the chance to explain to his face the reason I did what I had to do.

Molly Reid, Doncaster

Pause for thought

'I came across this in our local church magazine', writes Mr A E Wright of Great Chesterford, Essex:

If you have food in the refrigerator, clothes on your back, a roof over your head and a place to sleep… you are richer than 75 per cent of this world.

If you have money in the bank, in your wallet, and spare change in a dish somewhere… you are among the top 8 per cent of the world's wealthy.

If you woke up this morning with more health than illness… you are more blessed than the million who will not survive this week.

If you hold up your head with a smile on your face and are truly thankful… you are blessed because the majority can, but most do not.

If you can hold someone's hand, hug them or even touch them on the shoulder… you are blessed because you can offer a healing touch.

If you can read this message, you just received a double blessing, in that someone was thinking of you; and furthermore, you are more blessed than over 2 billion people in the world who cannot read at all.

TIP TIME

Use pieces of orange peel dotted around the garden to keep cats away.

March 24-30

TEA-TIME TREATS

Florentines

Makes about 30

- 3 oz/75 g flaked almonds
- 2 oz/50 g cut mixed peel
- 2 oz/50 g glacé cherries, quartered
- 2 oz/50 g butter, melted
- 2 oz/50g caster sugar
- 1 tablespoon double cream
- 4 oz/100 g plain chocolate, melted

1 Preheat oven to 190°C/375°F/Gas Mark 5. Mix together almonds, peel and cherries. Stir into butter, together with sugar and cream. Leave until cold.
2 Place teaspoonfuls of mixture well apart on greased and floured baking sheets.
3 Bake in oven for about 6 to 8 minutes until golden brown.
4 Reshape using a pastry cutter and leave on baking sheet until nearly cold. Transfer to a wire rack and spread thinly with melted chocolate.

I WISH I'D SAID THAT...

"God could not be everywhere and therefore he made mothers.
– Hebrew proverb"

Letter of my life

After several years of trying to start a family and ten months of waiting to see if we would be accepted by the authorities to adopt a baby, my husband and I received a one-paragraph letter that changed our lives. It told us they had a little boy for us.

The day after the letter arrived, we collected our little boy. Over the next 36 years, that tiny, 26-day-old bundle has made me the happiest and proudest mum on the planet. He gave me all the support a child at the age of nine could give, when I was going through a divorce.My son has now given me and my second husband, yet more love and devotion in the form of his lovely wife and adorable three-year-old son – who is now giving my son the love he gave me, all those years ago.

Name and address supplied

Pause for thought

'My mother used to sing this to my sister and me when we were small,' writes Mrs J Pearson of Bury St Edmunds, Suffolk. 'I'm now 73 and my sister, Hazel, is 78. It's a lovely song for Mother's Day.'

To watch over you when a baby,
To sing you to sleep with a song,
To try to be near you
To comfort and cheer you,
To teach you the right from the wrong.
To do all she can just to make you a man
And over a million things more.
She'll sigh for you, cry for you,
Yes, even die for you –
That's what God made mothers for.

Well, fancy that!

Riddle: What is broken when you name it? Answer: Silence

PIC: THE ROYAL COLLECTION – 2002 HER MAJESTY QUEEN ELIZABETH II

Treasured Photo

Joan Foster of Bolton sent in this photo and explains: 'I was a young mum when this snap was taken in 1959. We were dressed for the annual Trinity Sunday walks. My husband had agreed I could have the annual Co-op dividend of £5 to provide for myself and our two girls.

I bought remnants of Moygashel, to make outfits. Then to Woolworth's for two shapes for the girls' hats which I hoped to cover, and another for myself. I bought ribbon and buttons for trimmings, and some net to cut into strips that would be like flowers when gathered to cover my hat.

I was nearly defeated by the girls' hats. I had bought a tin of white enamel and applied a coat, but at first they softened. After a second coat they dried hard and shiny. A proud father took the photo. I am now a widow of 71 and this is my only memento of the day.

Tip Time

When measuring out honey, very lightly oil the spoon first. The honey will drop off easily.

Healthy Living

Diet and your crowning glory

- ❑ Dandruff and a dry scalp may signal a zinc deficiency. Eat more oily fish (tuna, sardines and mackerel), red meat and nuts and seeds (such as pumpkin)
- ❑ Lacklustre hair is often caused by a lack of vitamin A. Nibbling on dried apricots gives a good boost.
- ❑ Greasy hair can be exacerbated by eating too much sugar.

Beautiful Britain

Windsor Castle, Berkshire

The largest inhabited castle in the world, Windsor Castle, and its predecessors on this site, have been home to royalty for more than 900 years. This is where William the Conqueror relaxed after hunting in the surrounding forest, but it was with Queen Victoria that it became so central to the lives of the royal family. Windsor is the final resting place for many royals, including Henry VI, Henry VIII, his wife Jane Seymour, Charles I, Edward VII, George V, George VI and, more recently, his wife, Queen Elizabeth, the Queen Mother and their daughter, Princess Margaret.

The castle is said to house several ghosts, including those of Henry VIII, who is said to roam the corridors, groaning, and his second wife, Anne Boleyn, who has been seen in one of the windows.

King George III was kept at the castle while his mental state deteriorated. He died here on January 29, 1820, and it is said he has been seen at the window of the room where he spent his last days.

"You must be joking"

A man wrote in to a newspaper Agony Aunt for some advice. 'I must get this off my chest. I made this awful golf shot and the ball didn't go anywhere near the green. In fact it landed on this bloke's head and killed him. What should I do?'

Agony Aunt, 'Try and get more rhythm in your swing'.

DO YOU REMEMBER...

PIC: HULTON ARCHIVE

Arthur Askey and Richard Murdoch

...BBC Radio's Bandwaggon

BY the end of the 1930s, 98 per cent of the population could 'listen in' to the BBC's radio services. Nearly nine million 10s (50p) listening licences had been taken out.

Around this time, the BBC decided to broaden the scope of its dance band shows by adding a resident comedian. Arthur Askey and Richard Murdoch provided the comedy and their spots soon came to dominate the show.

Many of their sketches had Arthur and Richard sharing a top-floor flat in Broadcasting House, along with Lewis the goat and pigeons named Basil, Lucy, Ronald and Sarah. Other regular characters included Mrs Bagwash, the char, and her daughter, Nausea, both of whom were often referred to but never heard. Arthur was courting Nausea but he never seemed to be getting anywhere.

Their adventures often ended violently with the famous Bandwaggon crash – and it was the first show to use catchphrases in a big way. 'Big-hearted Arthur, that's me', 'Ah, happy days', and 'Ay thang yew' – a pronunciation that Arthur had picked up from London bus conductors.

The last show was broadcast on December 2, 1939, and featured the departure of Arthur and Richard from their famous flat which left many listeners in tears.

...Kunzle Cakes

DELICIOUS, melt-in-the-mouth Kunzle cakes with the jelly sweets on the top were sold in their thousands. Perhaps, we don't see them in the shops today because we're all too weight conscious!

Kunzles were created by Swiss born Christian Kunzle, who came to Britain in 1896, to train as a pastry chef. His fame as a cake maker and caterer grew nationwide.

GREEN FINGERS

Brits for all seasons

PIC: EMAP GARDENING PICTURE LIBRARY

IS your garden or allotment looking neglected? Well, spring is nearly here and excuses about the cold and damp won't work any more. Gardening is a rather British passion. In other European countries, a homeowner's land is his land and that's that – unless he has a vineyard or an orange grove to tend – but we Brits are happiest with a perfect lawn and weed-free borders.

Allotments have been around for longer than you might imagine. In fact, small Celtic fields in Land's End, Cornwall, dating from around 100BC, are still in use today as allotments.

Urbanisation of Britain following the Industrial Revolution heralded the suburban garden, and Victorian gardens reflected new wealth and an influx of exotic plants from overseas. The flowers in an 'English country garden' were immortalised in a 19th century song, composer unknown:

How many kinds of sweet flowers grow
In an English country garden?
We'll tell you now of some that we know
Those we miss you'll surely pardon
Daffodils, heart's ease and flox
Meadowsweet and lady smocks
Gentian, lupine and tall hollihocks
Roses, foxgloves, snowdrops, blue forget-me-nots
In an English country garden.

The potting shed is also a typically British retreat. There's something infinitely cosy about sheltering in a shed with the rain bouncing off the felt roof.

The British are famed for talking about the weather. But whatever happened to the natural progression of our seasons? It's just as well the supermarkets stock 'seasonal' produce all year round, as we often desire toasted crumpets in July and summer fruits in November given the unpredictability of the British climate!

And the winner is...

Relive the excitement of the Oscars without having to sit through the acceptance speeches.

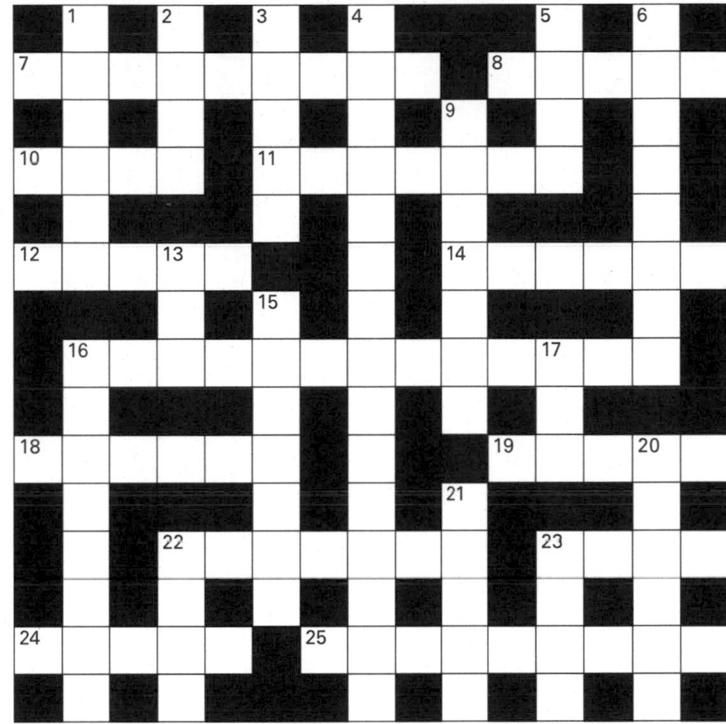

Solution on Page 159

ACROSS

7 Roman epic, starring Russell Crowe, which was voted Best Picture at the 2001 ceremony (9)
8 Surname of the actress who won Oscars for Dangerous and Jezebel (5)
10 The ___ in Winter, film for which Katharine Hepburn won a record-breaking third Oscar (4)
11 First name of actor Peck, winner for 1962's To Kill a Mockingbird (7)
12 Ben ___, screenwriter nominated for Wuthering Heights and winner for The Scoundrel (5)
14 Surname of Ron, who won the Best Director for A Beautiful Mind (2002) (6)
16 Star who won the Best Actress award for Roman Holiday (6,7)
18 Surname of Sissy, who has five leading actress nominations, and one win for Coal Miner's Daughter (6)
19 1955 film in which Oscar-winning Ernest Borgnine played a Bronx butcher (5)
22 Surname of Faye, winner for 1976 drama, Network (7)
23 1980 Alan Parker musical about performing arts students, whose score and title song won Oscars (4)
24 Surname of actress Tatum, whose film debut in the 1973 Paper Moon won her a Best Supporting Actress Oscar (5)
25 The Diary of ___, 1959 wartime drama for which Shelley Winters' supporting role won an Oscar (4,5)

DOWN

1 ___ Trevor, Oscar-winning supporting actress in Key Largo (6)
2 East of ___, 1955 film for which Jo Van Fleet won the Best Supporting Actress award (4)
3 1996 Coen Brothers film for which Frances McDormand won a Best Actress award (5)
4 1939 Hollywood classic which was showered with Oscars, including one for Vivien Leigh (4,4,3,4)
5 First name of actor Cooper, Oscar winner for Sergeant York and High Noon (4)
6 1931's Best Picture, a western saga starring Irene Dunne and Richard Dix (8)
9 Veteran comedian and actor who has hosted more than fifteen Oscar ceremonies (3,4)
13 1963 Paul Newman western for which Patricia Neal won a Best Actress award (3)
15 The Lost ___, Best Picture of 1945, starring Ray Milland and Jane Wyman (7)
16 Actor with six nominations to his name when he finally won an Oscar for 1992's Scent of a Woman (2,6)
17 First name of actress Thurman, nominated for her supporting role in the 1994 Pulp Fiction (3)
20 ___ Jerry, cartoon duo with eight Academy Awards to their name (3,3)
21 Surname of actress Winona, who was nominated for roles in The Age of Innocence in 1993 and Little Women in 1994 (5)
22 ___ Man Walking, 1995 drama for which Susan Sarandon won the Best Actress award (4)
23 Surname of John, four-times winner of the Best Director award, whose films include The Grapes of Wrath and The Quiet Man (4)

THE TEA DANCE SHOWDOWN

By Ariela Davis

Romance is in the air at a tea dance but tempers are set to flare...

On Friday afternoon Jim Spencer arrived at the Regal Hotel where he went directly to the men's room. He washed his hands, ran a comb through his neatly groomed hair and dusted imaginary specks off his dark grey suit. Jim gave himself a final check in the full-length mirror, clicked his heels smartly together, smiled at his reflection and congratulated himself on looking not half bad for a 72-year-old widower.

He walked towards the hotel's flower shop where he purchased a single red rose. Mary, the florist, helped him pin it to his buttonhole. "You're a one, you are – after the ladies again?" Jim gave her a wink. He'd been following this routine every Friday and it got him nicely in the mood for the hotel's tea dance.

Standing in the doorway of the restaurant, Jim took in the white-clothed tables laid out in a semi-circle around the highly polished dance floor. A white baby grand, double bass and drum kit stood on the raised platform in readiness for the musicians who would soon arrive with the rest of their instruments.

He smiled as he pictured himself dancing the tango with his favourite lady, then made his way to the table he always shared with his two pals, Steve and Derek.

"Hello, Jim," said Steve. "The usual faces again, except for that chap over there. Never seen him before!"

Jim didn't bother to look around. He was busy piling his plate with sandwiches and one of the cakes before his friends whipped the lot. "Yeah, and that woman you have a crush on, what's her name... Irene, Eileen? She's here too," said Derek.

"Her name is Eileen, and I wish you wouldn't talk about her like that, it's so common."

"Oh, stop being pompous! You like her, but haven't got the nerve to ask her out," said Derek. "I'm right aren't I?"

Jim sighed. It was true he did rather like Eileen Perry. He approved of the way she wore her hair pulled back in a bun at the nape of her neck and her blue eyes had an attractive twinkle He also appreciated the way she always wore a dress to the tea dance.

Every week he looked anxiously to see if she was there and would feel a warm glow when he saw her friendly face. He always danced with her but hadn't had the courage to suggest taking her home, and the idea of asking her out for a meal made him go all hot and clammy.

Eileen nudged her friend: "Look, Betty, Jim's arrived. Doesn't he look smart?" Eileen was so intent on admiring Jim, that it took her a moment to realise that Betty wasn't paying attention. "Who are you looking at?"

"That man," Betty inclined her head towards a newcomer who was making his way towards their table. "What's he doing coming over here?"

Dawn, who was just sitting down, followed Betty's gaze: "That's not on, he's got to wait for the music to start." Eileen could hear the others twittering at the break with protocol and glared at the advancing man. He stopped, turned and retreated.

Jim spluttered: "Did you see that? The cheek of the man, he's not been here five minutes and he's already flouting the rules."

"He was heading for Eileen's table. I wonder why he went back?" mused Steve.

Every week he looked anxiously to see if she was there and would feel a warm glow when he saw her friendly face

PIC: ARTVILLE

Jim sat scowling. This jumped up newcomer was holding her far too close

"He'd better not try anything on with Eileen or he'll have me to answer to," said Jim, now quite red in the face.

"Oh yeah?" said Derek. "You and whose army? He looks quite fit."

"Rubbish, he's a puny little devil." Jim eyed the new man. He looked as though he'd bought his suit at the Oxfam shop and his rather long, thinning hair was obviously touched at the sides with dye. Jim didn't like the look of him.

The musicians began to play the opening foxtrot. Jim pushed his way towards the dance floor. In his haste he almost trampled a waiter with a tray of empty glasses, and arrived at Eileen's table only to find the new man had beaten him to it.

Jim sat scowling. This jumped-up newcomer was holding her far too close. By their third dance together Jim was on the edge of his seat watching them like a hawk.

Then the bandleader announced there would be a Gentleman's Excuse Me. Jim shot out of his chair, heading straight for Eileen and her partner. He politely tapped the man on the shoulder. The man shrugged Jim's hand away and told him to 'clear off'. Jim pushed the man away from Eileen. The room went silent. Everyone held their breath as Jim drew back his arm, his fist clenched and eyes blazing. The man stepped back, holding up his hands. "I don't want a fight."

Jim turned to Eileen who smiled sweetly at him and placed her hand gently on his shoulder in readiness for the next dance. "That was rather dashing, it made me feel quite girlish." Feeling pleased with himself, he pulled her closer and whispered: "I'd do anything for you."

"You could buy me a drink, I could do with a rest."

While Jim was at the bar, Eileen turned to Betty and Dawn. "I thought that would do the trick."

"What do you mean?"

"Well, I'd have been in my dotage if I had waited for Jim to ask me out, so I thought I'd push things along. I asked John, an old friend, to come here today and pretend to be interested in me. I think he carried it off quite well."

Betty and Mary looked at Eileen open-mouthed. "You mean it was a set-up?"

"Of course, but don't ever let Jim know. Promise?" Eileen put her finger to her lips, as Jim came back from the bar with drinks for them all.

"Everything all right?" he asked.

"Everything is just fine." Eileen patted the chair next to her: "Come and sit by me."

April 2003

HIGH DAYS AND HOLIDAYS...

Easter time

These days, Easter is generally considered to span four days, Good Friday, Easter Eve, Easter Day and Easter Monday. The timing of these each year are determined by the day allocated to Easter Day, which is the Sunday after the first full moon following the Vernal Equinox on March 21.

Widow's Bun Ceremony (April 18)

A poor widow baked a bun to welcome her sailor son home from sea, but he never returned. To perpetuate her devotion, each Good Friday, a sailor or Wren adds a newly made 'hot crossed bun' to the netted cluster which hangs permanently from the ceiling of the Widow's Son pub at Bromley-by-Bow in London's East End, the site of the widow's cottage.

PIC: HULTON ARCHIVE

Easter Monday traditions

For more than a century, the Cart Horse Parade has been held at Regent's Park in London. Huge horses laden with brasses and regalia are put through their heavy paces.

The Coal Carrying Championships at Gawthorpe near Wakefield is a relatively new tradition, started in 1963, following an 'I'm the toughest' argument in a local hostelry. Men carry 55k of coal, women 20k up a slight hill for just under a mile.

TUESDAY	1	April Fool's Day
WEDNESDAY	2	
THURSDAY	3	
FRIDAY	4	
SATURDAY	5	
SUNDAY	6	
MONDAY	7	
TUESDAY	8	
WEDNESDAY	9	
THURSDAY	10	
FRIDAY	11	
SATURDAY	12	
SUNDAY	13	Palm Sunday
MONDAY	14	
TUESDAY	15	
WEDNESDAY	16	
THURSDAY	17	
FRIDAY	18	Good Friday (Bank Holiday)

SATURDAY	19	
SUNDAY	20	Easter Day
MONDAY	21	Queen's birthday Easter Monday (Bank Holiday, except Scotland)
TUESDAY	22	
WEDNESDAY	23	St George's Day
THURSDAY	24	
FRIDAY	25	
SATURDAY	26	
SUNDAY	27	
MONDAY	28	
TUESDAY	29	
WEDNESDAY	30	May YOURS on sale

This month don't forget to...

- ☐ Sow tender vegetables if the weather's mild.
- ☐ Watch out for those April showers – and don't forget your umbrella.
- ☐ On Easter Sunday, hide some eggs in the garden for the grandchildren and send them on an egg hunt!
- ☐ Wear a red rose to mark St George's Day.

The Beatles

PIC: HULTON ARCHIVE

It happened in April...

April 21, 1964: The BBC's second television channel started transmission.

April 9, 1970: The Beatles split up.

April 12, 1983: Sir Richard Attenborough's acclaimed film Gandhi scooped a staggering eight Oscars.

April 13, 1991: A man was jailed for three years after driving his mechanical digger into the front of a house, causing £45,000 of damage, when the owner refused to heat his lunch in her microwave.

March 31-April 6

I WISH I'D SAID THAT...

"Oh, to be in England
Now that April's there."
– Robert Browning, English poet

TIP TIME

To whiten the tips of your nails, plunge them in the flesh of half a lemon for a few minutes.

Letter of my life

In 1935 I was going out with the boyfriend who would become my husband. One day I overheard my parents say they weren't married. This shocked me as it was considered terrible in those days. I wrote my boyfriend a note, telling him I couldn't see him any more. The letter I received back changed my life because it said…'My Dear Anne, in the words of an old song, I don't care what you used to be. I know what you are today and I love you.'

I married him in 1939 and we had 52 years of happy marriage. He died in 1971 and I have never married again.

Anne Foley, Sheffield

"You must be joking"

In an office, 'Would the person who took the step ladder yesterday please bring it back or further steps will be taken.'

Pause for thought

'I saw the following in a café in Tenby, Wales,' writes Walter King of Bath. 'Unfortunately, I don't know who wrote it, but I think it's food for thought.'

The Clock of Life

The clock of life is wound but once
And no one has the power
To tell just when the hands will stop
At late or early hour.

Now is the only time you own;
Live, toil, love with a will,
Place no thought for tomorrow, for
The clock may then be still.

TEA-TIME TREATS

Mini Egg Crispies

Makes 16

- 7 oz/200 g Cadbury's Dairy Milk chocolate
- 4 oz/100 g butter, softened
- 1 oz/25 g desiccated coconut or crushed biscuits
- 3 oz/75 g crisped rice cereal

Icing:

- 1 lb/450 g icing sugar
- Finely grated rind and strained juice from 1 lemon
- 1 tube Cadbury's Mini Eggs

1 Melt chocolate, then stir in remaining ingredients.
2 Spread mixture in lightly greased 7 x 11 in/18 x 28 cm Swiss roll tin and set. Later, cut into 16 finger shapes but leave in the tin.
3 Sieve icing sugar into bowl, add lemon rind and juice and just enough water to make a coating icing. Spread over fingers.
4 Press three Mini Eggs on to each finger, then lift out, trim edges and leave to set.

PIC: CADBURY TREBOR BASSETT

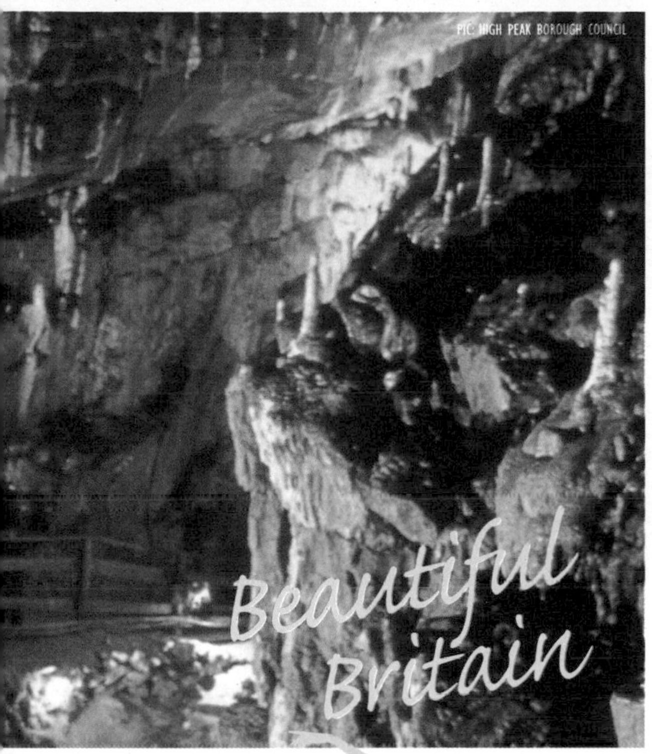

Buxton, Derbyshire

Buxton is a spa town on the edge of the Peak District. Although its natural spring was discovered by the Romans in 78AD, and was a popular spa in the time of Elizabeth I, its golden age was in the 19th century when visitors flocked to the area to use the town's thermal baths, aided by the arrival of a railway in 1863, which made access easier.

Nearby is Poole's Cavern, a spectacular limestone cave with masses of stalactites and stalagmites, and the source of Derbyshire's River Wye.

This region is home to Buxton spring water and, according to geologists, the water that we can buy in bottles fell as rain more than 5,000 years ago!

The water filters through a layer of limestone deep in the ground and emerges through a spring in the town itself, its warm temperature indicating that it has been pushed up 1,500m or more, propelled upwards by the heat of the rocks deep in the earth.

Healthy Living

Caffeine – the facts

A cup of coffee has 100-150 mg of caffeine; doctors recommend a maximum of five cups a day. By contrast, a cup of tea has 20-50mg of caffeine. This level may surprise you, but bear in mind that tea may guard against heart disease, due to the presence of naturally occurring chemicals called flavenoids, which prevent the build up of fatty deposits in the arteries.

Well, fancy that!

It's impossible to sneeze with your eyes open.

Treasured Photo

John Miles, writing from Chesterfield, well remembers a voyage from South Africa:

'It was on Friday, April 1, 1949, that I left Cape Town on board RMS Pretoria Castle bound for Southampton after completing my National Service with the Royal Army Pay Corps. After three days at sea a young woman stowaway was found, who turned out to be a communist sympathiser. It was quickly decided to deny her permission to land in the UK, so RMS Edinburgh Castle, already en route to the Cape, was ordered to meet us at an arranged venue so that the young woman could be returned to South Africa.

The photograph was taken on Thursday, April 7, at 11.05 am and shows the exchange of the stowaway and some hastily arranged mail. The occasion caused a lot of excitement – and was timed to perfection!'

April 7-13

Treasured Photo

Mrs G Broom of Bristol writes:
'I saw this Mini in Oxford Street, London around 20 years ago and couldn't resist taking a photo. It was for some charity or other and had gold-painted pennies (old money) all over it. I wonder what became of it?'

Well, fancy that!
The average person falls asleep in 7 minutes.

Tea-time Treats

Walnut scones

An easy recipe with no rubbing in, from Olivia Black from Riley, Yorks:

Makes 8
- 8 oz/225 g SR flour
- 1 level teaspoon mixed spice
- Pinch salt
- 2 oz/50 g caster sugar
- 2 oz/50 g walnuts, chopped
- 2 tablespoons cooking oil
- 1 egg, beaten
- 3-4 tablespoons milk

1 Pre-heat oven to 220°C/425°F/Gas Mark 7.
2 Sieve flour, spice and salt into a mixing bowl.
3 Stir in sugar, walnuts, oil, egg and enough milk to form a soft dough. Knead lightly.
4 Roll out on a floured surface to ½-¾ in/1-1½ cm thickness. Cut into 2 in/5 cm rounds.
5 Place on a greased baking tray and brush with milk. Bake for 10 minutes until well-risen and golden.

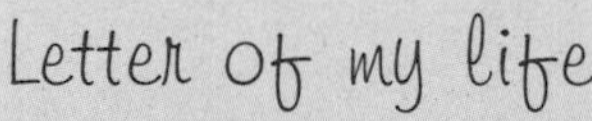

After my husband died three years ago I had a breakdown.

One day I was told about a workplace called Standen Enterprises, near Morecambe. It is for people like me who suffer a breakdown or have schizophrenia. My social worker helped me to fill in the form and eventually I had a letter inviting me to an interview. It changed my life.I started at Standen Enterprises a fortnight later.

Standen Enterprises is a very therapeutic place and I have also started a computer course.

But most of all, I've found sincere love and friendship.

Christine Nelson, Morecambe, Lancashire

Q Doctor, doctor, will you help me out?
A Certainly, which way did you come in?

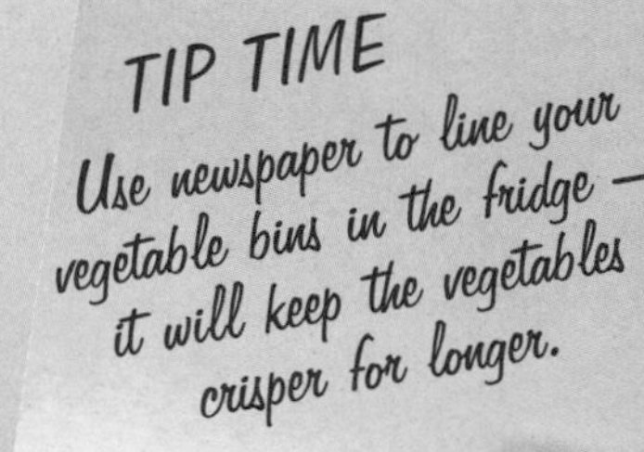

TIP TIME
Use newspaper to line your vegetable bins in the fridge — it will keep the vegetables crisper for longer.

Lyme Regis, Dorset

This pretty seaside town has a literary claim to fame – the ancient Cobb Harbour is where the French Lieutenant's Woman (played by Meryl Streep in the film adaptation) stood and stared out to sea in John Fowles's famous novel and it is also the setting for Jane Austen's novel, Persuasion.

Lyme Regis is also world-famous for its fossils. One of its most renowned 19th century residents, Mary Anning, found a plesiosaur (a marine dinosaur that grew up to around 35 feet long) and a pterodactyl (a flying dinosaur) when she was just 12 years old.

In the waters of Lyme Bay, you can find all sorts of sea creatures, including sharks and congers. And in this week last year Chesil Beach, a huge, beautiful sweep of shingle, made the national news when it was visited by a friendly dolphin, who frolicked near the shore with local swimmers in the early spring sunshine.

Pause for thought

'I cannot tell you how many kindred spirits share my copy of YOURS (as much as I would like to keep it for myself),' writes Doreen Wade, from Hereford. 'And so it travels a few miles – once I set it in motion. I am also inspired by readers' poetry. I have always loved the spring, and wrote this poem after a day spent strolling in a Sussex woodland with my late husband.'

The Bluebell Wood

Have you walked amidst the glory of an
English bluebell wood,
Felt serenity enfold you as you never
dreamt it could,
Breathed the haunting tender fragrance
borne upon a gentle breeze,
Gazed in wonder at the beauty spread
beneath protective trees?
Listened to a singing blackbird perched
upon a hazel bush
As the peace caressed your spirit – far
away from noise and rush?
If you have – then Nature beckoned,
bidding you to be her guest
To share these lovely gifts from Heaven –
my friend, you have been truly blessed.

I wish I'd said that...

"Rain – what taxi drivers pray for and pedestrians pay for."
– Lewis Grizzard

Healthy Living

Improve your posture

- ❏ Pay attention to the way you sit and stand. Sit with a straight back and your feet flat on the floor and stand up straight, shoulders back, tummy muscles pulled in and pelvis tilted forward.
- ❏ Focus on your breathing while gently contracting your stomach muscles. Do this several times a day.
- ❏ Stretching and regular activity such as walking helps to unlock tightened muscles that contribute to poor posture.
- ❏ Laugh! This will release tension in your tummy and back muscles.

April 14-20

TIP TIME

To remove scuff marks from lino, rub the marks away with a large eraser (rubber).

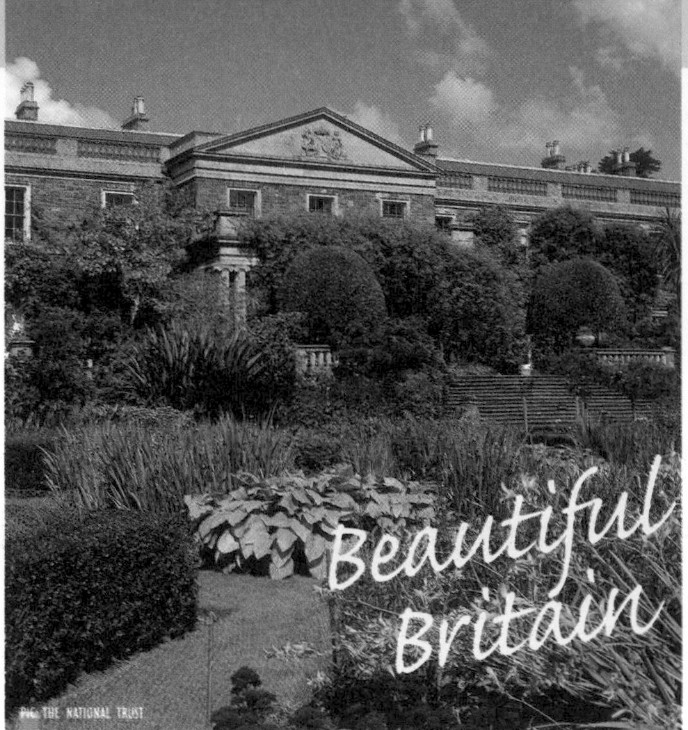

Mount Stewart House, Ards Peninsula, Northern Ireland

The gardens at Mount Stewart House, on the shore of Strangford Lough, are ranked among the National Trust's top six, and were designed as a series of outdoor 'rooms', where the mild climate of the Ards Peninsula allows many rare plants to thrive.

The garden was created by Lady Londonderry, wife of the seventh Marquess of Londonderry, in the 1920s and was influenced by various styles, including that of Gertrude Jekyll.

The famous Dodo Terrace contains stone figures of dodos, dinosaurs and other creatures – supposedly representations of family and friends in animal form. The gardens also feature some interesting topiary shapes – including an Irish harp!

Other areas of the gardens include: A Spanish garden, an Italian garden, a sunken garden and a shamrock garden and in the centre of the grounds is a picturesque five-acre lake.

Before the creation of these formal gardens, Mount Stewart House was the Irish home of Robert Stewart, who was the foreign secretary of England during the Napoleonic Wars.

Pause for thought

Easter

Hedgerows are waking,
Flowers open their eyes.
Songbirds are giving
Their song to the skies.

Sweet willow and catkin,
And daffodils bright,
Dispel gloom and sadness,
And put fears to flight.

Christ's passion is over.
The winter has gone.
Rejoice with the songbirds,
His victory is won.

Mrs M Peake, Stoke on Trent

"You must be joking"

Church bulletin howlers:

- At the evening service tonight, the sermon topic will be What Is Hell? Come early and listen to our choir practice.
- Don't let worry kill you, let the church help.

I wish I'd said that...

'Twas Easter Sunday. The full blossomed trees
Filled all the air with fragrance and with joy.

– Henry Wadsworth Longfellow, American poet

Letter of my life

Jessie Armitage, Trevarrian, Cornwall

The most important letter of my life was indeed a special delivery. A Humber car drew up at my gate and down the path walked a uniformed chauffeur who handed me a letter. It was from my boss – and very brief. It said, 'After you left the office your husband rang. He is safely back in England and will be with you tomorrow. Take two days off.'

As I remember that letter, my heart still flutters. We had been apart since the day after our wedding in December 1941 and this was April 1945. A wartime letter, of course. What emotion, what joy, what relief it brought. A letter to remember over the years.

HEALTHY LIVING

Sugar in disguise

Just because you can't see sugar on the list of a food's ingredients doesn't mean that it isn't there. The modern food industry uses many different types in the manufacturing process. So if you're trying to cut down on your sugar intake, look out for these names – sucrose, lactose, maltose, fructose, honey, molasses, glucose, dextrose, corn syrup and invert syrup. They're all the same basic ingredient, sugar.

TREASURED PHOTO

Lilian Fry writes from Wootton, Bedford: 'Here I am (*on the left*), with my friend Margaret Downing in Petticoat Lane in 1949. It was a cold Easter Sunday morning, hence my headscarf and big fur gloves – fashionable at the time. I'm also wearing my 'New Look' powder blue coat and black patent ankle-strap shoes. We both bought flowers from a barrow boy, two bunches for a shilling – too good a bargain to miss. We said we would go back the next Sunday but we never did. We went to the Kursaal at Southend instead!'

Well, fancy that!

Eskimos use fridges to stop their food from freezing.

TEA-TIME TREATS

Bunny Biscuits

Makes 10 to 20

- 4 oz/100 g butter, cut into small pieces
- 6 oz/175 g plain flour
- 2 oz/50 g light brown soft sugar
- ½ teaspoon ground cinnamon
- Grated rind of 1 lemon
- 1 large egg yolk
- 2-3 tablespoons milk

To decorate:

- Mini-marshmallows, currants, royal icing

1 Preheat oven to 180°C/350°F/Gas Mark 4.
2 Rub butter and flour together until resembles fine breadcrumbs. Stir in the sugar, cinnamon, lemon rind, egg yolk and enough milk to bind the mixture into a soft dough.
3 Knead lightly on a floured surface until smooth. Roll out ¼ in/5 mm thick. Cut out rabbit shapes using a shaped cutter and lift on to two ungreased baking sheets.
4 Bake for 10-15 minutes until golden. Cool, then place on a wire rack. Leave until cold.
5 Decorate with mini-marshmallow tails and currant eyes, fixed in place with a little royal icing.

PIC: TATE & LYLE SUGARS

April 21-27

I wish I'd said that...

"Advice is what we ask for when we already know the answer but wish we didn't."
– Erica Jong, American poet and writer

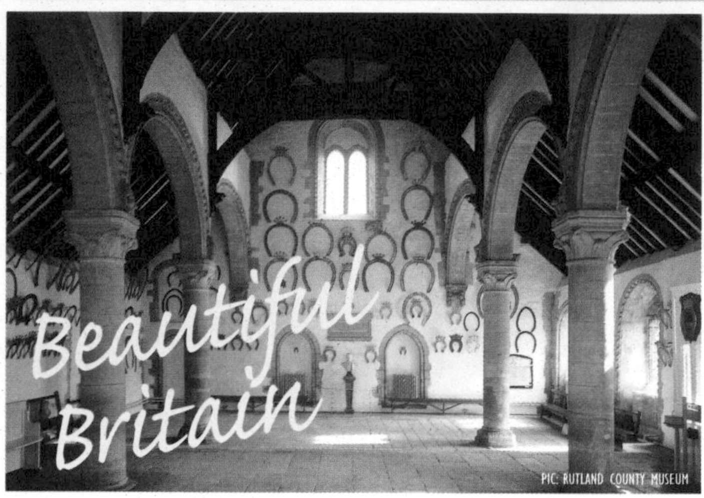

PIC: RUTLAND COUNTY MUSEUM

Oakham, Rutland

The Domesday Book records that the town of Oakham once belonged to Anglo Saxon queens, then passed to William the Conqueror following the death of Edward the Confessor's wife, Edith.

All that remains of Oakham Castle today is the Great Hall, which is hung with more than 200 horseshoes. A horseshoe, or sufficient funds for one to be cast, was the toll levied by the lord of the manor of Oakham on all royalty and peers who passed through the town.

The oldest surviving horseshoe is one put up by Edward IV in around 1470, and there are also horseshoes from prominent members of the royal family through the years including Elizabeth I, George IV, Victoria and Elizabeth II.

Nearby is Rutland Water, the largest man-made lake in Europe, where watersports, fishing and birdspotting are very popular.

Oddly, there is a semi-submerged church here, which now houses the Water Museum, 100 yards from the shore and reached by a causeway. This is because, when the lake was created as a reservoir, many buildings were submerged, but the church was saved by raising its floor level.

Letter of my life

Delia Tearrell, Southminster, Essex

In 1964 my husband and I had three young children under the age of three. We couldn't afford the deposit for a property of our own so we were renting a small house, which consisted of a living room and kitchen downstairs, two bedrooms upstairs and an outside toilet. We were desperate to find a bigger house and we would take the children out most weekends to get away from the cramped conditions.

Then one morning a letter dropped through our letterbox. It was from the local council informing us that we'd been allocated a new council house because our property had been condemned as unfit for human habitation. I was jumping up and down, crying tears of joy. The children must have thought I was going mad.

Our new home was a three-bedroom property with a downstairs cloakroom, central heating and a garage. We were in seventh heaven!

That letter from the council was the best letter we have ever received. It gave us the chance to give our three lovely children a happy and stable start to their young lives.

Healthy Living

Go on, smile!

Those blessed with their own teeth need to take extra care with them as the years go by. Use an electric brush for most effective cleaning. Otherwise, choose a small-headed, soft-to-medium brush and change it frequently. To make sure you don't apply too much pressure, hold the brush like a pen. Of course, most important of all are regular check-ups.

Well, fancy that!

It's easy to remember the order of the planets using this simple saying: My very eager mother just served us nine pizzas (Mercury, Venus, Earth, Mars, Jupiter, Saturn, Uranus, Neptune, and Pluto)

TIP TIME

If your honey has crystallized, stand the jar in a bowl of hot water. Stir when softened until smooth and runny.

TREASURED PHOTO

Among several photographs sent in by Mrs Sylvia Hancock of Addlestone, Surrey was this fascinating reminder of traditional grocery stores:
'The photo shows my Dad outside the International Stores in Peckham, where he was the manager, with his staff. In the First World War he was badly wounded at Cambrai.'

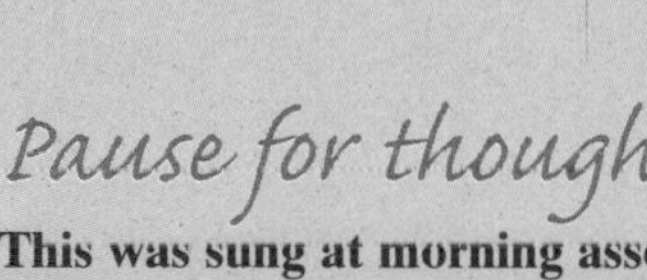

Pause for thought

This was sung at morning assembly at my school, Meanwood Road Council School, Leeds, about 1942, writes Mrs E Hall. I have never heard of it since but it brings back many happy memories and is especially appropriate to celebrate St George's Day (April 23):

England

Soft grey clouds on the dusky hills
are falling now.
Soft grey dreams to the lovers in
the vale.
For here and there the note of a bird
and everywhere so green.
Oh! England is the fairest land that I
have ever seen.

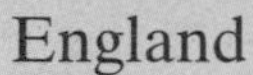

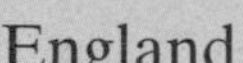

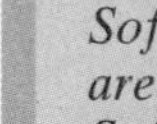

Oh, England I love you,
Your ever changing skies,
Your spinneys and your pastures
Your streams that wander wide.
A mother to be proud of
Wherever children roam;
There's joy in such an island
Forever she is my land.
Oh, England I love you,
England my home.

You must be joking

Three new potatoes were talking to their mother:
Potato 1: "When I grow up, I'm going to marry a King Edward."
Potato 2: "When I grow up, I'm going to marry a Jersey Royal."
Potato 3: "When I grow up, I'm going to marry Jimmy Hill."
"Oh no dear," says mother, "you can't do that – he's just a common-tater."

PERFECT PUDDINGS

Yoghurt Honeys

A favourite recipe from Rhiannon Evans of Llandrillo, Clwyd:

Makes 20-30

- 3 eggs, separated
- 2 tablespoons syrup
- 1 large tub yoghurt
- 6 oz/175 g plain flour
- 1 teaspoon bicarbonate of soda
- 2 teaspoons baking powder
- 2 oz/50 g butter
- Honey to serve

1. Beat egg yolks in a bowl. Add syrup and yogurt and beat well.
2. Sift flour with bicarb and baking powder, then mix thoroughly with egg yolk mixture to make a batter.
3. Melt butter and add to the batter.
4. Whisk egg whites until just stiff, then fold into the mixture.
5. Cook spoonfuls on a lightly greased griddle and brown on both sides. Serve hot with honey.

Do you remember...

Jimmy Savile established his career on Radio Luxembourg

...Radio Luxembourg?

FOR most listeners, commercial radio meant Radio Luxembourg, which was broadcast around Europe for 59 years, from 1933 to 1991. During the 1940s and '50s, thousands preferred its laid-back style to the more formal tones of the BBC. To listeners, pop music was a revelation – no speeches, gardening or cookery tips.

Roy Plomley became one of the first of many familiar voices who made their names on continental commercial radio. Another who appeared in the 1930s was a young Canadian, Hughie Green.

After the war, audiences were lured back by request shows and the chart countdown. And although there was still popular music in the schedules, there was also comedy, drama and quiz shows.

During the 1950s Jimmy Savile established his career on Luxembourg, as did David Jacobs who hosted the honeymoon show. With the advent of the 'swinging '60s', the radio station had to find a new, younger market. In doing so, millions of teenagers established the secret culture of listening to Luxembourg under the bedclothes!

... cleaning aids and elbow grease?

PURITAN soap, Parazone for snow-white linen and Bluebell Metal Polish – what did we do before them? Donkey soap for those deep-seated stains, Zeebrite for the cast-iron fireplace and Handy Andy for your paintwork.

With the surge of electrical appliances in the 1950s, new cleaning products appeared such as Daz and Omo, and Sqezy washing up liquid, which arrived in 1956. A new foaming cleaner from America rivalled the old scouring powders such as Vim and Ajax. And Flash powder had arrived to tackle the linoleum floors.

Brits for all seasons

The big spring-clean

The advent of spring spurs us on to have a good clear-out and get on with an old-fashioned spring-clean. It's probably something to do with the extra hours of daylight we've grown accustomed to.

All the unwanted Christmas gifts, the discarded magazines (YOURS excepted!) and the clothes which, for some inexplicable reason, no longer fit and have outstayed their welcome, need to be dispatched to pastures new.

PIC: BRIAN GIBBS

It's the new season of the bring-and-buy, the car-boot and the jumble sale. Any day now, Scouts and Guides will be calling, ready and willing to take away what we have sorted out.

It's an equally British trait – some might even call it an eccentricity – to rummage at those same sales. And, even if we don't end up re-buying our own discarded treasures, we'll probably come back laden with more knick-knacks and bargains that were just too good to miss. Well, it will give us something to clear out next spring!

We're always happy to do our bit for a good cause, whether it's to raise money at a bring-and-buy for church repairs or knit blanket squares for the Third World. The amount of cash raised annually by charities such as Children in Need and Comic Relief is testimony to the extraordinary generosity of which we are capable. British reserve means that we don't discuss such matters openly, but we do dig deep nonetheless.

Government statistics for the financial year 2000/01 state that the average weekly amount given by UK households was £46 million.

Code cracker

In this clueless crossword, every letter of the alphabet appears as a code number. All you have to do is crack the code and fill in the grid. We've decoded one letter to start you off, so you can write a 'B' wherever the number 25 appears in the grid. For a further clue, the word in the shaded squares is the name of the pictured spring flower. Use the smaller grid to keep track of letters you have deciphered.

25 B	21	2	23	25	23	21	21	■	3	26	15	10
2	■	12	■	3	■	15	■	16	■	4	■	23
8	15	17	23	14	■	18	2	3	14	14	23	21
12	■	2	■	24	■	2	■	19	■	1	■	3
22	3	14	10	■	13	15	13	3	26	15	16	22
■	■	1	■	9	■	10	■	25	■	■	■	23
11	23	23	10	23	14	■	3	21	8	4	7	10
2	■	■	■	3	■	25	■	23	■	12	■	■
14	15	25	3	21	10	14	22	■	6	15	17	12
7	■	3	■	4	■	23	■	8	■	7	■	14
15	7	26	21	2	10	23	■	3	21	15	25	15
17	■	4	■	17	■	20	■	17	■	4	■	20
5	4	7	23	■	17	23	7	16	23	7	26	23

A ~~B~~ C D E F G H
I J K L M N O P
Q R S T U V W X
Y Z

1	2	3	4	5	6	7	8	9	10	11	12	13
14	15	16	17	18	19	20	21	22	23	24	25 B	26

Solutions on Page 159

Logic problem

Give your powers of deductive reasoning a work-out.

Three youngsters decided to play April fool pranks on their unsuspecting families. Unfortunately, the victims failed to see the funny side of these tricks, and each child ended up with a punishment. From the six clues, can you work out each child's prank, the family member who fell for it, and the resulting punishment?

1 Tommy was not the child who put all the clocks in the house forward one hour.
2 The mother caught out by one of the pranks is not Molly's mum.
3 The child whose pocket-money was docked was being punished for putting salt in the sugar bowl.
4 One of the miscreants was sent to their bedroom in disgrace.
5 Jimmy, who played the trick on his brother, was not the prankster who was made to do the washing-up for a week as penance.
6 The father of one of the children was soaked by a bowl of water propped above the door.

Name	Prank	Victim	Punishment
Jimmy			
Molly			
Tommy			

HE WHO DARES, GRINS

By Patricia Hartman

We were all young once but that's often hard for today's youngsters to believe!

PIC: ARTVILLE

"Okay then, whose turn is it for a dare today?" asked Jody as she sat in the park, sipping cola with her school pals James, Peter and Lisa.

"Think it must be yours, James," said Peter, glad that it was his turn to laugh at someone else.

"I thought I had a go the time before last?"

"No, that was Pete."

"Okay," James sighed. "What do you dare me to do?"

"I know," said Jody. "How about doing what that bloke did on that advert?"

"What, spill sauce on his jumper?" joked Peter. "No, silly, run up to a total stranger and give her flowers!"

James liked the sound of that. Not too scary, couldn't get into trouble for it, and there was a cute 14-year-old girl from school he could see her not so far away on the swings!

"Okay, I'll do it," James agreed, trying to pretend this was really a scary thing to do but he was up to it.

"Of course," said Peter with a wicked grin, "we get to choose the woman."

"What?" James was aghast. "Hey, that's not fair!"

"Of course it's fair. You'd just pick someone you like the look of and that wouldn't be hard to do." Peter was enjoying the whole thing. "Ah yes, perfect! Over there in the pale blue hat and coat."

James scanned across the park. Finally he saw her, a small figure of an elderly woman. She was strolling along watching the children play. "Her!" exclaimed Peter.

Everyone laughed.

"Wow, an older woman!" teased Lisa. "Probably want you for her toy boy after this, Jim!" guffawed Peter.

"Okay, quit the jibes. I'm a man, I can do this." Everyone laughed even more.

Reluctantly James walked over to the nearest flowerbed. He checked that the park attendant wasn't looking and then grabbed a handful of carnations and some forget-me-nots. He found a piece of tissue in his pocket and wrapped it around the stems. Looking again to make sure that none of his classmates were around, he dashed off towards the woman.

She was watching children paddling in a small pool. James didn't know whether to run up to her and stuff them in her arms and run off again, or to casually approach her and risk having to explain.

No, he would approach her casually and offer them to her, and hope she didn't think he was going to mug her.

Gingerly he sidled up to her, trying not to make her

"Okay, quit the jibes. I'm a man, I can do this." Everyone laughed even more

jump. "Excuse me," he said nervously, "thought maybe you would like these."

He held the flowers at arms length and waited for a swipe around the ears with her handbag. It never came.

"Why, thank you very much," she said sweetly if somewhat surprised. "But why me?"

"I thought that maybe at your age you didn't get many nice surprises," he lied.

"You're right, young man, I don't! These are lovely flowers, thank you so much." A tear welled up in her eye.

"Are you okay?" He was suddenly concerned.

"Yes, yes... I'm sorry," she stammered, dabbing at her eyes with a handkerchief. "It just brought back a very special memory for me."

"Oh, I'm sorry." Now he felt guilty.

"No it's all right, young man. It's just that my dear late husband handed me flowers the day he asked me out."

James smiled at her, then surprised himself by saying: "Would you like a cup of tea?"

He felt sure that's what you

James just couldn't imagine Sylvia on a motorbike, and without a crash helmet!

did when someone was upset, offer them tea and sympathy.

"I'll tell you what," she smiled. "I'll buy you one and a cream cake too as a thank you for the flowers."

James was never one to miss a freebie, so he was delighted to accept. Together they walked to the little cafe near the lake. "I'm James by the way."

"And I'm Sylvia," she said and shook his hand. Inside the cafe they found a quiet corner and sat down. Sylvia ordered tea and cream cakes and then continued with her story. "My husband, Roland, came up to me with a bunch of flowers on the day we first met. He had seen me walking in the park on several occasions and had taken a fancy to me. Then one day he finally plucked up the courage to approach me. He gave me forget-me-nots. Rather symbolic, don't you think?"

"That's a lovely way to say hello," said James. "Yes – and you've had your first practice today!" They both laughed.

They eagerly tucked into their cakes.

"This is great, Sylvia," said James. "Tell me, was life very strict and proper when you where young? Didn't you find life boring?"

Sylvia laughed: "Good Lord, no! We knew how to have fun back then. I remember once my father was angry with me and grounded me for a week, I was 20 years old too! I was so desperate to see Roland that I shinned down the drainpipe to be with him. I had a heck of a job trying to climb back up later. Luckily my sister heard me and let me in by the back door."

"Did your father ever find out?"James was amazed.

"If he did, he never said."

"Cool.What else did you do?"

"Well, not many people had cars then but my brother had a motorbike and I loved to ride on the back. He would go at top speed down the straight roads and my long hair would fly wildly in the wind. We felt so free."

James just couldn't imagine Sylvia on a motorbike, and without a crash helmet!

She saw the look on his face and smiled. "You're like a lot of younger ones, James, you think that the old 'uns have always been old. You forget, we were young once too, we knew how to be daring."

"Did you ever do a dare?"

"Many a time. I was once dared to hang my knickers on the top of the village flagpole the night before the carnival"

"And did you?" "Of course!"

James burst out laughing. He knew what she'd said was right. He liked Sylvia.

"Do you always come to the park on a Friday?" he asked.

"Yes, do you?" "Yes, I meet my friends and we play dare or forfeit." He asked: "Can we have tea together again sometime?" She reminded him of his granny whom he had known only briefly.

She smiled. "Yes, that would be lovely, James."

James looked at his watch. "I'll have to get back to my friends now, they will wonder where I've been."

"Yes, you'd better, and it's been very nice meeting you." He stood up and shook her hand once more and then walked to the door. Turning, he said: "Thanks for the tea and cake."

"It has been my pleasure, and thanks for the flowers." "Maybe I could bring my friends next time?"

She laughed: "If you dare!"

May 2003

HIGH DAYS AND HOLIDAYS...

PIC: HULTON ARCHIVE

May Day (May 1)
This day marked the great festival to celebrate the coming of summer. Fairies were at their busiest, putting changelings in place of mortal babies, barriers between the 'other' world and our own being at their most permeable. The power of water was at its most potent today and in Somerset, May Day dew could wipe away freckles.
The hymn Te Deum Patrem Coilmus is sung from the tower at Magdalen College in Oxford at 6am on May Day. The bells then ring out and Morris Men dance, along with street music and entertainment.

Cheese rolling (first Sunday in May)
From 6pm, hardy competitors scramble down the three-in-one slope of Cooper's Hill, Brockworth in the Cotswolds – after a wood-encased cheese. Anyone can enter but it is not for the faint-hearted, as progress is usually by tumbling, sliding and turning head-over-heels to the bottom. First to the bottom of the hill wins the cheese.

Weighing in (late May)
The jocular custom of weighing the incoming and outgoing Mayors of High Wycombe, Bucks, takes place annually in May. This custom is said to have stemmed from a remark made by Queen Elizabeth I about the corpulence of High Wycombe's civil dignitaries.

THURSDAY	1	
FRIDAY	2	
SATURDAY	3	
SUNDAY	4	
MONDAY	5	May Day Bank Holiday
TUESDAY	6	
WEDNESDAY	7	
THURSDAY	8	
FRIDAY	9	
SATURDAY	10	
SUNDAY	11	
MONDAY	12	
TUESDAY	13	YOURS Summer Special on sale
WEDNESDAY	14	
THURSDAY	15	
FRIDAY	16	
SATURDAY	17	
SUNDAY	18	

MONDAY	19
TUESDAY	20 Chelsea Flower Show
WEDNESDAY	21 Chelsea Flower Show
THURSDAY	22 Chelsea Flower Show
FRIDAY	23 Chelsea Flower Show
SATURDAY	24
SUNDAY	25 Whitsunday
MONDAY	26 Bank Holiday
TUESDAY	27
WEDNESDAY	28
THURSDAY	29
FRIDAY	30 June YOURS on sale
SATURDAY	31

This month don't forget to...

- [ ] Harden off bedding and container plants. Sow some parsley outdoors. And when you've done that...

- [ ] Find a sheltered sunny spot in your garden and take time out with a cup of tea and the monthly YOURS Puzzles magazine!

Princess Margaret

PIC: MIRROR

It happened in May...

May 24, 1902: Empire Day was celebrated for the first time.

May 9, 1932: Piccadilly in London was lit by electricity for the first time.

May 13, 1940: Winston Churchill made his famous 'blood, toil, sweat and tears' speech.

May 24, 1977: Princess Margaret and Lord Snowdon were divorced.

April 28-May 4

TREASURED PHOTO

This photo was sent in by Mrs Kathy Jackson (née Bethell) of Newport, who writes:

'This was my first school, in Oldham, and I am seated, third from right, in the second row. The school was closed when the war started, to use the premises as a first-aid post, and we were all sent to other schools. On either side of me are my two best friends, Barbara Fielding (now Barker) and Judith Whitehead (later Atkinson). Another friend, May Broom née Rowbottom is standing on a chair, top left.'

Pause for thought

Things that mean the most

It's little things in life that make the memories
It's little things in life that warm the heart.
You may be someone popular or famous
You'll make a lot of money if you're smart.

But it's little things in life that you'll remember
When you sit and reminisce of days gone by.
The happiness you shared with your family
You'll remember that until the day you die.

Just to think of walks and picnics in the summer
And games you played in winter with the snow.
You can turn the pages in your book of memories
To any time or place you used to know.

You'll remember with affection your dear old mum and dad.
It's worth more than any money you'll possess.
The way they used to say goodnight at bed-time,
With a tender hug and kisses, then 'God Bless'.

It's little things in life that make the memories
You can share them with your friends and even boast.
If they're lucky just like you they'll have memories too.
It's little things in life that mean the most.

Hazel Rose, Basingstoke, Hampshire

PERFECT PUDDINGS

Banana Puffs

Makes 24

- 1 lb/500 g sweet potatoes, cooked and mashed
- 2 ripe bananas, mashed
- ½ oz/10 g butter, melted
- 2 eggs, separated
- ¼ teaspoon salt
- 5 fl oz/150 ml hot milk or cream
- ¼ teaspoon nutmeg

1. Preheat oven to 200°C/400°F/ Gas Mark 6.
2. Mix the potatoes and bananas together, then add the melted butter, egg yolk, salt, milk or cream, nutmeg and beat together.
3. In another bowl, beat the egg whites until stiff. Gently fold into the potato mixture.
4. Spoon the mixture in tablespoonfuls, well apart, on to a greased baking sheet.
5. Cook the puffs for 12-15 minutes or until golden brown. Dust with icing sugar.

Well, fancy that!

Half the world's population has seen at least one James Bond movie.

"You must be joking"

Bald man: "I say Inspector, my wig has been stolen. Has it been handed in?"
Policeman: "Not yet, sir, but we are combing the area."

Letter of my life

The letter of my life was written many years ago by my mother, in a moment of great worry.

It begins with my birth, a difficult one, which meant my mother was unable to have any further pregnancies. And I myself became very ill with various life-threatening ailments, finally entering hospital with rheumatic fever.

As time went on, doctors advised my mother that her only child did not have a future (I am now 75).

Perhaps now I can look back and see that my mother, fearing the worst, was trying to hold fast with a desperate plea that I would be spared. Her words conveyed her innermost feelings, not really to be sent to me but written to ease her own suffering.

It was found after her death, many years later, among a parcel of items from my baby days that had been kept lovingly. But nestling among them were the words that I have treasured so deeply since…a mother's cry for help:

To You from Mother
– And I shall think of you
Whenever I am most happy
Whenever I am most sad
Whenever I see a
beautiful thing.
You are a burning lamp to me,
a flame
The wind cannot blow out, and
I shall hold you
High in my hand against
whatever darkness.

John R Eachus, Wirral

TIP TIME

Clean your bathroom mirror and then apply a mixture of water with a tiny bit of soap in it. Wipe dry. Now you won't have to keep wiping away the 'fog' on the mirror when getting ready.

HEALTHY LIVING

Fruit and veg

Snack on raw vegetables – pop a few in your mouth as you prepare them for cooking.

- ❑ Don't chop veg until you're ready to cook, and don't chop too finely.
- ❑ Don't leave chopped vegetables standing in water.
- ❑ Make sure the water is boiling before adding veg – the shorter the cooking time the higher the vitamin and mineral content.

I WISH I'D SAID THAT…

"April showers bring forth May flowers."
– Proverb

TOTNES, DEVON

Totnes is an ancient market town, built on a hill above the River Dart. It has a long history as a borough, having been given a charter of independence by King John in 1206. Medieval legend has it that, following the ancient war between Greece and Troy, the defeated Trojans, led by a prince named Brutus, set out to find a new home. Arriving at a beautiful, virtually uninhabited island, Brutus leapt ashore on to a boulder and proclaimed this place, which he called Totnes, his new home. According to the myth, the island was then named Britain, after Brutus himself.

Totnes was very wealthy in medieval times and the remains of its Norman castle and town walls can still be seen. Totnes has a reputation as the alternative centre of the south-west – those interested in the arts and in all things New Age, come here.

Each spring, nearby Blackawton hosts what must be one of the most unusual competitions in Britain – the International Wormcharming Festival. Teams have five minutes to 'worm up', by damping the ground, then 15 minutes to catch as many worms as they can. All worms are returned to the ground after the contest!

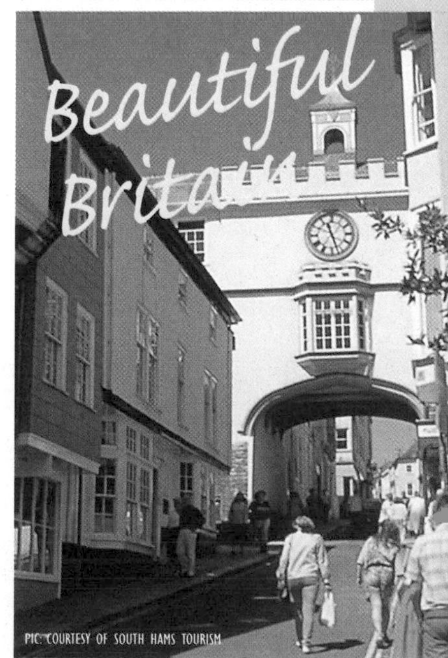

PIC: COURTESY OF SOUTH HAMS TOURISM

May 5-11

I WISH I'D SAID THAT...

"Blow trumpet, for the world is white with May. – Alfred Lord Tennyson, English poet"

TEA-TIME TREATS

Two-choc Brownies

Makes 12

- 2 oz/50 g plain chocolate, chopped
- 4 oz/100 g butter
- 2 large eggs, beaten
- 7 oz/200 g soft dark brown sugar
- 2 oz/50 g plain flour
- 1 teaspoon baking powder
- 2 oz/50 g toasted hazelnuts, roughly chopped (nuts optional)
- 2 oz/50 g white chocolate chips

1 Preheat oven to 180°C/350°F/Gas Mark 4. Grease a shallow rectangular tin 11 x 7½ in/ 28 x 19 cm and line with parchment.

2 Melt chocolate and butter together in a bowl over a saucepan of simmering water.

3 When melted, stir well, then remove bowl from saucepan and stir in eggs, sugar, flour, baking powder, hazelnuts (optional) and chocolate chips, mixing well.

4 Spoon mixture into the tin and level. Bake for 25-30 minutes. Cool slightly, then cut into 12 equal pieces. Cool on a wire rack.

PIC: TATE & LYLE SUGARS

PIC: THE NATIONAL TRUST PHOTOGRAPHIC LIBRARY/ROBERT THRIFT

GRASMERE, CUMBRIA

Grasmere is famous as the home of the poet William Wordsworth, who lived there in the first half of the 19th century and is buried in the village churchyard along with his sister, Dorothy, and his wife, Mary.

William and Dorothy would take walks together, and she would describe the sights in her journal. Some of the things she described were also the subjects of her brother's famous poems.

Grasmere is also home to an annual rushbearing ceremony, which dates back to ancient times when church floors were made of bare earth and covered with rushes. Parishioners would bring sweet-smelling rushes at the feasts of dedication to freshen the air (it was common at this time to bury the dead in the church, as well as in the churchyard) and help keep out the cold.

This became known as 'rushbearing'. The practice stopped in the 19th century, when stone floors were laid, but in a few villages, including Grasmere, the tradition continues, with a procession bearing wild flowers and rushes that ends at the church. Traditionally, Grasmere children who have carried rushes are given a special piece of gingerbread.

Well, fancy that!

The most populated city in the world is Tokyo, with 30 million residents.

HEALTHY LIVING

Beating middle-age spread

- ❏ Switch to healthier eating habits that you can stick with for life.
- ❏ Exercise increases your metabolism, which means you will burn more calories.
- ❏ Eat a varied diet.
- ❏ Aim to drink two litres of water each day.
- ❏ Stock up on healthy nibbles – grapes, dried fruit, celery, apples and carrot sticks.

Pause for thought

'A few years ago I spent some time in hospital, feeling I might never be well again,' writes Joyce Swinburn from Cramlington, Northumberland. 'One day my husband visited me, bringing with him a card from a dear friend. On the front of the card was the following prayer. I read it every day and believe it paved the way for my better health.'

I Said a Prayer for You Today

I said a prayer for you today
And know God must have heard.
I felt the answer in my heart
Although He spoke no word.
I didn't ask for wealth or fame
I knew you wouldn't mind.
I asked Him to send treasures
Of a far more lasting kind.
I asked that He'd be near you
At the start of each new day
To grant you health and blessings
And friends to share the way.
I asked for happiness for you
In all things great and small
But it was for His loving care
I prayed the most of all.

"You Must be joking"

A young lad was working at a farm during the school holidays and the farmer told him to count the sheep in a field. Quick as a flash, the youngster replied: "There are 517 sheep in the field." The farmer was amazed. "How did you count them so quickly?" he asked. "Easy," said the boy. "I just counted their legs and divided the total by four."

Treasured Photo

This group of children, evacuees from Butler Street School, Liverpool, were photographed in 1941 in Abererch, a village near Pwllheli, North Wales. Redvers Bucknell, now living in Cornwall (2nd row, 3rd from the right), writes:

'We were evacuated to Abererch in 1941 after the May Blitz. We had our lessons with Miss Forbes in the village hall. I lived with Mr and Mrs Evans and had a good time there. I kept in touch with them, and with their son and his wife, until they died.'

Letter of my life

The letter that changed my life arrived in a large manila envelope bearing a Boston, Lincolnshire, postmark and was accompanied by several photographs.

I had been waiting for a particular letter for a fortnight but I knew no one in Lincolnshire. It had been a long wait – 53 years to be precise. That was how long ago my younger brother had been given up for adoption. I had never seen him. He had been adopted at birth, and not long afterwards, due to the early death of my father and my mother's ongoing illness, I had been placed with foster parents. I had no knowledge of other family members, and it was not until my own children grew up and left home that I decided to research my birth family. I then discovered I had a brother.

Unknown to me, while I was making inquiries about him he was seeking information on his birth parents. At some stage, by a million to one chance, my brother's file and mine landed up on the same desk in the Social Services Department and a sharp-eyed worker made the connection. The authorities passed on a letter from me to him.

As I read his letter from Lincolnshire I knew he was indeed my brother.

John was a retired teacher, living in Boston. From photographs that he sent it was obvious that we were related and I lost no time in replying and giving him further details.

Since then we have met on many occasions but John's first letter was probably the best one I have ever received, and it changed my life for ever. Having spent 50-odd years thinking I had no one, suddenly I had a brother I could confide in and look to for support.

Lyn Lowe, Hornchurch, Essex

TIP TIME

Stop hayfever by putting a smear of Vaseline just inside each nostril. It works!

Mrs J Courtney, Bristol

May 12-18

Letter of my life

Mrs M E Hortopp, Camberley

This is a letter from my granddaughter, Becky. I'm so proud of her. She is a lovely girl, so caring, and likes to make everyone happy.

'To My Dear Nan,

Thank you for making this weekend so special for me. Recently I've realised it's a myth that there will always be a tomorrow, so I want you to know today that I love you with all my heart. You are truly an inspiration to me, with your strength, courage, restlessness for life and sense of fun. Thank you for knowing just what to say to make me feel loved and cherished. Thank you for the laughter and fun you bring to my life.

You brighten up even the darkest cloud and I am honoured that this beautiful, kind, loving person is my Nan. I love you.

Your granddaughter, Becky

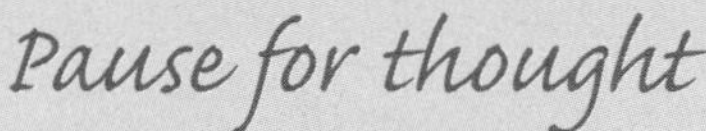

Nothing

We are always being told to do something with
Our lives, and 'don't end up being a nothing'.
As for myself, I've always done nothing.
Nothing to hurt my family,
Nothing to upset relatives or friends,
Nothing to betray true friendship.
Nothing to embarrass people of other colours.
Nothing to deride those of different
Religions or creeds.
Nothing to hurt the creatures of our planet,
Nothing to damage earth's God-given beauty
That's so precious to our very being.
So when anyone tells me I've done nothing
In life, I say, 'Yes, that's exactly right'.
Because, after all, that is what really
Makes me something.

H J Young, Oldham, Lancashire

Well, fancy that!

The muscles that allow you to blink are the fastest in the human body, allowing you to blink up to five times a second. On average, we blink 15,000 times a day.

Tea-time Treats

Date Sponge

If you're a fan of dates and walnuts, then May Oldrey from Harold Hill in Essex has a recipe to fit the bill:

- 6 oz/175 g caster sugar
- 6 oz/175 g margarine
- 6 oz/175 g self-raising flour
- 1 teaspoon bicarbonate of soda
- 3 eggs
- 2 oz/50 g walnuts
- Small packet dates
- ½ pint/275 ml stewed apples
- Juice of 1 lemon

1. Preheat oven to 190°C/375°F/ Gas Mark 5. Grease and flour two 7 in/18 cm round tins.
2. Beat sugar and margarine. Separate egg white from yolks and add both gradually to mixture.
3. Gradually add flour, bicarb and walnuts. Add 2 tablespoons tepid water and mix well. Divide mixture evenly and bake for 25 minutes.
4. Meanwhile, chop dates into a saucepan. Add lemon juice and stewed apples and boil until water evaporates. Spread on to cooked sponge and sandwich together. Leave in a tin for a day, then dust sponge with icing sugar.

I wish I'd said that...

"The grand essentials of happiness are: Something to do, something to love, and something to hope for."
– Allan K Chalmers

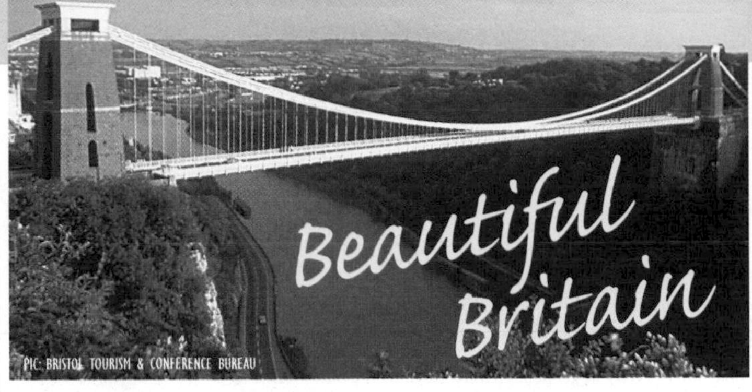

Clifton suspension bridge, Bristol

In 1829, a competition was held to design a bridge that would span the Avon gorge. Isambard Kingdom Brunel, who was already a known and respected architect, submitted four designs and the Egyptian-inspired design that actually won. Despite now being world-famous, it was not Brunel's favourite. The bridge measures 702ft across and is 250ft above the river, offering some breathtaking views.

Work on the bridge began in 1836, but sadly it was not completed until 1864, five years after Brunel's death.

The location and nature of the bridge inevitably attracts suicides, and one story goes that in the 1880s a young woman, having jumped from the bridge, was saved by her petticoats, which acted as a parachute. She landed safely and subsequently lived to a ripe old age! Most, however, are not so lucky.

A couple won £250,000 on the pools. They were obviously delighted but the wife had one worry. "What about all the begging letters?" she asked her husband.

"Continue sending them, my dear."

TIP TIME

Oil stains on clothes? Rub on talcum powder. Leave for one hour. Wash as normal.
Mrs S Kay, Blackpool

Treasured Photo

Writing from Skegness in Lincolnshire, Violet Hankin (formerly Bond, née Kember) describes her wartime service:
'I was one of the first NAAFI girls to go abroad in wartime, to take over from the men in charge of canteens in Egypt. As we were civilians we had to do ATS training before going out and were given appropriate ranks (I was Sergeant Kember). We went out in May 1943, not knowing where we were going, and took three months to reach Alexandria. In the photo I am second from the right, as we leave for our unknown destination.'

Healthy Living

Make exercise fun

- ❏ Join a group – exercising in a group is a great motivator.
- ❏ Tell everyone you're starting an exercise programme. It'll make it much harder to quit.
- ❏ Start slowly – if you overdo it, you'll run the risk of injury.
- ❏ Be realistic – this is a programme for life.
- ❏ Maintain interest by altering your routine.
- ❏ Set short-term targets – set achievable goals.
- ❏ Reward yourself – when you achieve a target, take time to treat yourself.

May 19-25

I WISH I'D SAID THAT...

"The easiest thing to grow in a garden is tired. – Anon"

TIP TIME

Us a bar of soap as a pin cushion. It makes sewing easier as the needle just slides through.

PORTMEIRION, NORTH WALES

Portmeirion is a privately owned village in Tremadog Bay, surrounded by sub-tropical gardens, woodlands and sandy beaches.

Sir Clough Williams-Ellis, the Welsh architect, wanted to show that it was possible to develop a naturally beautiful site without spoiling it and he created Portmeirion in the 1920s with this aim in mind. It is now a thriving cluster of cottages with restaurants, shops and its own pottery.

Portmeirion is often referred to as a home for fallen buildings, as all sorts of buildings from different countries were dismantled, transported here and rebuilt. The village is based on a Mediterranean piazza, with lots of archways, and is painted in a range of pastel colours.

Portmeirion attracts a variety of visitors and Noel Coward spent some time writing there in the 1940s – but the most famous resident has to be Patrick McGoohan, who played No. 6 in the cult TV series The Prisoner, which was filmed on location here in the 1960s.

Letter of my life

YOURS magazine was instrumental in changing my life. Back in 1995 you published an article I had written.

A lady called Josie read it and wondered if I was related to her – because of the rare surname. She wrote to me via the YOURS office and it soon became evident she was my cousin – the daughter of one of my father's younger brothers. This led to my finding my long-lost sister, Shirley (pictured below), whom I had last seen 51 years previously in 1944.

My father and I hadn't seen eye to eye and we parted acrimoniously. I spent 12 years in the Royal Navy.

It transpired my father had died in 1969, always saying that I had been killed during the war, so you can imagine my sister's joy when I contacted her! Our first meeting was a tearful and emotional occasion but our lives had been changed for ever, thanks to Josie's letter!

Mr G W Girt, Blackpool, Lancashire

HEALTHY LIVING

Our pick of the nut crops

- Almonds: Excellent source of calcium.
- Brazils: A rich source of selenium, thought to be a protector against cancer and heart disease.
- Cashews: Packed with iron (ounce for ounce, more than beef!) and zinc.
- Peanuts: High in fibre and protein.
- Walnuts: Rich in linoleic acid, for healthy skin.

Pause for thought

Honey for Tea

"Honey for sale", the notice said,
On a tree, by the cottage door,
And an old dog followed me up the path,
Where kittens played, three or four.
The beehives under the orchard boughs
Stood in a shining row,
While petals around their slatted walls
fluttered like pale pink snow.
The air was full of the scents of spring,
And a cheerful, industrious hum,
While a blackbird sang in a lilac bush…
Oh, I felt so glad I'd come!

For the countrywoman, pinafore-clad,
Who greeted me, seemed to match
Her snug little house, with its diamond panes
Twinkling beneath the thatch.
Her smile was warm; with sturdy gait,
The jar of honey she brought,
And the price, though rather high, I paid
Without a second thought.
For I knew I was taking back with me
To the city, not merely honey,
But a glimpse of a lovely forgotten world,
Too precious to buy with money!

Kathleen O'Farrell

Proud of his grasp of classic foreign phrases, a lad gave his teacher a translation of '*Honi soit qui mal y pense*'. (Shame to him who thinks ill of it.)

"It means, 'Honestly, sir, I think I'm going to be sick'."

Well, fancy that!

Predictions that missed the mark…

- In 1894, President of the Royal Society, Lord Kelvin, predicted that radio had no future. Today there are more than one billion radio sets in the world tuned into more than 33,000 radio stations.
- In the early 20th century, a world market of only four million cars was predicted – because the world would run out of chauffeurs.
- Irish scientist Dr Lardner didn't believe that trains could ever be an effective means of transportation. People, he said, would suffocate at high speeds.

Tea-time Treats

Flapjacks

Makes 12

- 6 oz/175 g butter
- 1 oz/25 g golden syrup
- 4 oz/100 g soft brown sugar
- 8 oz/225 g porridge oats
- 2 oz/50 g desiccated coconut

1. Preheat oven to 180°C/350°F/Gas Mark 4. Grease a 7 x 11in/18 x 28 cm Swiss roll tin
2. Melt butter and syrup in a pan. Take off the heat and stir in remaining ingredients.
3. Turn into greased tin and spread evenly. Bake in oven for 15 mins.
4. Cool slightly, cut into fingers and remove from the tin.

Treasured Photo

There was an elegantly-dressed visitor to Stonehenge in 1934… Mrs E Bray of Thornbury, Bristol, remembers:

'Way back in nineteen thirty-four
A time of peace before the war
On a fine and sunny day
To Stonehenge we made our way.
A photo of the stones and me
To take back home for folks to see.
Stonehenge, unaltered, rules the skyline
But extra stones have changed my outline!'

May 26-June 1

Well, fancy that!

In the old days, sea captains used to keep pigs on board because they believed that, should they be shipwrecked, pigs always swam towards the nearest shore.

TREASURED PHOTO

Those were the days! Barbara Roper of Bradford says:

'This charabanc trip set off from Kensington Street, Girlington, West Yorkshire, about 85 years ago, bound for Harrogate and Knaresborough. In the photograph are my cousin (the baby) held by my grandma, and my father (on the back seat, far left, wearing a hat).'

Letter of my life

When I was 11 years old I sat the scholarship for the local grammar school. It was a day-long exam involving arithmetic, problems and English, and was held in the grammar school itself.

During the morning I began to feel unwell but soldiered on and then went home for lunch. By this time I had a headache and felt generally 'achey'. My mother thought I was starting a cold and, although I didn't want to go back for the afternoon exams, my mother urged me to go. Reluctantly I went back, but I can't remember the rest of that day.

The following day I came out in a rash. I had developed scarlet fever which, at that time, was a serious illness requiring six weeks in isolation.

But my efforts in the scholarship exam must have paid off because the Education Officer wrote to my parents on May 31, 1935, confirming that I had been awarded a 'special place' in the Wheelwright Grammar Schools. This letter changed my life as it led to my staying at school until I was 16, followed by two happy and successful careers.

If I had not passed the exam I would have left school at 14 and perhaps gone to work in a shop or as an office junior.

I shall always be grateful to my mother for her encouragement during the lunch hour on the day of the scholarship exam, enabling the pattern of my life to take a completely different turn.

Muriel Bowers, York

TIP TIME

To warm dinner plates quickly, dip them in water, then stack the wet plates and place in the microwave on full power for one minute.

I WISH I'D SAID THAT...

Youth would be an ideal state if it came a little later in life. – H H Asquith, British Liberal statesman

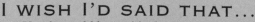

Pause for thought

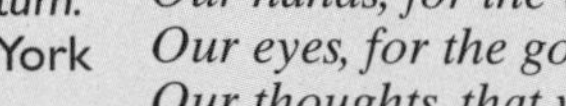

'I wrote this prayer for our parish magazine,' writes John Dunn of Boston in Lincolnshire:

Morning Prayer

Lord, we thank you for
guiding us through the night,
Into the new day's hours
of light.
Please guide our prayers that they are
faithful and true;
Our hands, for the work they must do,
Our eyes, for the goodness they may see,
Our thoughts, that we may think of Thee,
Our words, that they neither sting nor scold,
Our actions, that they are correct and bold,
Our steps, to tread the righteous way
Until the end of the present day.
Then guide us, Lord, through the night
Into the next day's hours of light.
Thank you, Lord. Amen

TEA-TIME TREATS

Banana Fruit Bread

- 6 oz/175 g sugar
- 4 oz/100 g butter
- 2 eggs, well beaten
- 3 tablespoons sour milk
- 1 teaspoon bicarbonate of soda
- 12 oz/350 g self-raising flour
- 2 very ripe bananas, mashed
- 6 oz/175 g sultanas
- 1 teaspoon vanilla essence

1. Grease a 2 lb loaf tin. Preheat oven to 180°C/350°F/Gas Mark 4.
2. Cream butter and sugar. Add remaining ingredients to mixture and stir well to combine.
3. Bake for 40-45 minutes until firm.

HEALTHY LIVING

This is the best time of your life because…

- ❑ Retirement means the end to the daily grind of earning a crust.
- ❑ The mortgage is likely to be paid off.
- ❑ Your marriage has fewer pressure than ever before – there's plenty of time for companionship and independence.
- ❑ Your relationship with your adult children grows stronger as they have families of their own.
- ❑ Grandchildren are a pleasure.
- ❑ Your friendships are secure – you've tackled life's roller coaster ride together.

"You must be joking"

Did you hear the one about the St Bernard that went up a mountain to take some brandy to a lost climber? They thought the dog had died because he was gone for days, then suddenly he turned up with a note around his neck. 'Great brandy. Can you send up the bottle?'

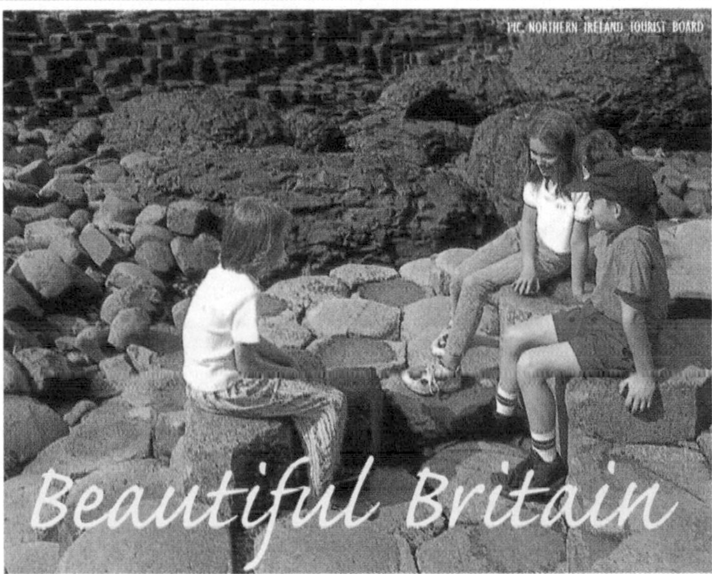

PORTRUSH, ANTRIM, NORTHERN IRELAND

Portrush, a very popular seaside resort, is close to The Giant's Causeway, a world heritage site. The causeway is a mass of basalt columns, packed together, that were formed by volcanic rock contracting as it cooled – or, as ancient myth would have it, by a giant named Finn McCool! Finn McCool was General of the King of Ireland's armies and, when he fell in love with a giant who lived on Staffa, an island off the Scottish coast, he built this causeway as a road to bring her to Ireland. There are around 40,000 of these columns and the tallest of them are around 40ft high.

Each year, around May or June, the town hosts the Portrush Raft Race, where the aim is to get down the river as fast as possible in the most bizarre floating contraption possible. All the proceeds go to charity and entries have included aquatic elephants, pirate rafts and amphibious cars – not to mention the outlandish costumes worn by the crews.

DO YOU REMEMBER...

PIC: MIRROR

The Dome of Discovery

...The Festival of Britain?

ONE hundred years after the Victorians' Great Exhibition, crowds congregated on the South Bank in London, in May 1951, for the long-awaited Festival of Britain. While conditions in Britain had improved, people's daily lives were still affected by continuing post-war shortages and rationing.

After such a trying time, the Festival was viewed as an opportunity to demonstrate and celebrate Britain's resilience and achievements.

Its organisers also wanted to offer people a much-needed good time.

Twenty-seven acres of bomb-damaged London near Waterloo were transformed into the exhibition site, much of the area given over to the Dome of Discovery, a huge inverted aluminium saucer, featuring a planetarium, a Polar Theatre and a life-sized repro of Captain Cook's Endeavour. The 300ft Skylon – a slender, luminous rocket of steel and aluminium – lit up the skyline at night and there were themed festival pavilions. The only exhibition structure still to survive is the Royal Festival Hall.

Just like the Millennium Dome, the cost of the Festival of Britain – more than eight million pounds – was heavily criticised, the public's chief complaint being that a cup of coffee cost 9d.

...Mr Pastry?

RICHARD Hearne's madcap, bowler-hatted creation, Mr Pastry, complete with walrus moustache and flapping coat-tails, was hugely popular on children's TV in the 1950s.

He was born in Norwich in 1908 into a theatrical family. His father was an acrobat and his mother a dramatic actress; Richard made his stage debut in her arms at the age of six weeks. As a youth, he appeared in circus and later went on tour developing his 'dumb' act, its visual humour going down well.

The character of Mr Pastry came from a stage show that he and Fred Emney were in, called Big Boy and was developed by Hearne as the bungling, optimistic clown. He was to star in slapstick sketches on stage, TV and film. He was awarded the OBE in 1970 and died in 1979.

Brits for all seasons

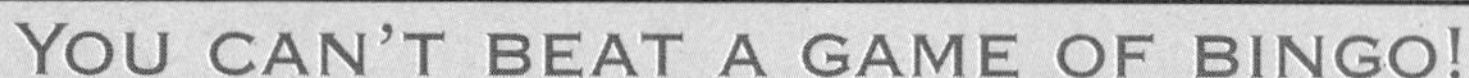

YOU CAN'T BEAT A GAME OF BINGO!

FOR a great night out with good company and a few laughs, it's hard to beat a game of bingo. What is it about this fast-moving game that brings us Brits to the bingo halls in droves? Is it the camaraderie or the thrill of chasing a possible big win? Whatever it is, it's been drawing us in for decades. Mecca Bingo alone has three million members and 124 clubs across the UK.

The origins of bingo can be traced back to 16th-century Italy, where a state-run lottery game called Lo Giuco de Lotto originated. The game is still held every Saturday in Italy. 'Lotto' migrated to France in the late 18th century in a form similar to today's bingo, with a playing card, token and numbers called aloud.

PIC: MIRROR

In New York bingo really took off and, by 1940, thousands of games were being played every week all over America. The game soon spread to Britain.

Perhaps the ultimate night out is a game of bingo followed by a fish-and-chip supper. Fish became a popular national dish during the industrial revolution. Today, we have 9,000 fish-and-chip shops in Britain, turning over a staggering 60,000 tonnes of fish each year.

The first chips were actually made from fried bread. It was as a result of wheat shortages that potatoes were substituted, so perhaps it is no coincidence that we have married bread and chips together into that British culinary masterpiece – the chip butty!

Skeleton

With just the bare bones of a grid, see if you can work out the grid pattern, which is fully symmetrical, and complete the crossword.

					■					
								17		
31										
									■	

ACROSS
1 Discussion theme
5 Social call
9 Avoidance
10 Gemstone
12 Bring into force
14 Type
15 Not many
17 Furrow
18 Additionally
20 Depend
21 Flabbergast
22 Practise boxing
24 Smear
27 Buffoon
28 Fuss
30 Mineral aggregate
31 Gauge
33 Uninteresting people
35 Apparent
36 Expressed openly
37 Bread ingredient

DOWN
1 Bone of the leg
2 Fringe benefits
3 Climbing plant
4 Young cow
5 Panorama
6 Charged particle
7 Entrap
8 Threadbare
11 Oval
13 Refinement
16 African antelope
19 Rowing blade
20 Primary colour
22 Brazilian dance
23 Michaelmas daisy
25 Main artery
26 Assail
28 Dry and barren
29 Comply
32 Night before
34 A single

Solution on Page 159

Lost for words

Some of the letters in this quotation from Charlton Heston have been left out, as well as all punctuation and word spaces. See how quickly you can fill in the missing letters.

I			V	E	P			Y		D	T	H		E	
P	R			I	D		N			T		R		E	S
A			T	S		N		T	W		G			I	U
	E	S		F	T			T	D		E		N	T	
R		A	T		A			G	O	P		O	B		
M	N			H		N	G		O	E					

Solution on Page 159

Mrs Cooky's Camp

By Tony Quaife

PIC: HULTON ARCHIVE

Scout camp was a rare treat for those young lads lucky enough to go, even if their teachers went with them. But who wanted a soppy woman interfering in the world of men versus the elements?

IN the late 1940s and into the early 1950s I was lucky enough to belong to the 24th Hastings Grammar School Scout Troop – a grand title for what was some 40 lads, each keen to abandon academia for two weeks of the year to become embryonic Davy Crocketts at the annual scout camp.

One of these forays into the wilderness was a camp in the New Forest in 1950, when I was 14. By this time, my career progression in the Scouts had taken me to the dizzy heights of Patrol Leader of the Seagulls and I had charge of six other aspiring Baden Powells.

As a Saturday dawned in early summer, we gathered with our parents in Castle Square, Hastings, awaiting our transport. We were surrounded by kitbags, tents, cooking utensils and other paraphenalia deemed necessary for our survival and safe return two weeks later.

No air-conditioned coach with loos for us. Instead, three open lorries hired from Ricketts Premier Coal Merchants who considered it unnecessary to remove the coal dust for a one day outing!

Our parents waved farewell with a mixture of anxiety and relief as our imaginary wagon train began its journey west.

Arrival at the selected spot in the New Forest was followed by a frenzy of activity such as one might witness in a disturbed ants' nest. Although it appeared chaotic, by evening our camp was fully established with the Union Jack proudly flying over bell tents, kitchens, washing areas and latrines set out exactly as prescribed by BP in his manual, 'Scouting for Boys', which recommends a Scout should 'smile and whistle under all difficulties'.

Ah, the beauty of that first morning… waking to the smell of dew-soaked grass and the sight of sunrays filtering through the trees followed by a wash in clear, cold water from the river. Soon all six patrols had lit their fires with delicate curls of silver birch bark and the air was filled with the smells of wood smoke, porridge and bacon.

By evening our camp was fully established with the Union Jack proudly flying over bell tents, kitchens, washing areas and latrines

Being a school Scout Troop our Scout leaders were also our schoolmasters. At first it was difficult to accept the masters, who usually dressed in gowns and mortarboards and were treated with respect and fear, were human and could change overnight into jolly, avuncular men ready to tease and be teased, play silly games and introduce us to so many of the wonders of the countryside.

The three who will remain forever in my mind – and in my heart – were, in order of seniority, Mr Baker (senior maths), Mr Cookson (junior maths) and Mr Dennison (senior French). In Scout uniforms they became Com, Cooky and Denny and between them they managed to occupy our every waking hour with fun, work and activities. We were praised, cajoled, punished, nursed and counselled and, as an adult now, I marvel at their patience and energy.

I remember lots of little things about that fortnight. The time the whole camp fell silent as a rainbow appeared to touch a neighbouring field of corn, turning it into a multi-coloured fairyland. Then there was the time in early morning when Cooky had boiled some water for a shave and then couldn't decide whether to use it for shaving or indulge in the ultimate luxury of soaking his feet in hot water. By the time we had convinced him to shave first and then soak his feet the water had gone cold!

So many memories come flooding back over the years. On the second day, the 'tenderfoot', or youngest member of the Seagull patrol, suddenly dissolved in tears. Luckily Denny recognised the signs of homesickness and led him quietly away from the rest of us. He sat talking with him beneath a huge elm tree and I knew that Mr Dennison – the Genghis Khan of Upper School French – would never be the same to me again.

Two or three times each week the day ended with a camp fire. These were the highlights of the fortnight. Nothing could surpass the excitement of seeing the fire spring into life and then walk from our tents through the darkness of a country evening to assemble around it, our knees wrapped in blankets and an enamel mug of cocoa or soup to warm our hands.

Songs were sung as the fire crackled, sending sparks to join the stars above us. Each patrol had to sing a song of its own, tell a story or act a play.

As the fire died the younger Scouts would fall asleep, overcome by fresh air, exercise and happiness. We older ones, feeling quite grown up, would carry them back through the darkness to their tents to sleep soundly until the dawn would signal the start of another day.

During this camp it was announced that Cooky's wife would be spending some time with us. I must admit that this news was not received with much enthusiasm. After all, who wanted soppy women interfering in our world of men versus the elements?

Her arrival was met with a cool politeness but we noticed the twinkling eyes, the ready smile and a certain air of fun and motherliness. Within a few days we came to admire and respect 'Mrs Cooky', as we called her, and we even vied with each other to do little jobs for her and to join the parties she took on nature rambles. We sat entranced as she talked, and we soon came to understand why Cooky had fallen in love with this special lady.

On camp fire night she was the star attraction and told us stories in such a way that we were held spellbound. The next morning, Cooky told us sadly his wife had returned home as the result of an insect bite which had turned septic. The last few days of our camp were greyer and colder as though, in some way, the summer had ended with her leaving.

Some time later I discovered that this special lady's full name was Catherine Cookson and her stories were published in books read by millions of people. But to me, she will always be 'Mrs Cooky' and her stories were written just for a troop of ragamuffin Boy Scouts.

I saw her in a TV interview 40 years later when she was an elderly lady fighting pain and illness. She described how she was supported throughout by her 'Tommy', and the love in their eyes for each other was as bright as it was when a young woman played the guitar and sang quietly to her husband and a bunch of young lads on a still, summer night in the New Forest.

As the fire died the younger Scouts would fall asleep, overcome by fresh air, exercise and happiness

June 2003

HIGH DAYS AND HOLIDAYS...

Morris Men

Although Whit Monday used to be the biggest day of the year for Morris dancing, many gather to dance in June, notably in Thaxted, Essex.

White is the colour of the White goddess, the earth mother in her gown of daisies and Queen Anne's lace. It is in her honour that the Morris men don their white garb and deck their hats with flowers. Their bells and ribbons banish harm and bring fertility.

PIC: HULTON ARCHIVE

St Barnabas' Day (June 11)

This day is the traditional start of hay-making, hence the memory-jogger, 'By St Barnabas, put scythe to grass'.

Summer Solstice (June 21)

At Midsummer, St John's Eve or the longest day, which all fall between June 21 and 24, there has been a tradition of lighting bonfires on beacon hills, especially in Cornwall and the West Country. This was to celebrate the power of the sun and to implore it not to wane.

Midsummer Day (June 24)

Tin miners had a paid holiday today, for it was unlucky to work on Midsummer.

SUNDAY	1	
MONDAY	2	Golden Jubilee of Queen's Coronation
TUESDAY	3	
WEDNESDAY	4	
THURSDAY	5	
FRIDAY	6	
SATURDAY	7	
SUNDAY	8	
MONDAY	9	
TUESDAY	10	
WEDNESDAY	11	
THURSDAY	12	
FRIDAY	13	
SATURDAY	14	
SUNDAY	15	Father's Day
MONDAY	16	
TUESDAY	17	
WEDNESDAY	18	

THURSDAY	19
FRIDAY	20
SATURDAY	21
SUNDAY	22
MONDAY	23 Wimbledon Tennis Championships start
TUESDAY	24
WEDNESDAY	25
THURSDAY	26
FRIDAY	27
SATURDAY	28
SUNDAY	29
MONDAY	30 July YOURS on sale

This month don't forget to...

- Make your elderflower wine – the fruit will be in plentiful supply now but don't pick those from the side of the road, near exhaust fumes.
- On a warm day, if possible, get your mattress outside for a good airing. A light breeze will freshen it up.
- Run your central heating now and again for three to four minutes to forestall any problems in the autumn.

Marlon Brando

It happened in June...

June 3, 1937: The Duke of Windsor married Mrs Wallis Simpson in France.

June 30, 1953: An eclipse of the sun was visible across Britain.

June 12, 1973: An angry Marlon Brando punched a photographer who was annoying him and broke his jaw.

June 20, 1991: A man who spent his redundancy money on building a bungalow in County Durham, without first obtaining planning permission, shot dead a local authority planning officer as he attempted to serve a demolition order on the building.

June 2-8

Well, fancy that!

The movie The Madness of King George was released in England under the title The Madness of King George III. Then the III was dropped because it was believed that American movie-goers would think it was a sequel and wouldn't go to see it because they'd missed parts I and II.

TREASURED PHOTO

The vehicle in this picture was a bit special, according to the sender, Enid Lewis of Dursley:

'The photo shows my cousin Doreen (*right*) and myself, both aged six, at Great Yarmouth in September 1939. Behind us is my grandfather's camper van. We believe it to be the first of its kind, built by Bedford in 1938 to grandfather's specification. The photo was taken on a family holiday from Nuneaton, a day before war was declared. I remember we made a very quick departure.

Pause for thought

Contentment

Are you, like me, content to be,
in rain or sun, beneath this tree?
Togetherness is all I'll ever ask,
While drinking from a common flask,
That I can always be with thee.

Did you, like me, give loving thought
to things we found, or things we bought?
Or songs of youth, so seldom heard,
Or song of wind, or song of bird?
Or being two as one for this life so short?

And will you, like me, still be content
to stay with me till life be spent?
And drink with me from common spring,
To hear your voice when e'er you sing
That voice, that love, both heaven sent.

And will you, my love, like me, repent
The passion of those long nights mis-spent?
Or evenings that we spent alone
When the seeds of lifelong love were sown
While in each other's arms, content?

If this be love, then I shall be
Content to spend this life with thee
Beneath this heavy laden bough,
The fruit of life to share with thee.
Then shall we both contented be!

Gwyn Tilley, Pontypool, Gwent

TEA-TIME TREATS

Canadian Malt Loaf

Monica McInerney from Milford Haven sent us this recipe which, she says, has been well-used:

- 12 fl oz/330 ml hot water
- 2 oz/50 g butter or margarine
- 13 oz/375 g dried fruit
- 13 oz/375 g self-raising flour
- 9 oz/250 g sugar
- ½ teaspoon bicarbonate of soda
- 2 eggs, beaten
- Mixed spice (optional)

1 Preheat oven to 180°C/350°F/Gas Mark 4. Line a small bread tin.
2 Put dried fruit and butter into a saucepan with the hot water. Bring to boil and simmer for 4 minutes. Allow to cool.
3 Place fruit mix into a mixing bowl, add flour, sugar, bicarb, beaten eggs and mixed spice. Mix well.
4 Put into bread tin and bake in middle of the oven for about 1 hour.

Chester, Cheshire

Chester, on the River Dee, began life as the Roman city of Deva. After the Romans withdrew in the 5th century, it was a Saxon town, a Norman fortress, a medieval walled town, and finally a city that became a tourist attraction the first guidebook being published in the 18th century.

There are two miles of walls around the city, built in Roman and medieval times, which have survived virtually intact. In 1785, some steps were added to the wall and are known as the 'wishing steps' – the legend being that, if you can run up and down them while holding your breath, your wish will come true.

Chester claims to have more ghosts than any other city in England, among them a Roman soldier and a Cavalier from the Civil War. Another Chester ghost is a monk in a grey habit who is said to walk around the cathedral.

Tip Time

Break lettuce leaves off by hand. Never cut lettuce with a steel blade as it causes the leaves to wilt and go brown.

Letter of my life

I was born in 1940, one of 18! My eldest brother, Jack, was away at sea and it was during this time he thought he might never see us again so wrote a loving letter to our mother, Winifred…

'I have no premonition or any feeling of getting killed, but this is just in case, and there are a few things that I feel I would like you to know. Can I express my thanks or my love? I do not think that is possible. I thank you for all the love, sympathy and understanding which you have always shown me. I have always been able to lean on you, and you have never let me down. You fed me, clothed me and gave me a comfortable home. Knowing all this, perhaps you will understand why I feel happy to be doing my bit for King and Country. Really it is for all the things you have brought me up to respect.'

Shortly after writing this he was taken prisoner. Luckily he returned home safe and was at home when his letter arrived, three years after he'd written it. Our mother was overcome.

Unfortunately Jack returned to sea and, in 1944, only a year after his letter arrived, the submarine he was on went down. His body was never recovered. My mother treasured the letter from her loving son whose very fitting nickname was 'Gentle John'.

Patricia Brown, Northwich, Cheshire

I wish I'd said that…

"Hope for the best, but prepare for the worst." – Proverb

"You must be joking"

A boy was crying on the beach. "What's the matter?" asked his dad.
"A crab just bit my toe."
"Which one?"
"How do I know, Dad, all crabs look the same."

Healthy Living

Keep your heart healthy

- ❑ Stop smoking – a high risk factor for heart disease.
- ❑ Watch your weight.
- ❑ Exercise regularly – walking and swimming is good.
- ❑ Cut down on fat.
- ❑ Eating oily fish two or three times a week.
- ❑ Aim to eat five portions of fruit or veg a day.
- ❑ Watch your alcohol intake. A couple of units a day are thought to be good but don't overdo it.

June 9-15

I WISH I'D SAID THAT...

"There is nothing – absolutely nothing – half so much worth doing as simply messing about in boats.
– Kenneth Grahame, Scottish children's writer"

WOBURN ABBEY, BEDFORDSHIRE

The first building on this site was a monastery, dating back to 1145. In 1538, the Abbot was found guilty of treason – he was hanged and the monastery was confiscated.

The lands were granted to Sir John Russell, later the 1st Earl of Bedford, in 1547, although the property didn't become established as a family home until 1616 when Francis Russell, later the 4th Earl, built a house on the site of the old monastery. Nothing remains of the original building.

Woburn Abbey remains in the family to this day and has had many famous visitors, including Elizabeth I, Charles I and Queen Victoria. It is also famous for its animal residents, both in the park itself, where nine different species of deer roam free, and in the Safari Park, where you can see lions, rhinoceros, monkeys and many endangered species, including the Asian elephant.

Letter of my life

The letter landed on my doormat one morning 35 years ago. I was alone, my husband and children were out at work, and I knew I had to open it. I held the letter in my hands for a while, afraid of what I might read. Would it be good news or would I be devastated?

I sat down with a cup of tea to steady my nerves and at last opened it. As soon as I read the first line 'I am pleased to inform you...' my world was transformed! I had, at the age of 49, been successful in passing my final exams and was now a State Registered Nurse – an SRN!

Even now, aged 84, I can still feel my sense of pride and elation when I look back and remember that letter and what it meant to the rest of my working life.

Mrs B Mellor, Oldham, Greater Manchester

"You must be joking"

Headline bloomers:

- Something went wrong in jet crash, expert says.
- Drunk gets nine months in violin case.
- Red tape holds up bridge.
- Two Soviet ships collide, one dies.

Tea-time Treats

No Bake Raisin Squares

Makes 15

- 5 oz/150 g sweet digestive biscuits
- 2 oz/50 g raisins
- 2 tablespoons golden syrup
- 3 oz/75 g butter
- 2 oz/50 g drinking chocolate powder

1 Crush biscuits and add raisins.
2 Melt syrup and butter; stir in chocolate powder. Add to the biscuits and mix well.
3 Press into a shallow Swiss roll tin. Leave to harden, then carefully cut into fingers.

Pause for thought

When to the flowers so beautiful
The Father gave a name
Back came a little blue-eyed one,
All timidly it came.
And standing at his Father's feet
And gazing at His face,
It said 'Dear Lord
The name Thou gavest me
Alas I have forgot.'
Kindly the Father looked him down
And said 'Forget Me not'.

Sister Denis, St Peter's Convent, Herne Bay, Kent

Tip Time

My Grandma gave me this tip on my marriage in 1962. Never put anything down, always put it away. This has proved to be wonderful advice.

Pauline Cooke, Nottingham

Treasured Photo

Mrs S Mitchell of Mottingham, London couldn't resist sending us this photo. She writes:

'I've been going through some very old family photographs and came across this one of my Grandma holding a baby. It's the sign on the shop behind her that is interesting. She would be 128 years old now, so I think a guinea was probably worth a lot of money back then.'

Healthy Living

All about antioxidants

You may have heard of 'super' vitamins and minerals called antioxidants, which are thought to play a big role in disease prevention. But what are they? When oxygen is used in various processes within the body, it creates potentially harmful by-products called 'free radicals'. Antioxidants are thought to help fight them. For a diet rich in antioxidants, choose green leafy vegetables, tomatoes, carrots, vegetable oils, wholegrain cereals and nuts.

Well, fancy that!

The shortest scheduled airline flight is made between the islands of Westray to Papa Westray off Scotland. The flight lasts two minutes.

June 16-22

Treasured Photo

Broadstairs in Kent was the setting for this picture, sent in by Molly Phillips of London: 'I'm on the right of the photo, which was taken in the 1940s. Also enjoying the day at the beach were my two friends Mary Hood (*on the left*) and Nina Hickey (*centre*). We have been good friends since childhood and are all now in our seventies.'

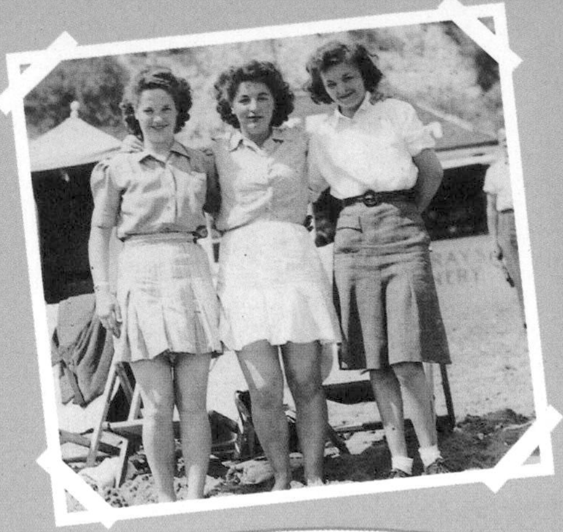

Well, fancy that!

Riddle: A doctor has a brother who is a lawyer in London, but the lawyer in London does not have a brother who is a doctor. Who can it be? Answer: His sister.

Perfect Puddings

Chocolate Dipped Fruits

- Summer fruits: Strawberries, kiwi, mango etc chopped or sliced
- 1 bar milk chocolate, melted

Dip half of a piece of fruit into melted chocolate and leave on wire rack to harden. Eat within one hour.

Pause for thought

'I have a book that must be about 100 years old, entitled Consult Me,' writes N Cannon from Leeds. 'It contains weird and wonderful cures and recipes, as well as rules and regulations for all sorts of things – including how to speak correctly! Here's a quaint poem from the book – unfortunately, I don't know who wrote it':

Dancing

At first they move slowly, with caution and grace,
Like horses when just setting out on a race;
For dancers at balls, just like horses at races,
Must amble a little to show off their paces.

The music plays faster; the raptures begin;
Like lambkins they skip; like teetotums they spin;
Now draperies whirl, and now petticoats fly,
And ankles, at least, are exposed to the eye.

O'er the well-polished Ballroom in circles they swim;
He smiles on her, and she smiles on him,
Her hand on his shoulder is tenderly placed;
His arm quite as tenderly circles her waist.

They still bear in mind, as they're turning each other,
The proverb… 'one good turn's deserving another'…
And those bodily turns often end, it is said,
In turning the lady's or gentleman's head!

I wish I'd said that...

"Airline travel is hours of boredom interrupted by moments of stark terror."
– Al Boliska, from Quotations for our TIme

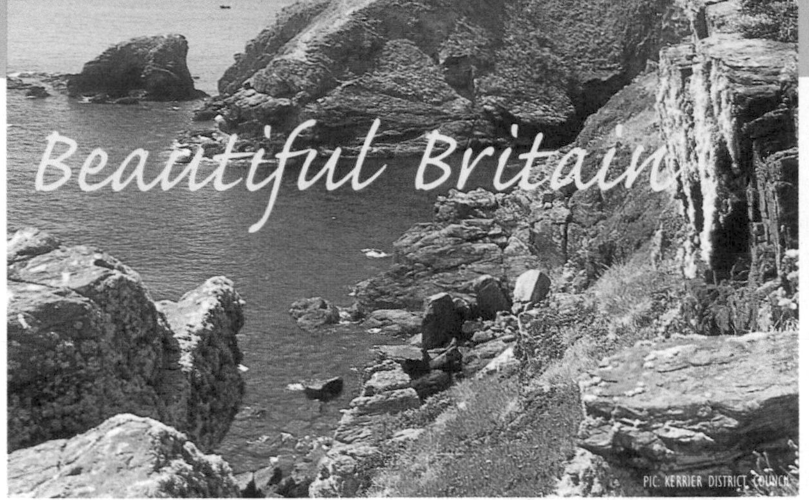

Lizard Peninsula, Cornwall

This is the most southerly part of Britain and, warmed by the Gulf Stream, it enjoys a mild climate. The area is one of outstanding beauty and is popular with ornithologists as well as visitors wanting to explore the dramatic scenery to the south and the gentler, picturesque woods and rivers of the north.

Among its many claims to fame, it was from this area of Cornwall that Marconi made the very first transatlantic radio transmission in 1901.

To the north of the peninsula, the landscape of the Helford River appears in Daphne du Maurier's famous novel Frenchman's Creek, and she also set her books Jamaica Inn and Rebecca in her beloved Cornwall.

The spectacular coastline has some beautiful sandy beaches, but these waters are also notorious for shipwrecks, especially when the coast is lashed by gales in the winter – and the lighthouse on Lizard Point has one of the most powerful beams in the world.

"You Must be joking"

A man was given the job of painting the white line down the middle of a road. On day one he painted six miles, the second day three miles and the third, less than a mile. When the foreman asked him why he was painting less and less each day, he replied: "I just can't do any better. Each day I keep getting further and further away from the paint can."

TIP TIME

If a recipe calls for butter and yours is too hard – grate it.

Healthy Living

Good digestion

- ❑ Chew food slowly – it helps break down the food for digestion.
- ❑ Eat your main meal at lunchtime. If you do eat in the evening, don't go to bed for three hours to give your stomach time to digest the food thoroughly.
- ❑ Avoid lots of processed foods.
- ❑ Sip on a peppermint or chamomile tea after a meal.
- ❑ Take some exercise – it boosts the digestive system.
- ❑ Avoid spicy or rich, fatty foods late at night.
- ❑ If you get indigestion when you sleep, try propping the head end of the bed up slightly.

Letter of my life

If only there was more love in the world today, the world would be more at peace.

My dear husband and I were married in 1949. We loved each other devotedly and over the years I always kept birthday, anniversary and Valentine's Day cards in a special place.

Sadly I lost my dear husband six years ago and have recently moved house to be closer to my daughter and family. During the process of packing I spent some time going through all of my cards and, to my great delight, I found a letter in one of my old anniversary cards that I will always cherish. The letter is only short, but it means so much to me…

'Thank you my darling wife for just being you, and for everything you do for me and looking after me for all these years. If I didn't have you I would have nothing. I am the luckiest man in the world. I love you.'

Reading his letter moved me to tears, once again! Love is a very splendid thing, don't you agree?

Mrs G M Pead, Bexley, Kent

June 23-29

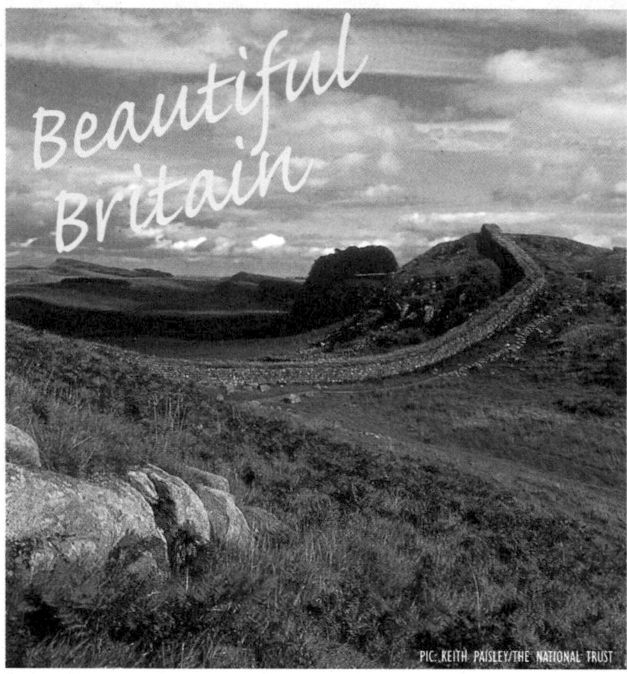

PIC: KEITH PAISLEY/THE NATIONAL TRUST

Hadrian's Wall

This wall, built from around 122AD, ran across the whole width of Britain, stretching 73 miles from Newcastle to the Solway Firth. It is now a World Heritage Site.

The wall was originally 15 ft high, with 6ft battlements on top of that and it was the biggest engineering task undertaken by the Romans –taking more than six years to complete. The wall was the northern frontier of Roman Britain for 250 years, with ditches, stone and turf walls, including forts and signalling turrets, a road system and earthworks, known as 'vallum'.

Every mile there was a fort called a milecastle, and in between them were watchtowers, so that messages could be passed rapidly along the wall in the event of an attack.

There is a story, dating from the 19th century, that tells of a phantom hunt that used to be seen near the remains of Hadrian's Wall. It was said that the sight of the ghostly animals galloping past used to terrify the local cats and dogs – which would all run away.

I wish I'd said that...

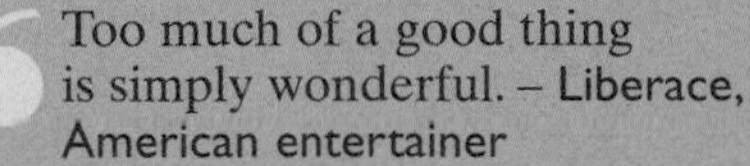

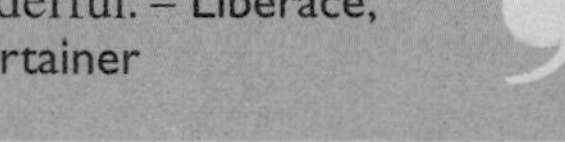

Too much of a good thing is simply wonderful. – Liberace, American entertainer

Tip Time

One rose in full bloom can look as good as a whole bunch. Cut its stem really short and float it in a little water in a wine glass.

Letter of my life

The letter arrived at 8.30am on June 29, 1940. It was in an official envelope and the first thing I saw on opening it was 'Killed in Action'.

We were both nearly 21. We'd met at work, AG Spalding – sports equipment manufacturers. He was an industrial chemist and worked in the lab; I wrapped golf balls. Jim was a territorial at Putney Bridge Barracks in the 1st London Signals and was mobilised in August 1939.

We intended to get engaged at Christmas 1939. However, as war was imminent, our parents gave their consent for us to marry.

We had our wedding organised for 3pm, Saturday September 23. At the last minute Jim was told he was in the advance party to France, so we had to get the vicar out of bed to marry us by 9am so that Jim could return to Sutton, Surrey where the company was billeted.

The CO removed him from the advance party and allowed him to come home for the next six days. I had a letter every day until January 1940 when he was given ten days leave. By then I had rented a flat opposite my family home.

I shall never forget the last time I saw him. It was at Victoria Station as he disappeared into the darkness of the platform.

We wrote every day. In April he was due for leave, but it was cancelled at the last moment. Our boys had to march for days until they reached the beach at Dunkirk.

Each evening I went to Addison Road station where trains full of Army evacuees were being brought back. I hoped Jim would be one of them.

Jim never came home and I had to wait another month before that letter arrived, and a further month before I received a letter from the padre who found my Jim with five other boys, washed up on the beach. He very kindly told me all that had happened to them in the 24 hours beforehand. My life changed that day.

Eve Middleton, Brickhill, Bedford

TREASURED PHOTO

Mrs J Lewer of London writes:
'This family photo was taken at Land's End in 1959. We always took our holidays together. This was a camping holiday and great fun, especially for the children, as they had lots of safe areas to play in. We spent many memorable holidays in Cornwall.'

Well, fancy that!

Footballing howlers...

- *If you don't believe you can win, there's no point getting out of bed at the end of the day.* Neville Southall
- *I'd like to play for an Italian club; like Barcelona.* Mark Draper
- *You've got to believe that you're going to win. I believe that we'll win the World Cup until the final whistle blows and we're knocked out.* Peter Shilton
- *I can see the carrot at the end of the tunnel.* Stuart Pearce
- *I couldn't settle in Italy. It was like living in a foreign country.* Ian Rush
- *It was like the ref had a brand-new yellow card and wanted to see if it worked.* Les Ferdinand

TEA-TIME TREATS

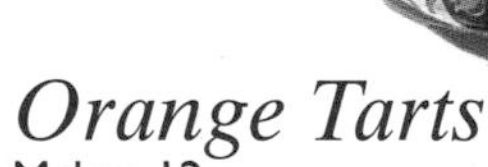

Orange Tarts

Makes 12

- 6 oz/175 g pastry
- 2 oz/50 g caster sugar
- 1 egg
- 2 oz/50 g butter
- ½ oz/10 g ground almonds
- Finely-grated rind of one orange

1 Preheat oven to 190°C/375°F/Gas Mark 5.
2 Roll out the pastry thinly and use to line 12 tartlet tins.
3 Put sugar and egg in a bowl and stir until evenly mixed. Melt butter and stir into egg mixture. Stir in almonds and orange rind.
4 Half fill the pastry cases with the mixture and bake for about 15 minutes. Cool on wire rack.

HEALTHY LIVING

Alternative cures for a headache

- ❑ A headache is one sign of dehydration. Drink a few glasses of water to see if it works.
- ❑ Lie down in a darkened room with a cool cloth on your forehead.
- ❑ Ask your partner to massage your back and shoulder. If you're on your own, gently massage your temples.
- ❑ Take a warm shower – many sufferers swear by it.

Pause for thought

A favourite poem sent in by Mrs E Abbott, Church Accrington, Lancashire:

Losing the One You Love

On the day that we were married
They told us we were one,
But no one told us what to do
When half of one is gone.
What to do with half a heart
Or half a will to care?
What do you do with half a life
Now the other half's not there?
You were the other half of me,
A heart linked with my own.
What do I do with half a life,
Now I am on my own?

'You must be joking'

"Did you hear about the lion tamer who had a nasty accident?"
"No, what was his name?"
"Claud Bottom!"

DO YOU REMEMBER...

PIC: MIRROR

...the Sinclair C5?

WITH traffic congestion in towns and cities becoming an increasing problem, electronics expert Sir Clive Sinclair thought he had the answer. In January 1985 he invented a one-seater electric tricycle called the Sinclair C5. Powered by a battery, it was capable of travelling 20 miles before it needed re-charging and cost £399.

But the lightweight C5 was no match for London's lorries and buses and looked rather vulnerable on our congested roads. But Sir Clive predicted that by the end of the 20th century, the petrol engine would be extinct. Unfortunately, it was the C5 that expired after just two months.

...the Kodak Brownie?

FOR most of us, our first photographs were taken with a box Brownie. Some are still tucked away at home today.

The Brownie box camera was manufactured by the Eastmann Kodak Company in America in 1900 and for the next 50 years, it was the most famous camera in the world.

The first model was made of jute board, stiffened with wood and covered with imitation leather. But it was too flimsy, so before it went on general sale, alterations had to be made to make it more sturdy.

The Brownie was a great success, its cheapness and simplicity of use ('can be operated by any schoolboy or girl') inspiring many imitators. But the Brownie remained popular until it gave way to the Instamatic in the 1960s.

Brits for all seasons

TIME FOR TEA

SUMMER is upon us and one of the delights of the season is to take a trip into the countryside and sample the delights of a British tea room. The idea of afternoon tea is said to have been introduced by Anna, 7th Duchess of Bedford, in the early 1800s, who devised the idea of a light meal to stave off hunger pangs before dinner. The Earl of Sandwich had already put a filling between two slices of bread and this was an ideal snack for tea, taken from four to five o'clock in the afternoon.

Today a perfect tea consists of home-made scones with a dollop of summer fruit jam and topped with a generous helping of clotted cream – this isn't the time to count calories! It should be accompanied by a pot of freshly-brewed tea, served in bone china cups. The pot should hold enough for two good cups each, and a jug of milk should be provided (not those irritating plastic cartons that are the devil to open). Extra boiling water should be provided to freshen the pot after your first cup. If this isn't forthcoming, don't be too British to ask!

We Brits still drink twice as much tea as coffee, with the majority being consumed in the Midlands, the regional king of the cuppa for the last 20 years. Our favourite brand is Tetley, followed by PG Tips. On average we drink around three cups of tea a day, and drinking it can do you the power of good? The milk provides calcium, zinc and potassium as well as vitamins.

Substances in tea, called polyphenols, are also thought to lower rates of heart disease and cancer. We think that calls for another brew!

PIC: PHOTODISC

The grocer's shop

By Maureen Brown

Forest Stores stood at the end of Surrey Street; Littlehampton. It was a double-fronted grocer's shop and had three steps leading from the pavement to the door. In the flat above the shop lived the manager and his wife, Mr and Mrs Scott. Below the shop was a cellar, the entrance to which was at the end of the bacon counter where a wooden trap door could be lifted up, revealing a flight of uneven steps. In this cellar was the coffee roaster. Coffee was delivered as sacks of green beans and then roasted, filling the shop with a delicious aroma.

I started work in the shop in 1950 when I left school, and my wage was £1 10s a week (£1.50). The shop opened at 8.30am and closed at 5.30pm, with one hour for lunch Monday to Friday, except Wednesday when it closed at one o'clock.

The staff wore thick white overalls and white hair bands held on with clips. The overalls had no buttons, just little round holes into which we had to insert a button and hold it on with a split ring.

My first counter was dry goods. Everything came in bulk and was kept in wooden drawers behind the counter, ready to be weighed on request – split peas and lentils were the worst to handle because they would slip off the scoop. Tea, sugar and soap powder were the only goods rationed. Tea came loose and had to be weighed – no tea bags back then. There were no sweet biscuits available, only cream crackers.

Customers were greeted with a smile and, 'Good morning Madam, can I help you?' Chairs were available for customers, but the staff never sat down or had a tea break. If there were no one to serve, I stocked shelves.

At the end of the counter was the coffee grinder. After the green beans were roasted brown, they were fetched and ground for the customers. Next to the grinder stood the brass scales, polished every day in readiness for a visit from the Weights and Measures man who came to check that the weights were correct.

Every summer, 2 1b of jam sugar was allowed on each ration book for housewives to make jam from the fruit in their gardens. Sugar came in 56 1b sacks and was weighed into blue bags. There were no tills on the counters – the customer's money, plus a ticket showing the amount, was put into a wooden container that was attached to overhead wires. Pulling a handle sent the little dish to the cashier's office; it was returned with the customer's change.

The shop cat wandered about as he pleased, something that would never be allowed in these days

Another job was to make up the orders that came from the big houses out in the country. Goods were packed carefully into boxes, making sure that nothing could be damaged, for the van driver to deliver. No one had to carry their shopping home – local deliveries were made by a boy on a bike.

After a few months I was moved on to the provisions counter and was taught how to cut up a side of bacon, cut a cheese and sell the wines, spirits and beers. I can still remember the price of a bottle of gin – it was 32 shillings (£1.60). The weekly amount of rations for one book was 3 oz of butter, 5 oz of bacon, 4 oz of cooking fat and 1oz of cheese, plus one egg. Farm workers and those in the building trade were allowed an extra 14 oz of cheese a week for packed lunches.

The cheese came in large blocks weighing about 56 lb. They were cut through the centre by a wire with wooden handles, and then quartered. After that it could be cut on the cheese board into smaller portions ready for the customers, making sure there was no waste and everyone got their fair share of the rind.

The bacon came as a whole half or side of pig and was always smoked. No waste was allowed – every piece of bone had to be removed clean.

The bacon was now ready for the machine to cut into rashers. Bacon was always cut on demand. The bacon machine wasn't electric but the blade rotated at great speed, so you had to watch out that you didn't lose a finger!

At the end of each day this machine had to be cleaned with scalding-hot water because it got very greasy. The counter top, made of marble, also had to be scrubbed down every day. Cooking fat came in 28 lb blocks that had to be cut with a knife, another greasy job. Trying not to get grease all over the customers' ration books when you marked off their ration was a work of art.

The shop cat wandered about the shop as he pleased, something that would never be allowed in these days of pre-packaged food and check-out tills. I suppose it's all a lot more efficient now, but I do miss the personal service of the old grocers' shops, when customers paused to swap news while their order was made up by staff who took great pride in their work.

July 2003

HIGH DAYS AND HOLIDAYS...

PIC: HULTON ARCHIVE

Well-Dressing

In July one of the old customs which combines a religious work with floral decorations is the art of Well-Dressing, when the village well or source of water is dressed. This usually takes the form of biblical scenes on beds of damp clay, with flowers, petals, leaves, mosses and plants.

The Bale (July 4)

This date is Old Midsummer Eve and at Whalton, near Morpeth in Northumberland, it is the day of The Bale, or Baal Fire. 'Bale' is a Saxon word meaning bonfire and at 7.45pm, the fiddlers and pipers play and children dance around a great bonfire on the village green.

St Swithin's Day (July 15)

St Swithin died in AD862, a champion of the poor and church builder of Winchester. He once helped a woman whose eggs had been knocked to the floor by using magic to restore them to their shells. This is why his shrine and the cathedral altar screen at Winchester have an eggshell motif.

According to his wishes, after his death, he was buried outdoors so that humbling rain could fall on him. He sent his 40 days of rain to those who wished to bury him indoors. To this day the legend says if it rains on St Swithin's Day it will continue for 40 days.

TUESDAY	1	
WEDNESDAY	2	
THURSDAY	3	
FRIDAY	4	
SATURDAY	5	
SUNDAY	6	Final day of Wimbledon Tennis Championships
MONDAY	7	
TUESDAY	8	Hampton Court Flower Show
WEDNESDAY	9	
THURSDAY	10	
FRIDAY	11	
SATURDAY	12	
SUNDAY	13	
MONDAY	14	
TUESDAY	15	
WEDNESDAY	16	
THURSDAY	17	
FRIDAY	18	The BBC Proms begin

SATURDAY	19
SUNDAY	20
MONDAY	21
TUESDAY	22
WEDNESDAY	23
THURSDAY	24
FRIDAY	25
SATURDAY	26
SUNDAY	27
MONDAY	28
TUESDAY	29
WEDNESDAY	30
THURSDAY	31 August YOURS on sale

This month don't forget to...

- Drink plenty of water to avoid dehydration.
- Give your thirsty hanging baskets a daily drink, too! But don't forget to enjoy yourself in the garden – sit back and enjoy the fruits of your labour.

- Tune into Radio 3 for the start of the Proms.
- Head off to the Bristol Community Festival, one of the country's best summer music and arts events (14/15, to be confirmed)

PIC: MIRROR

World Cup win

It happened in July...

July 1, 1937: The 999 emergency telephone service comes into operation.

July 30, 1966: England beat rivals Germany to win football's World Cup on home ground.

July 19, 1983: The remains of a new species of dinosaur is discovered in a clay pit in Surrey.

June 30-July 6

"Why are you looking so miserable?"
"I've just lost my dog."
"Well, why not advertise for him in the paper?'
"It wouldn't do any good. He can't read."

Letter of my life

Ros Glickman, Barton on Sea, Hampshire

Thirty years ago I was given a book, 84 Charing Cross Road, by Helene Hanff. I felt I had to write to the author. I contacted the publisher and asked if they would forward a letter.

A correspondence with Helene Hanff started which lasted more than 20 years. I would write occasionally and Helene always responded – and always written by hand.

One day, the phone rang and a voice said, 'Ros this is Helene Hanff'. She was in London for a few weeks and wondered if we could meet up.

She was a marvellous person – tiny but feisty and very funny. We went to Keats's House, and then had lunch at a nearby hotel. A few days later, Helene returned to New York and our correspondence continued intermittently.

Sitting in my doctor's surgery one day, I glanced through a newspaper and read, 'Helene Hanff, author of 84 Charing Cross Road, died on July 4, 1997'.

A few years passed and I was in the process of moving house. I found the small box containing Helene's letters. I reread them before deciding they should be auctioned.

Sotheby's sold my letters for £395. I decided to write an article about my correspondence with Helene and submitted it to a journal who printed it two months later.

Well, fancy that!

A 'jiffy' is an actual unit of time for 1/100th of a second.

Beautiful Britain

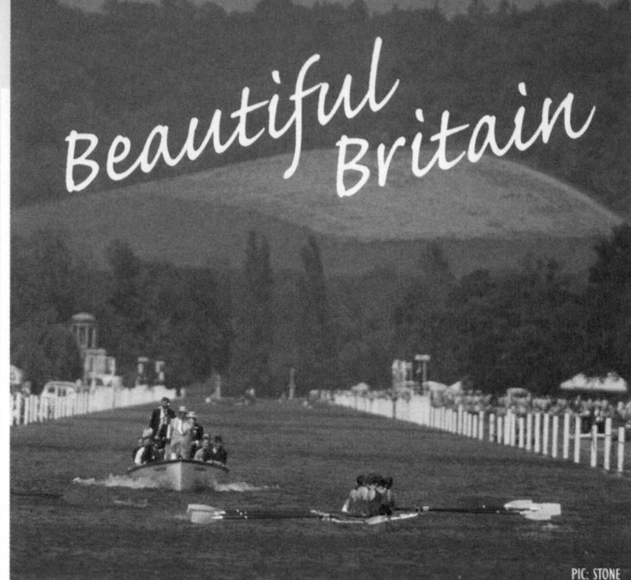

PIC: STONE

HENLEY-ON-THAMES

In 1829, the first Oxford versus Cambridge boat race took place along the River Thames between Hambledon Lock and Henley Bridge, and since 1839, Henley has held its Regatta in the first week of July (it became a Royal Regatta when Prince Albert became its patron in 1851).

Henley-on-Thames has a long history, from its medieval beginnings as a port supplying wood and grain along the river to London. And the 13th century nave arcades in St Mary's Church, in the main part of the town, can still be seen.

There is now a River and Rowing Museum at Henley, displaying artefacts and pictures associated with the sport and its history, as well as exhibitions about the town itself.

In the 18th century, Henley-on-Thames was a hotbed of artistic achievement and innovative engineering. Among others, non-conformist minister the Reverend Humphrey Gainsborough was also an inventor, and believed to be responsible for the development of a steam engine with a separate condenser. His brother was the artist, Thomas Gainsborough.

And local socialite Anne Damer, was also a sculptress and carved the keystones for Henley Bridge

HEALTHY LIVING

Stay safe behind the wheel

- ❑ Have your eyes checked regularly.
- ❑ Avoid driving at night where possible – our night vision deteriorates as we grow older.
- ❑ Take plenty of breaks on any long journey.
- ❑ Consider buying a mobile phone – essential in an emergency.

TIP TIME

Use soothing garden herbs in your bath. Put them into a leg from a pair of tights, tie them to the tap and immerse in water. Let the herbs infuse for a few minutes before getting in.

Pause for thought

'A friend I've known for over 50 years recently 'qualified' as a senior citizen,' writes Mrs J Smith from Rugby, Warwickshire. 'To welcome here into the clan I wrote this poem':

Instructions on becoming an OAP (sorry, 'Senior Citizen')

The time has come (as the Walrus said) to discard many things,
To instigate the changes that OAP-hood brings.

Here is a list of things that on you I must impress,
Mainly all the changes concern your mode of dress.

Starting with your lingerie (which becomes your underwear)
It's cover up every piece of flesh and leave not a morsel bare.

The 'push-up, push-out, round-'em-up' bra will have to go;
It's front-fastening, boned and DD cups now; no cleavage must you show.

Bikini briefs, eye-watering thongs, and lacy things that tease
Are suddenly interlock with gussets, and elastic round the knees.

15-denier nylons, lacy hold-ups, and stockings sheer and fine
Become ribbed wool, or something that resembles knotted twine.

Stiletto shoes and strappy sandals with heels so thin and high?
These change to brogues and fluffy slippers; it's enough to make you cry.

Those sparkling Lurex boob tubes and the belt you called a skirt?
Well, say hello to lambswool twin-sets – with pearls you'll be a cert!

Well, this is all you need to know, and I'm sure you will agree
That we say 'Knickers' to the lot of them – and go out on a shopping spree!

TREASURED PHOTO

Sheila Garrett of Burton on Trent writes: 'I am the middle one of three sisters. Audrey, the eldest, now lives in New Zealand and Jean, the youngest, lives in Strood, Kent. Jean and I loved dressing up but I've no idea where the clothes came from. In the photo I'm dressed in Dad's cap, shirt and trousers – held up by an old tie.

Jean's wearing a beautiful hat and I will never forget her dress – it was like organza and all frills (I think she loved that dress) – and she wore a smock over it. Dad always had a good vegetable garden and kept a few chickens, so we had fresh eggs and the odd boiling fowl. They were happy, carefree days. Jean is now 71 and I'm 73; we were about 10 and 12 in the photo.'

I WISH I'D SAID THAT...

Blessed are they who can laugh at themselves, for they shall always be amused. – Anon

PERFECT PUDDINGS

Strawberry Swirl

- 8 oz/225 g strawberries
- 2 eggs
- 6 oz/175 g double cream
- 3 oz/75 g icing sugar

1 Pureé strawberries.
2 Beat eggs to a froth and stir in icing sugar. Add strawberry pureé.
3 Whip cream until thick but not stiff. Fold into strawberry mixture, but don't beat too vigorously.
4 Pour into a plastic container and freeze for at least two hours.

July 7-13

TREASURED PHOTO

Joan Hammond of Wickham Market in Suffolk treasures this picture. She writes:

'My friend Dorothy Williams and I met in the ATS when I was stationed in Naples. As a lorry driver, I would take groups to Sorrento and Amalfi at weekends and Dorothy was always there. We have remained friends for 56 years. (Dorothy is on the right in the photo, taken in Naples.)'

A man inserted an ad in the classifieds: 'Wife wanted.' Next day he received 100 letters. They all said the same thing: 'You can have mine.'

HEALTHY LIVING

Face savers

- ❑ If you have oily skin, eat a diet rich in vitamin A – melons, spinach and broccoli are excellent sources.
- ❑ For dry skins, eat foods rich in essential fatty acids such as salmon and tuna.
- ❑ Don't clean your face more than twice a day – even if you have an oily skin. Oil is the skin's natural barrier – not a sign that it's dirty. Too much cleansing can even make it more oily!
- ❑ Try to go without make-up every now and then, to give your skin chance to 'breathe'.

Letter of my life

The first half of 1941 was not a happy period of my life. The war was on, I had been called up, leaving my home for the first time, had finished my Army training and been posted far away from home with no hope of leave for some time. I was at a low ebb when the letter arrived. It was an ordinary day in July, but it was to change my life.

I looked at the unfamiliar writing and eagerly opened the envelope. It was from a young lady who worked at the Council House, Coventry. It appeared she had been talking to a friend of mine and asked him if he knew of a soldier who needed cheering up – and he had given her my address.

Naturally I replied and soon we were writing to each other every week, which eventually became every day. On my first leave I asked her to meet me. We decided on Northampton railway station – she would be wearing a Royal Artillery badge (which I had sent her) in the lapel of her coat. What a wonderful occasion that turned out to be, for very soon the seed of love had been sown and we were radiantly happy. I will never forget her smile as we met, the thrill of our first kiss, the wonderful joy of being together.

On March 21, 1945, we were married and were blessed with a son in July 1946. But through that letter I can honestly say I found the joy of living, for she gave me so much love.

Not only was she my wife, she was a wonderful companion and the greatest friend anyone ever had. For 53 years we were together, sharing each other's joys and sorrows, until she was called home. I miss her so much but I still have the letter she wrote some 60 years ago. Today it is a bit the worse for wear, but as I read it at this moment, my life is surrounded by so many memories that I pause and thank God that she wrote the letter which, to me, was the letter of my life.

Francis James, Brackley Northamptonshire

TIP TIME

To get more juice from lemons, first soak them in hot water for a few seconds. Then roll them on your board or work surface, under the palm of your hand.

Pause for thought

Joyce Phillips from Littlehampton, West Sussex, sent in this photo of herself and her brother, and also her favourite prayer. "It brings me comfort and peace," she says.

This My Prayer

Bless me, heavenly Father,
forgive my erring ways,
Grant me strength to serve Thee,
put purpose in my days...
Give me understanding
enough to make me kind
So I may judge all people
with my heart and not my mind...
And teach me to be patient
in everything I do,
Content to trust your wisdom
and to follow after You...
And help me when I falter
and hear me when I pray
And receive me in Thy Kingdom
to dwell with Thee some day.

TEA-TIME TREATS

Lemon Curd

- 3 lemons, rind and juice
- 3 oz/75 g butter
- 3 eggs, well whipped
- 9 oz/250 g sugar

1 Put all ingredients in a bowl over a pan of boiling water, stirring continuously until butter melts.

2 Carry on stirring for a further 5 minute until mixture thickens slightly. Pour into sterilised jars. Cool, then seal jars. Use within two weeks.

I WISH I'D SAID THAT...

"Ensnared with flowers, I fall on grass. – Andrew Marvell, English poet"

Well, fancy that!

The elephant is the only mammal that can't jump.

PIC: PORT SUNLIGHT VILLAGE TRUST

PORT SUNLIGHT VILLAGE, BIRKENHEAD, MERSEYSIDE

Port Sunlight Village is a picturesque, much visited place, but did you know that it takes its name from the famous Sunlight Soap?

William Lever chose this site for his expanding soap business in the 19th century. He wanted to build quality housing for his workers, as well as a factory, and he helped to design it as a garden village, employing nearly 30 different architects to help create his vision.

Port Sunlight is now a conservation area and is still contained within its original boundaries. It is home to the famous Lady Lever Art Gallery, which has a famous collection of pre-Raphaelite paintings and Wedgwood china. There is also a Heritage Centre, where you can see a scale model of the village and of a Victorian house, as well as the original plans for the village buildings and displays of the packaging and advertising of the time.

The architect who designed the Port Sunlight Heritage Centre also designed another magnet for tourists – Blackpool Tower.

July 14-20

I WISH I'D SAID THAT...

Music is the only language in which you cannot say a mean or sarcastic thing. – J Erskine

PIC: LLANWRTYD WELLS TOURIST BOARD

LLANWRTYD WELLS, POWYS, WALES

Llanwrtyd Wells developed as a spa town in the 18th century due to its sulphur spring, which still flows today. It is set in glorious countryside but for visitors who've had their fill of exploring and soaking up the scenery, there are a number of interesting events, including a man versus horse marathon and a cycling event held in conjunction with the local beer festival, known as the Real Ale Wobble!

The most famous of them all, though, has to be The World Bog Snorkelling Championships, where contestants 'swim' through a 60-yard trench and back, without using conventional swimming strokes.

Wearing snorkels and flippers, these brave souls have to contend with freezing cold water as well as the mud, which reduces visibility below the water to zero, and they are allowed to surface only twice during the contest – for navigational purposes.

Competitors come from all over the world to join in the fun.

Letter of my life

Mrs I A Rickard, Tywyn, Gwynedd

On July 15, 2000, my father passed away. When I went to register his death I noticed his mother's name wasn't that of the Grandma I knew.

I soon discovered that he had been fostered when he was three. It also gave his place of birth – Louth. I wrote to all the Kingswoods in the Louth area, his place of birth, enclosing stamped, addressed envelopes. One day in August I came home from work and found one of my SAEs on the mat. It was a letter from my dad's half-sister, Hilda. She told me that my father's mother was still alive, aged 96. She also told me there were two older brothers.

I just sat and cried, so sad that I found all this out too late for Dad to meet his lost family. Also, I was crying because I was so happy that I had such a big family, after thinking I had only one cousin left.

I have since met my new family, which once again had me in tears, because Uncle George is so much like Dad in all ways.

TIP TIME

Before spending money at a video shop, check whether you can borrow the film from your local library.

Well, fancy that!

Where is there a flag that is never saluted? The only place where a flag flies all day, never goes up or comes down, never flies at half mast and does not get saluted is the moon. It is of course, the American flag after the successful moon landing on July 20, 1969.

QWhy don't bananas like sunbathing?
ABecause they have a tendency to peel!

Treasured Photo

Seaside memories are rekindled by this photo, sent in by Kathy Jackson from Newport, South Wales:
'It was taken on Bournemouth beach in 1965. It shows my parents, husband, myself and our two sons. I knitted their sweaters and they were much admired. Just look at the clothes the adults were wearing! It seems incredible now that men would wear jacket and tie on the beach. And look at my Mum's hat!'

Healthy Living

In-flight exercise

Health experts recommend a few simple exercises, which can be performed from your airline seat:

- Press down on the balls of your feet, with your heels raised off the floor. Gently push the heels back down to the floor and then lift your heels up. Repeat four times.
- Lift your right foot a couple of inches off the floor. Gently rotate the ankle by drawing a circle in the air with your toes. Do four circles to the right; then four to the left. Repeat with the left foot.

Tea-time Treats

Yoghurt Cake

This makes a deliciously different cake, says Mollie High of Morton, Lincolnshire

- 5 oz/150 g carton yoghurt
- 6 oz/175 g self-raising flour
- 5 oz/150 g sugar
- 2 oz/ 50 g butter, softened
- 2 eggs
- Dried fruit and cherries, to taste
- Peel and flaked almonds, to sprinkle

1 Preheat oven to 180°C/350°F/Gas Mark 4. Grease and flour a 2 lb cake tin.
2 Mix together yoghurt, flour, sugar, butter and eggs until smooth.
3 Stir in dried fruit and cherries (as much as you prefer) and pour mixture into prepared tin.
4 Sprinkle peel and almonds on top. Bake for 45 minutes.

Pause for thought

My Garden

Does your calendar quote, like mine,
'A garden is a lovesome thing, God wot'?
I look out, as the weather is fine,
And a lovesome thing my garden is not!

It's home to snails and also to slugs,
Greenfly and lice are prolific,
Small boys call to study the bugs.
In fact, it's really horrific,

The grass is long and full of moss,
And flowers need dead-heading.
I'm in despair and at a loss,
I'll have to buy plants for bedding.

I'll invite Alan Titchmarsh to tea
And ask him to landscape my plot
Which later, when shown on TV
Will be a lovesome thing, God wot?

Sylvia Stilts, London N20

July 21-27

TEA-TIME TREATS

Nutty Choc Bites

- 12 oz/350 g milk chocolate chips
- 5 oz/150 g butter
- 3 oz/75 g soft dark brown sugar
- 4 oz/100 g Greek yoghurt
- 4 oz/100 g pecan nuts, chopped
- 5 oz/150 g raisins
- 5 oz/150 g sultanas
- 4 oz/100 g Nice biscuits

1 Lightly grease and line a 2 lb/200 g loaf tin.
2 Melt chocolate and butter in a bowl over a pan of steaming water. Stir in the sugar.
3 Remove from heat and stir in yoghurt, pecans, raisins and sultanas until evenly combined.
4 Spoon one quarter of mixture into the tin and press a layer of biscuits on top. Continue layering the biscuits and chocolate mixture, ending with a chocolate layer.
5 Press a piece of parchment on top and cover the tin with foil. Chill in fridge until firmly set. Turn out, peel off the lining paper and cut into thin slices.

PIC: TATE & LYLE SUGARS

I WISH I'D SAID THAT...

"If you want to eat well in Britain, eat three breakfasts. – Somerset Maugham, British writer"

"You must be joking"

Getting married is very much like going to the restaurant with friends. You order what you want and when you see what the other fellow has, you wish you'd ordered that.

TREASURED PHOTO

There's a touching tale behind this photo. Vera Hilton of Weston-super-Mare writes:

'The picture was taken when I was eight years old (I'm now 83). The Teddy came from a fun fair while I was on holiday with my sister. We went every day to try to win him and on the last day I cried my eyes out because we'd spent all our pocket money and couldn't ask for more. The kind man behind the stall told me I could take the Teddy because he'd miss me!

Later, during the War, poor Teddy and all my dolls were stolen during an air raid while we were down the shelter and were bombed. And Granddad's little dog Kitty ran away and was never found. This upset us more than the air raid. My daughter was a baby then and I'd kept all my toys for her, so I was upset to think I'd treasured them for so long, only for them to be stolen.'

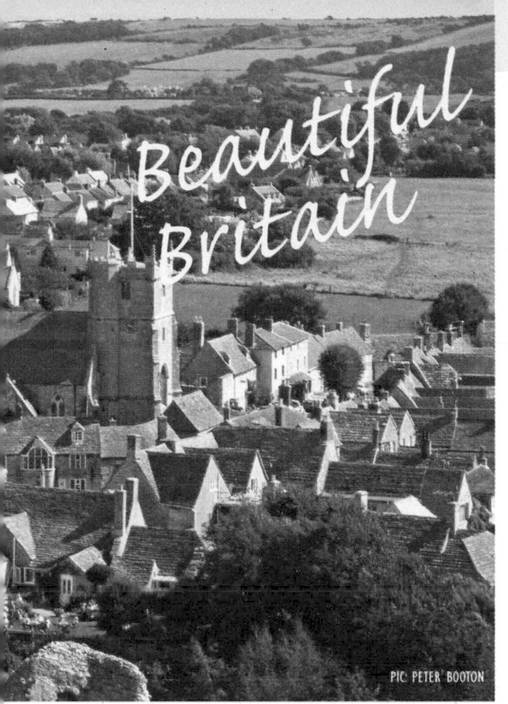

PIC: PETER BOOTON

WAREHAM, DORSET

Bounded by the River Piddle (yes, really – although it is now known as the Trent on one side, and the Frome on the other), Wareham is a pretty market town that was a major port until medieval times.

Historical interest includes massive earth ramparts that were built by King Alfred the Great for protection, a Saxon church, St Martin's, dating back to the 11th century and a mixture of stone cottages and Georgian town houses. In 1762, thatched roofs were banned in Wareham after the town was badly damaged by a succession of fires.

Nearby Corfe Castle watches over the town. This is where the young King Edward was murdered in 978 by his brother, Ethelred the Unready. The castle was beseiged twice during the Civil War, as the last Royalist stronghold between London and Exeter, and finally succumbed in 1646 when it was looted, then blown up, on the orders of Parliament.

There is an annual carnival when revellers take part in events over several days to raise money for charity.

TIP TIME

Nightdress cases are difficult to find. I use a round, zipped cushion cover. My bed looks smart, it didn't cost the earth and it does the job!

Mrs V M Fuller, Worthing

Letter of my life

The letter that changed my life came in July 1939 when I was just 19. It stated that I had been accepted into the Women's Land Army and was to report to a farm at Eashing.

I'd had a strict upbringing with church three times on Sunday, and was working as a housekeeper. Of course this changed drastically– directly after reporting for duty I was given a stool and promptly positioned under a cow! I'd never been near these animals in my life so it was a rude awakening!

I enjoyed six years of work on the farm, with all sorts of farm work and various animals, even working with huge shire horses.

I still keep in touch with the farming folk I worked with. I now appreciate what hard work goes into producing food.

Gwen Lawrence, Woking, Surrey

Pause for thought

"Do other mothers feel as I do, I wonder?" asks Mary McCuster, from Ipswich. "Should we have done things differently where our children are concerned?" She sent in this lovely poem:

If I had my child to raise all over again,
I'd finger paint more, and point the finger less.
I'd do less correcting and more connecting.
I'd take my eyes off my watch, and watch with my eyes.
I would care to know less, and know to care more.
I'd take more hikes and fly more kites.
I'd stop playing serious, and seriously play.
I would run through more fields and gaze at more stars,
I'd do more hugging, and less tugging.
I would be firm less often, and affirm much more.
I'd build self-esteem first, and the house later.
I'd teach less about the love of power, and more about the
power of LOVE.

Well, fancy that!

Ernest Vincent Wright's 1939 novel Gadsby has more than 50,000 words – none of which includes the letter 'e'.

HEALTHY LIVING

Best foot forward!

Summer's here and it's time to put on your sandals but are your feet fit for public display?

- Soak them in warm water with a few drops of almond oil, plus peppermint or other essential oil.
- Use a pumice stone to get rid of hardened skin. Dry thoroughly, then moisturise feet. Cut nails straight across, to prevent ingrowing.

July 28-August 3

Healthy Living

Terrific tomatoes

Tomatoes in your salad or a dollop of ketchup on the side of your plate can do you the power of good, thanks to the pigment lycopene, which gives the tom its red colour. Many health experts believe it is this pigment that gives the humble tom its health benefits against cancer, heart disease and osteoporosis. Baked beans in tomato sauce, pizza toppings and tomato ketchup get the thumbs up, too.

"You must be joking"

A Boy Scout was at summer camp when he was stung by a wasp. "I'm in agony," he told his pack leader.

"Don't worry, we'll put some cream on it."

"You'll be lucky. It'll be miles away by now."

Treasured Photo

Mrs E G Archer of Stoke-on-Trent sent in this charming studio portrait, typical of the time, with its idyllic backcloth, heavy drapes and ornate stool. She writes:

'This photo is of my mother in 1932, when she was still Miss Gertrude Tilson. She and my father were married for 68 years. Mother was 88 when she died.'

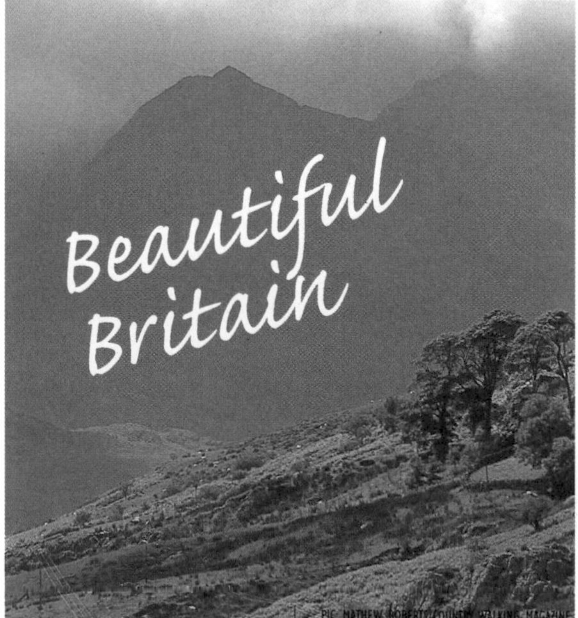

PIC: MATHEW ROBERTS/COUNTRY WALKING MAGAZINE

Snowdonia National Park, Wales

The Welsh name for Snowdonia is 'Eryri', which means 'place of eagles', and the mountain range in this area, including Snowdon and Cader Idris, is spectacular.

There are many signs of ancient peoples in Snowdonia, including stone-age burial chambers and bronze-age burial cairns, as well as Roman forts, and Welsh and Norman castles.

The beautiful, wild countryside, with its looming mountains, lends itself to stories and the whole area is steeped in ancient myths, including Arthurian legends. The Welsh name for Mount Snowdon is 'Yr Wyddfa', meaning 'great tomb', and legend has it that this is the burial place of a giant who was killed by King Arthur. It is also said that anyone who spends a night on Cader Idris will awake a madman or a poet – or not at all.

TIP TIME

These days most suitcases look very alike. When travelling, tie a handkerchief or some ribbon to the handle of each piece of your luggage. This makes it easy to spot.

Joyce Thurston,
Clacton-on-Sea

Letter of my life

Mrs D Bee,
Yaddlethorpe,
Scunthorpe

I didn't receive the letter personally, but the nuns in the home I was in did. The letter said I could leave. There was a job for me in service at Uppingham School. I couldn't take it in as, after 15 years, I was free. I would have a name at last and not a number. I was known as Number 7. All my clothes and brush and comb had CHI 7 (Children's Home number 1, followed by my individual number 7) on them.

This was 1950. I was put in the home when I was one because my mother died. I was known as a bastard and was continually reminded of this. We had prayers morning, noon and night and had to learn a verse by heart from the Bible each day, and on Sundays the Collect for the week. I had two sisters but they put us in separate homes so we couldn't mix. We had a terrible time as the least infringement was punishable.

I remember I was a bed wetter so in the mornings, from five years old, I had my sheets wrapped round me and had to walk round the yard till they dried. I can laugh now, but it wasn't funny then. We had three rounds of bread a day, one in the morning after porridge and two at night. We had either marg or jam, not both.

The nuns were not kind. There was no sympathy, no cuddles. I can't remember a kindness, just laws that had to be obeyed. That letter giving me a job was a miracle.

I WISH I'D SAID THAT...

"What dreadful hot weather we have! It keeps me in a continual state of inelegance."
– Jane Austen, in a letter

PERFECT PUDDINGS

Curd Cheese Tart

- 6 oz/175 g shortcrust pastry
- 3 oz/75 g butter
- 2 oz/50 g sugar
- 2 eggs, beaten
- Few drops almond essence
- 4 oz/100 g curd cheese
- 2 oz/50 g ground almonds
- Juice of ½ lemon
- 2 oz/50 g sultanas

1. Roll out pastry and line 7 in/18cm diameter flan dish. Bake blind for 5-7 minutes. Remove from oven.
2. Cream butter and sugar, then add eggs a little at a time, and the essence.
3. Add curd cheese and ground almonds, finally lemon juice and sultanas. Mix well.
4. Fill pastry case and cook in a moderate oven until pale brown.

Well, fancy that!

The shortest full sentence in the English language is 'Go'.

Pause for thought

Jesus is Everything

I've never seen my God and King…
But I know he is in everything.
He's in the beauty of the flowers,
Leaves on trees and in the showers.
The sand on the beach, the vast ocean around.
He's the day and the night and in every sound.
He's the smile on the faces of people I meet.
He's the autumn, winter, summer and spring.
In short, He is every real thing.
My God is no stranger to me when I pray.
He's my friend to the end of my days.
So, please show me the way to spread the great story,
That His is the Kingdom, the Power and the Glory.

Julia Prytherck-Jones,
Aberdare, Glamorgan

Do you remember...

Harold Larwood bowling for England

...the 'bodyline' cricket scandal?

EVEN if England's controversial 'bodyline' bowling strategy was before your time, most people remember the scandal!

It was a tactic adopted by the England captain, Douglas Jardine, to contain the prodigious scoring abilities of Australian batsman Donald Bradman in the 1932-33 Ashes series.

The theory was simple and involved using fast bowlers Harold Larwood and Bill Voce, to bowl on the line of the batsman's legs and body and restrict their stroke-playing options with a mass of close-in fielders on the leg side.

If the batsman couldn't play the ball, as they often couldn't, it could fracture his skull or ribs, and break the wickets. The bowler had to be quick and very accurate. Larwood could bowl on a penny and was fast.

Aussie Bill Woodford accused the England team of 'not playing cricket', after twice being hit by bouncers. Australia lost the series 4-1.

...having your hair permed?

OH, the dreaded permanent wave and smell of peroxide! First, your hair was divided into sections and perm solution dabbed on with a sponge or brush. Then it was tightly wound up with perm papers and rollers. More solution was dabbed on, then left to 'take', leaving 'madam' with a towel to mop up the drips. (And years ago, you'd then be hooked up to electric perm rollers!)

Then the solution was washed off and neutraliser applied. Out came the rollers and, oh, what bliss, as warm water washed your head! A squeeze of Estolan rubbed in to give your hair a shine, hair rollers in and off you went under the dryer!

But the arduous process was worth it in the end because didn't you look the bee's knees?

Brits for all seasons

Fun for all beside the seaside

THIS month we'll be heading to the seaside by the coachload.

In 2000, Blackpool was as popular as ever with 6,800,000 visitors to the Pleasure Beach, while in 2001, Brits took 27.9 million seaside holidays in the UK, spending £5.1 billion.

We've all heard of global warming but don't think that a long weekend in Skeggy will be just like sunning yourself in the South Pacific. The rest of the country might be baking, but by some climatic quirk, there always seems to be a stiff northerly wind whipping across the seafront.

But we can't be deterred by a bit of discomfort. All we need is a mac and a wind-break to see us through the worst of it. Even in the worst weather, you'll find a few brave souls paddling or in the swim!

PICS: HULTON ARCHIVE

And we're not afraid to spend a bob or two, either: in 2000, we Brits spent £32 billion on day trips alone!

Packed lunches always taste better by the sea – it puts the sand in sandwiches! Fish and chips or a pot of winkles on the pier is another great British tradition. Pier resorts are popular with all age groups. Thanks to The National Piers Society, founded in 1979 under Sir John Betjeman, more piers are being preserved although some face an uncertain future.

Pier amusements range from darts to rifle ranges and slot machines to the merry-go-round. Some gaming machines that take 2p pieces – winning the jackpot may only mean scooping 20p but it's still exciting.

It's a pleasure to browse around the shops along the prom. You'll still find 'kiss-me-quick' hats, children's windmills, bucket-and-spade sets, sticks of rock, flip-flops, suntan cream and those saucy postcards.

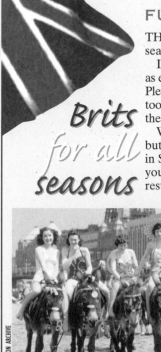

Jigsnip

With the help of just three rows of Across clues, see if you can fit the blocks into the empty grid to form a complete, symmetrical crossword. All of the Down words are associated with summer holidays.

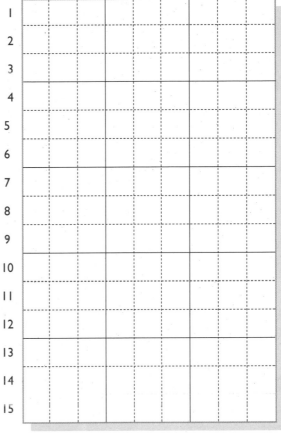

1
2
3
4
5
6
7
8
9
10
11
12
13
14
15

ACROSS ROWS
1 Had an inkling
3 Close • Wreck
5 Peninsula of Spain and Portugal

Solution on Page 159

U	S	H	T	E	N	B	R	B	R	I
R	T	R	R	A	C	Y	E	O	B	G
N	P	O	G	M	R	O	M	G	N	H
O	O	T	A	L	C	H	O	N	O	T
T	R	E	E	W	A	T	R	R	E	S
E	D	S	A	L	B	R	O	P	G	I
B	U	T	B	A	P	O	T	H	R	A
N	E	N	O	C	K	O	U	O	M	Y
O	B	R	U	O	T	L	G	N	E	T
T	R	I	D	R	A	Y	E	S	S	A
G	N	I	L	Q	U	S	K	G	R	E

Pathfinder

Starting from the red letter 'B', and moving up, down or sideways (but not diagonally), one letter at a time, can you find a continuous path through the names of fifteen UK seaside resorts? The pictured resort is the first on your trail.

Solution on Page 159

PIC: MIRROR

SUMMER FATE

By Polly Stephens

Holiday romances never last, so they say. But a group of pals went away together with the highest of hopes

If I hadn't gone to Blackpool that summer, everything would have been different. It wasn't where London girls usually went for their holiday. And to think it was Josie who suggested it.

We'd all heard of Blackpool and its Tower, of course. My mum knew someone who'd been up it. Lovely dance floor, they said, and a good tea for 1s 3d.

So when Josie suggested we go up north for our week's holiday, we all agreed. Dol's mum asked why we didn't we go to Clacton or Southend, but we'd made our minds up by then. In any case, Evie's dad, who was a long-distance lorry driver, was going to give us a lift.

The four of us had managed to get the same week off from work in Hackney, where we all worked as machinists. My dad called it a sweatshop but we felt lucky to have a job back then in the early 1930s, when so many were out of work. We'd just finished a major order for a big store and were ready for a break.

It was a lovely Saturday morning when we set off for Evie's house, lugging our suitcases. Dol came over all sentimental as we passed a wedding, saying she'd always wanted to be a summer bride. Josie said she needed a summer bridegroom first and we all started giggling. We'd stop and then someone would start us off again.

Josie was always quick. She was one of those girls who always looked smart whatever she was wearing. She was slim with nice legs, so knee-length skirts looked good on her. I kept hoping longer skirts would come back into fashion to hide my chubby calves.

Then we kissed each other and I thought my heart would burst

Blackpool didn't seem such a good idea after about five hours in the back of the lorry. There was only room for one of us up in the cab with Evie's dad. At first we took turns but, after a while, Josie said if she didn't sit there all the time, she'd be sick.

It was quite late when we reached Blackpool. Evie's dad drove slowly along, past all the 'No Vacancies' signs until we came to Sea View Guest House. We didn't have one, of course – a sea view – just rooftops and pigeons, but as Evie said, it was just like home, back in Bethnal Green.

The landlady, Mrs Billington, was a right old battleaxe. She was stout with buck teeth and a faint moustache, and wore a hairnet all the time. She read us the Riot Act before we'd even started: No stopping out late, no noise and no chaps in the bedrooms. ("We should be so lucky!" whispered Josie.)

When we'd unpacked, Dol came over all weepy. She'd never been away from home before and was missing it a bit. So I told her to hurry up and get her dance dress on or 'Kaiser Billington' would be locking the door on us. She cheered up a bit then.

We were all in good spirits when we got down to the local Palais and were soon enjoying a good dance session. Josie was a wonderful dancer, the sort people stop and look at. We all got partners, though. Dol was never a wallflower, with her sweet face and blonde hair. Evie and I had to wait a bit longer, chatting to each other while all the time keeping one eye open for any chap coming our way.

Suddenly Tom was standing in front of me, smiling and

The landlady, Mrs Billington, was a right old battleaxe. She was stout with buck teeth and a faint moustache, and wore a hairnet all the time

asking me to dance. It sounds silly, but I knew there and then he was Mr Right. I didn't say so, of course – he'd have run a mile! He said he worked for an engineering firm in Huddersfield, Yorkshire. I said: "Oh yes, you've got a good football team, haven't you, in the First Division?" He looked really pleased at that. He said people usually asked him if he sang in the Choral Society.

We stopped dancing after a while and sat down with a drink. We talked and talked. Everything he said was fascinating and, in turn, he seemed to hang on my every word. But then we were interrupted by Josie. She was in a bad mood so Tom fetched her a drink. She perked up a bit then, teasing him about the way he spoke, calling him 'Ee, bah gum'. But he didn't mind.

Tom and his friends were staying in Blackpool for a week, just like us, so we arranged to meet the next day. We had a lot of fun, splashing about in the sea, playing cricket on the beach, catching a tram to the south shore, going up the Tower.

And then all of a sudden it was our last day. I felt terribly upset at the thought that I wouldn't see Tom again; Yorkshire was such a long way from London. But Tom was behaving strangely. He was very quiet and I wondered if I'd offended him. To make matters worse, he seemed to be keeping away from me. Josie was all over him, flirting, making him laugh. I could have killed her.

That afternoon Tom and I found ourselves sitting in a shelter facing the sea – or where the sea would have been if the tide had been in! Josie had dragged Dol and Evie back to the shops to get spent up and the others were kicking a ball about.

I remember thinking 'It's now or never', so I asked Tom if I'd said or done something to upset him. He went a bit red and said Josie had told him I had a regular boyfriend at home – that I was as good as engaged. I was furious! I told him it wasn't true and that the only boyfriend I wanted was him.

Then he looked at me, really looked, and everything seemed to stop. It had gone dark, a big grey cloud blotting out the sun. We could hear shouts from people on the beach but they seemed miles away. Then we kissed each other and I thought my heart would burst. I don't know how long it was dark for – we sat holding hands, close together, kissing again and again. And then everything was bright again, with dazzling sunshine.

Josie and the others came back but we took no notice of them and after a while they went away again. Later Tom walked me back to the boarding house. It was the end of the beginning.

You asked me why Granddad and I speak so differently. "He talks like someone in Emmerdale," you said, "but you sound like Pauline in EastEnders." Well, now you know why.

August 2003

High days and holidays...

Lammastide (August 1)
To the Anglo-Saxons, the start of August was known as Hlafmas of Loaf-mass, or in Scotland, Lughnasad, the Feast of the Celtic Sun God, Lugh, who was seen as a God of Light whose spirit was the life of the growing corn. The Lammas Feast was seen as a celebration and a commemoration of this energy.

The Burryman (early August)
On the second Friday in August in South Queensbury, West Lothian, an extraordinary figure parades around the town, covered from head to foot with the sticky burrs of the burdock plant. Crowned with roses and carrying two staffs of flowers, he walks a nine-mile course around the town's boundaries to collect alms. The origins of this curious custom have never been fully explained although he was probably a pagan figure – a sea or fish god.

Music, poetry and crafts
August is the time for the Royal National Eisteddfod (the 'sitting down place') and each year its seat moves to a different venue in Wales. The proceedings are all in Welsh and the event is very popular; the 1993 Eisteddfod in Llanelwedd attracted more than 150,000 people.

PIC: HULTON ARCHIVE

Friday	1
Saturday	2
Sunday	3
Monday	4 Bank Holiday (Scotland)
Tuesday	5
Wednesday	6
Thursday	7
Friday	8
Saturday	9
Sunday	10 Edinburgh International Festival starts
Monday	11
Tuesday	12
Wednesday	13
Thursday	14
Friday	15
Saturday	16
Sunday	17
Monday	18

TUESDAY	19	
WEDNESDAY	20	
THURSDAY	21	
FRIDAY	22	
SATURDAY	23	
SUNDAY	24	
MONDAY	25	Bank Holiday (except Scotland)
TUESDAY	26	
WEDNESDAY	27	
THURSDAY	28	
FRIDAY	29	September YOURS on sale
SATURDAY	30	Edinburgh International Festival ends
SUNDAY	31	

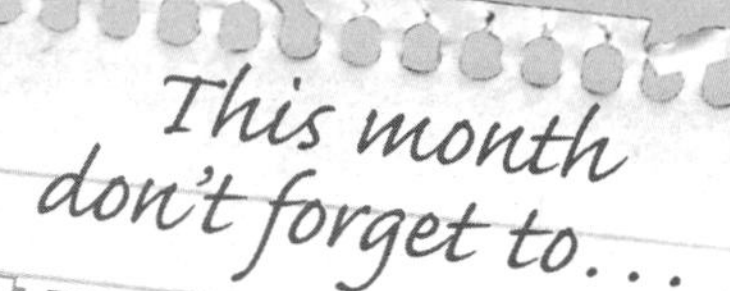

This month don't forget to...

- ☐ Wash and sterilise your jam jars in preparation for the preserves!
- ☐ Do a bit of work in the garden, even if the weather turns hot. Watering, grooming and weeding should be your priorities.

- ☐ Visit Edinburgh International Festival to enjoy three weeks of music, theatre and dance.
- ☐ Cancel the milk and the papers if you're going away. And get a kind neighbour to keep an eye on your home.

MORRIS MINOR
It's one of the family now

It happened in August...

August 30, 1916: Ernest Shackleton's crew was rescued from Elephant Island, after their terrible Antarctic expedition.

August 1, 1927: The Morris Minor first appeared.

August 30, 1940: Laurence Olivier and Vivien Leigh were married in New York.

August 12, 1964: Three women in London were found guilty of indecency after wearing topless dresses.

August 4-10

Pause for thought

Don't Pass Me By

I may be a bit hard of hearing,
and my eyesight decidedly dim,
But I try to be happy and cheerful,
being old is not really a sin,
It's true that I'm slow on the trigger,
and some modern things make me sigh,
But I still feel the same inside of my brain,
so please don't pass me by.
My voice has become harsh and croaky,
I suppose it's worn out through the years,
I've talked every day to folk round our way,
but now I am old they have nothing to say.
I won't waste your time, which is precious,
just a few words will brighten my day,
I have no-one else to talk to,
so don't look the other way.
A kindly smile and the touch of your hand
will brighten the gloomiest day,
It will bring some sunshine into my life,
and vanish the clouds of grey.
So the next time you go out walking,
remember the words of this rhyme,
If you see someone old and lonely,
just give them a bit of your time.

Mrs E Spencer, Portsea, Hampshire

Well, fancy that!

To make 1lb of honey, bees have to visit four million flowers, travelling a distance equal to four times around the world.

Healthy Living

Sensible snacking

Eating little and often may be healthier than three large meals a day, as long as you snack on healthy foods. Research has shown that eating small snacks throughout the day can benefit the heart by reducing cholesterol levels. Advocates of snacking urge replacing main meals with up to eight smaller snacks, spread evenly throughout the day.

Letter of my life

I was a WAAF during the war. The letter that changed my life began, 'I don't suppose you remember me but I am the soldier you met on the train some time ago'. I did remember him and happily began a penfriendship that grew warmer as the number of letters grew. Then I was stunned to get a letter that read, 'I don't know how to tell you this, but I am not the soldier you met on the train'. I was very angry that I had been deceived and began a very irate reply, but I suddenly realised that, whoever the writer was, I did not want his letters to stop and I forgave him. After several months we arranged to meet and fell in love.

We had 48 years of happy marriage before he died.

Joan Packham, Orpington, Kent

I wish I'd said that...

"The way to ensure summer in England is to have it framed and glazed in a comfortable room." – Horace Walpole, English writer and connoisseur

Tea-time treats

Picnic Slices

Makes 15

- 8 oz/225 g plain or milk cooking chocolate
- 2 oz/50 g butter
- 4 oz/100 g caster sugar
- 1 beaten egg
- 4 oz/100 g desiccated coconut
- 2 oz/50 g sultanas
- 2 oz/50 g glacé cherries

1 Grease a Swiss roll tin. Set oven to 150°C/300°F/Gas Mark 2.
2 Break chocolate into pieces and place in bowl over pan of simmering water. When melted, pour into bottom of Swiss roll tin and leave to set.
3 Cream butter and sugar, add egg, coconut, sultanas and chopped cherries. Mix well and spread evenly over chocolate.
4 Bake 30 minutes until golden brown. Leave to cool, then cut into slices with a sharp knife.

Bognor Regis, West Sussex

This popular seaside resort on the south coast claims to be the sunniest town in Britain. It was a small fishing village in medieval times, but in the 18th century, the London hatter, Sir Richard Hotham, decided to make Bognor a resort to rival fashionable Brighton and Bath.

Although the town gained the word Regis in its name in 1929 from George V, and Queen Victoria referred to it as 'dear little Bognor', it didn't attract wealthy guests and royalty to the extent that Sir Hotham had hoped.

Bognor is now a popular holiday destination and, each summer, it hosts the Bognor Birdman Competition, in which contestants build their own flying machines and attempt to take off from Bognor Pier. The idea is to jump 30 ft off the pier and 'fly' through the air for 100 metres. The winner gets £25,000 and, for those so inclined, it costs £25 to have a go.

More than 20,000 people come to watch the weird and wonderful flying machines and all sorts of designs have been entered in the contest over the years, including flying horses, a large-eared elephant, an inflatable spaceman – and even a naked man called John!

Treasured Photo

Here's a happy little girl – and what a lovely dress she's wearing! Mrs Audrey Child of Horsham writes: 'This is a photo of myself taken about 1933 when I was eight years old. I was so proud of my new pram and baby doll!'

"You must be joking"

A lady with a large flowery hat was stopped at the church door by the usher. "Are you a friend of the bride?" he asked. "Certainly not," she snapped. "I'm the bridegroom's mother."

TIP TIME

Rub lemon on cutting boards and utensils to get rid of fishy smells.

August 11-17

I WISH I'D SAID THAT...

I must go down to the sea again, to the lonely sea and the sky. – John Masefield, English poet, from Sea Fever

KINVER EDGE, STAFFORDSHIRE

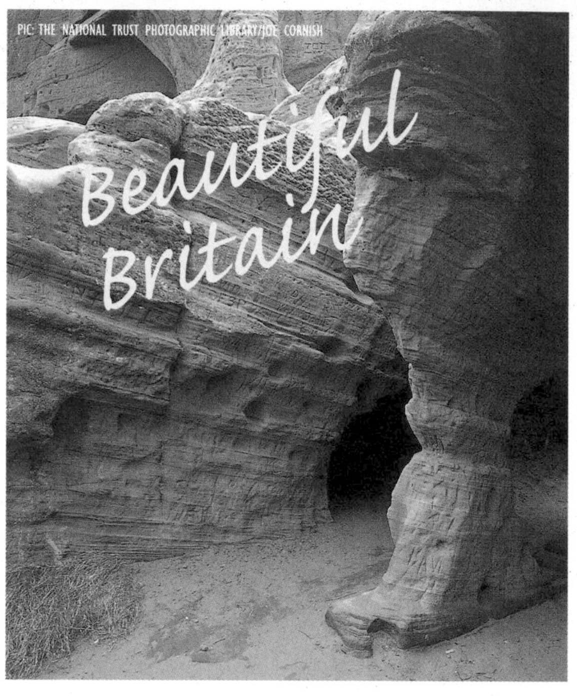

PIC: THE NATIONAL TRUST PHOTOGRAPHIC LIBRARY/JOE CORNISH
Beautiful Britain

Kinver Edge is a red sandstone escarpment, towering above the small town of Kinver. A famous local beauty spot, the views from the top of Kinver Edge are amazing – five other ranges of hills can be seen from here: The Clees, the Clents, the Cotswolds, the Habberleys and the Malverns.

The huge outcrops of sandstone here were formed in the Triassic era and were inhabited by iron-age tribes as long as 2,500 years ago. The sandstone suited early settlers as it was relatively easy to carve out dwellings in the soft rock. There are many cave dwellings and rock houses here, and some of them were used right up to the 1950s, notably at Holy Austin Rock, where houses were occupied by local families from around 1850, some of which had brick fronts, tiled gables and chimney flues. The caves are currently part of a National Trust restoration programme.

Well, fancy that!

Each year, more movies are produced in India than Hollywood. About 800 movies are made in India (or Bollywood, as it's known); about twice the output of Hollywood.

"You must be joking"

A cricket fan's wife was having a baby but he couldn't tear himself away from the Test Match on TV. He kept on phoning the hospital for news of his wife. Finally, he ended up phoning the cricket scoreline number by mistake and fainted when he heard the message, 'It's 160 all out – and the last one was a duck'.

Letter of my life

Linda Brabrook, Woking, Surrey

I had been a home help for several years to a lovely couple, Mr and Mrs Park. I used to visit them last so that if my allotted hour ran out, it didn't matter. Mr Park always bought me a bar of chocolate and, while I was working, they would sing all the lovely old music hall songs and tell me stories of their wonderful lives.

Alas, after 60 years of marriage Mrs Park died and, although I was no longer their home help I continued to visit Mr Park.

The letter I received from him is very close to my heart. He was becoming very forgetful – often he didn't even know who I was – and I don't know how he managed to write it or even discover my address. The letter changed my view about people – despite their physical condition, I am now totally convinced that the real person is still inside.

This is what he wrote:

'Dear Linda,

You not only were a friend to me and my wife when we were both in health, but when she became sick you found time to try and cheer us up and stayed right to the end when she sadly left us. We are all deeply grateful.

Yours truly, Mr Park and Family'

Treasured Photo

James Smith of Pinner writes:
'Just two old codgers but Harry and I met through YOURS magazine, via the Music Searchline. Harry (*right*) lives in Manchester but he came down to London in the summer of 2000 and this photo was taken at our lunch together. I'm married with family and Harry lives on his own, but he's a happy man who travels about here and there. He certainly makes the most of his life. We've maintained a solid friendship, which we hope will last the rest of our lives.'

Tip Time

To stop your vegetables boiling over, drop a pea-sized knob of butter into the cooking water.

Healthy Living

Going into hospital

By taking a few simple steps, you can make your stay on the ward a more pleasant experience.

- Take any medicines with you.
- Take plenty of things to do – books, magazines, cross-stitch, writing paper.
- Jot down any questions you might have for the doctor when he makes his rounds.
- Don't make plans around your discharge date – it's common for minor complications to require a change of plan.

Perfect Puddings

Rhubarb Fool

Serves 4-6

- 1 lb/450 g rhubarb, trimmed and chopped
- 2 oz/50 g pale brown sugar
- 2 oz/50 g butter
- 1/2 pt/275 ml double cream

1. Put rhubarb, sugar and butter in a saucepan over gentle heat until butter melts. Simmer gently until rhubarb is pulpy and thick, stirring occasionally. Transfer to a non-metallic bowl and chill in the fridge until cold.
2. Whip the cream until it holds its shape, then fold in the rhubarb.
3. Spoon into individual glass dishes. Serve chilled.

Pause for thought

Over Chips and Tea
(can be sung to 'Ye Choirs of New Jerusalem')

The glittering inviting aisles
The gently chiming bell
Herald not the Eucharist
But Sunday shopping tills.

Is this the God I knew when young,
Who tempered childhood days?
Is this the faith my parents loved,
And followed with their praise?

I saw Him in a young man's eyes
Care for his family
Not in a cold, unyielding pew
But over chips and tea.

Scorn not the nose ring nor the stud
('Though you may wince with pain)
The scooter and the skateboarder
All to our Lord obtain.

Rise from your knees, look outwards, see,
Don't patronise, don't shout
But gently smile the Christian word
Your neighbour is without.

Christine Peach, Norwich

August 18-24

I WISH I'D SAID THAT...

"Cheer up! The worst is yet to come!
– Philander Johnson, American journalist"

Letter of my life

The letter arrived. It didn't look very interesting, just a plain brown envelope, possibly even a bill, if I hadn't known better.

I had waited seven long years for this letter. During those years I'd had three children to add to the two I already had. I had moved house three times and learned to drive. My husband had left me. The years had been busy, happy, sad, long, arduous, but through all that time I had been waiting for this longed-for letter.

The children gathered. 'Is it here?' they asked. I couldn't speak. I ran up the stairs and locked myself in the bathroom. I caught sight of myself in the mirror. My face was white. My hands shook as I opened the envelope. I scanned the page – there was the word I was looking for...PASS. I had passed my Open University Degree! The rejoicing and partying were a sight to behold!

That result enabled me to change my life. I became a teacher in Further Education. I was able to independently support my children. I could have a rewarding, satisfying job. It was a life-changing moment and all the studying and hard work had paid off.

That letter arrived 18 years ago but I can still recall the moment as if it was yesterday.

Sheila Brown,
Lichfield,
Staffordshire

Pause for thought

Betty Bainton of Bournemouth, Dorset, writes: 'My daughter writes poems for pleasure. Here's one she wrote for me. I think it's very good':

A Man's Life

Said the child of three,
'Have you seen my ball?'
Said I to he,
'Not at all.'

Said the child of eleven,
'Must I learn more?'
Oh, what heaven,
Don't close the door.

Said the man of twenty,
'Which way do I go?'
Choices are plenty,
Just don't say no.

Said the man of forty,
'Am I happy now?
Or shall I be naughty?'
How much is allowed?

Said the man of sixty,
'Is that all there is?
To gamble is risky,
My home, my business.'

Said the man near to death,
'Life's been a ball!
This is my last breath,
I've enjoyed it all.'

Ruth Bainton

TEA-TIME TREATS

Seed Cake

- 8 oz/225 g self raising flour
- 8 oz/ 225 sugar
- 8 oz/225 g butter
- 4 eggs, separated
- 1 oz/25 g caraway seeds
- ½ teaspoon nutmeg

1 Grease and line a 7 in/18 cm round cake tin. Set oven to 180C/350°F/Gas Mark 4.
2 Cream butter and sugar.
3 Beat egg whites to stiff peaks; beat the yolks. Add whites and yolks to butter mixture. Gradually add flour, seeds and nutmeg.
4 Spoon in tin and bake for one hour.

Well, fancy that!

The word 'checkmate' in chess comes from the Persian phrase 'shah mat', which translates as 'The King is Dead'.

"You Must be joking"

Q "Waiter, waiter, why is this pie squashed?"
A "Well, you said, 'I want a pie, and step on it'."

Beautiful Britain
PIC: ARGYLL, THE ISLES, LOCH LOMOND, STIRLING & TROSSACHS TOURIST BOARD

DOUNE, SCOTLAND

Doune is a small, picturesque village seven miles from Stirling, which was once a famous centre for the manufacture of sporrans and pistols. It has a rich history dating back at least as far as the Romans, who – archaeological finds suggest – probably had a fort and a hospital here. The fort was on the site of Doune Castle, a 14th century building, which has been host to several royal guests, including Mary, Queen of Scots.

Today, Doune has as its centre the Mercat Cross, where the main streets intersect and where fairs used to be held throughout the year. However, it has a gruesome history, dating back to when King Charles I declared that public executions should take place at the Mercat Cross, rather than at the castle, where they had always happened before.

Doune is also known for its Motor Museum, which has a collection of vintage cars such as Rolls-Royce and Morgan models, as well as more unusual cars.

TIP TIME

To avoid talcum going all over the floor I put a small amount of talc in a screw-topped tin (like an old Nivea or Atrixo tin) with a small face puff. It lasts longer and the carpet stays clean!

Emily Turton, Widnes

HEALTHY LIVING

Fat facts

- ❑ Saturates – these are solid fats, such as butter, cheese, lard, and the fat on red meat – the bad guys for cholesterol levels.
- ❑ Polyunsaturates – vegetable oils. We are advised to use in moderation. An exception to this is the omega-3 oil found in fish.
- ❑ Monounsaturates – the 'good guy' oils, thought to help reduce heart disease. They include olive, hazelnut and rapeseed oils.

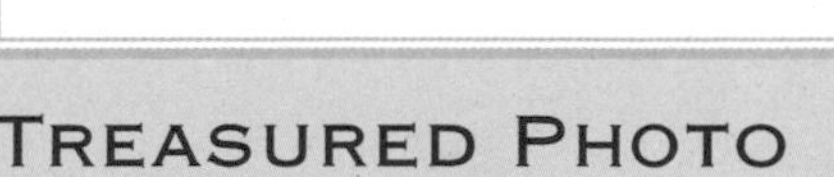

TREASURED PHOTO

Mrs Joan Lewer (neé Thirkell) of London writes:
'This photograph is of my mother, Dolly, myself, my two brothers Len and John, and Len's friend Larry. As children we went hop picking every year until the machines took over. This was our only holiday as such, and we always looked forward to it. We used to have great fun but it was hard work, up very early when it was quite chilly and a quick wash – just our face and hands. We have lots of happy memories, and when we meet up my brothers and I still talk about hop picking.'

August 25-31

TEA-TIME TREATS

Buttery Hazelnut Shortbreads

Makes 8-10

- 4 oz/100 g plain flour
- 1 oz/25 g cornflour
- 2 oz/50 g icing sugar
- 4 oz/100 g butter, cubed
- 1 teaspoon vanilla extract
- 1 oz/25 g chopped hazelnuts

1 Preheat oven to 190°C/375°F/ Gas Mark 5.
2 In a food processor, mix flour, cornflour and icing sugar. Add butter and vanilla extract and process until mixture resembles fine breadcrumbs. Add hazelnuts and process until the mixture comes together in a ball.
3 On a floured surface, roll into a large round (about ¼ in/5 mm thick). Stamp out rounds with a 3 in/7.5 cm cutter and place on non-stick baking tray. Bake in oven for 10-12 minutes.

PIC: ANCHOR BUTTER

Beautiful Britain

PIC: HISTORIC ROYAL PALACES

KENSINGTON PALACE AND GARDENS, LONDON

Diana, Princess of Wales, who died on August 31, 1997, lived in Kensington Palace after her marriage to Prince Charles. Princess Margaret also lived there until her death last year.

Queen Victoria was born in the palace and grew up there in rooms overlooking the gardens, which are full of special landmarks and curiosities, including:

- The elfin oak, a hollow log carved by Ivor Innes with gnomes and small animals, which look as if they are living in the bark. In 1996, the comedian Spike Milligan successfully campaigned to have it restored.
- Peter Pan monument, which was a project initiated by J M Barrie, and kept secret – so that on May 1, 1912, the statue appeared in the gardens as if by magic.
- Queen Anne's alcove, an arch by Sir Christopher Wren that stands beside Marlborough Gate. It was originally in the formal gardens, but was considered to attract the 'wrong kind of people', so it was moved.

It is interesting to note that, although the gardens were opened to the public in the 18th century, entry was forbidden to soldiers, sailors and servants!

TIP TIME

If you are stressed or can't sleep, drink a mug of hot milk with honey and a pinch of cinnamon or nutmeg to help you relax.

Well, fancy that!

No piece of dry paper can be folded in half more than seven times.

TREASURED PHOTOS

Sylvia Stilts of Whetstone, North London, remembers family holidays during the 1930s:

'In 1932 we stayed in a cliff-top bungalow at Selsey, Sussex (*above left*) that has since surrendered to the sea. It had a leaking roof and when it rained we had to shunt the beds around to avoid the drips.

'There was an ancient, fiercely roaring gas cooker and light was provided by smelly paraffin lamps.

'In 1934 we had a holiday at Jaywick Sands in Essex. I am pictured with my mother and brother, David. It was newly developed and regarded as posher than nearby Clacton. All the bungalows were new and had electric cookers. The thing that pleased my brother and me was the ladder up to a very small verandah around the roof. We used to go up there just before bedtime and lie flat, knowing that Mum wouldn't venture up to look for us.'

I WISH I'D SAID THAT...

"Weekends are a bit like rainbows; they look good from a distance but disappear when you get close up. – J Shirley"

Letter of my life

In 1972 I received a letter telling me I'd been awarded a Royal Humane Society Certificate for saving the life of a five-year- old child.

I was then as a beach attendant and groundsman at a quiet resort on the Isle of Wight. On August 30, 1972, I was selling deckchair, tickets etc, when I heard a call for help coming from the seaward side. I rushed over, to see a body floating face down about 15 metres out in the sea. With a little help from two young boys we got the child to dry land where I gave mouth-to-mouth resuscitation. To my joy the young girl responded – I had brought her back to life!

I received the certificate for my prompt action and I was thrilled. It now hangs on my bedroom wall.

David Yeates,
Cowes,
Isle of Wight

"You must be joking"

Bizarre instructions...

- On a hair dryer: Do not use while sleeping.
- On a frozen dinner: Serving suggestion – defrost.
- On a shower cap: Fits one head.
- On a sleeping aid: Warning... May cause drowsiness.

Pause for thought

My Healing Prayer

Ill health can come to all of us,
It really is no joke.
'There but for the Grace of God'
Occurs to many folk.
No matter what the suffering
And aches and pains we bear,
There's always someone who's worse off,
Who needs a little prayer.

My Prayer List gets quite full at times,
That makes me very sad;
To realise so many folk I know are feeling bad.
I am convinced that prayer can help
(it acts like healing water)
Then I can see my Prayer List shrink
And get a little shorter.

The Lord is always there to hear
The many prayers we send,
He always lends a listening ear,
He is our one true friend.
So if ill health should strike you down
And fill you with despair,
Put yourself atop the list
And pray a little prayer.

Mrs B M Tipper, High Peak, Derbyshire

HEALTHY LIVING

The alternative way

If you are interested in alternative treatments, follow these pointers:

- ❑ Seek your GP's advice. In some cases you can be referred on the NHS.
- ❑ Before you start treatment, check the cost and for how long you'll need it.
- ❑ Never stop any conventional treatments you are receiving.
- ❑ Report any side effects at once.

DO YOU REMEMBER...

PIC: HULTON ARCHIVE

...the Fosbury Flop?

BEFORE the 1968 Olympic Games, nobody had heard of American high-jumper Dick Fosbury, but by the end of the games in Mexico, he was a star.

Fosbury didn't like the traditional scissors technique when he jumped, so he devised a different style which lowered his centre of gravity as he crossed over the bar – he thought it would allow him to jump higher. He ran up to the bar, then he turned his back on it and went over head first. This was called the Fosbury Flop.

In the Olympics, he was against 11 other jumpers, all of whom adopted the 'straddle' style. One by one, they dropped out and Fosbury took the gold medal clearing 2.24 metres.

Today's leading high jumpers now all use the Fosbury Flop.

...hot pants?

THE mini skirt had made its impact in the mid '60s and died a death in 1969 – probably from natural causes, although the severe winter that year might have had something to do with it!

By 1970, the height of fashion was the maxi skirt. But then along came hot pants!

Hot pants were tight fitting shorts that left little to the imagination. Satin hot pants were favoured by disco divas, worn with the platform shoe.

The new fashion upset many. Princess Anne commented: "People complain one isn't 'with it', but honestly... that's the limit!" And in 1971, ladies in hot pants were only allowed to enter the Royal Enclosure at Ascot if the 'general effect was satisfactory'.

Brits for all seasons

BANK HOLIDAY MADNESS

MENTION the August Bank Holiday and images of traffic gridlock and overheating engines spring to mind.

Whatever strategy you adopt – getting up and out of the house as dawn breaks or waiting until lunchtime before setting off – you can almost guarantee to run into a traffic jam as others do the same. The return journey is likely to be as bad.

If you've had enough of this madness, you may decide to boycott a day out and put the time to good use. A spot of gardening or DIY can bring its own rewards, but beware these are the next most popular venues for Bank Holidaymakers, who flock to them.

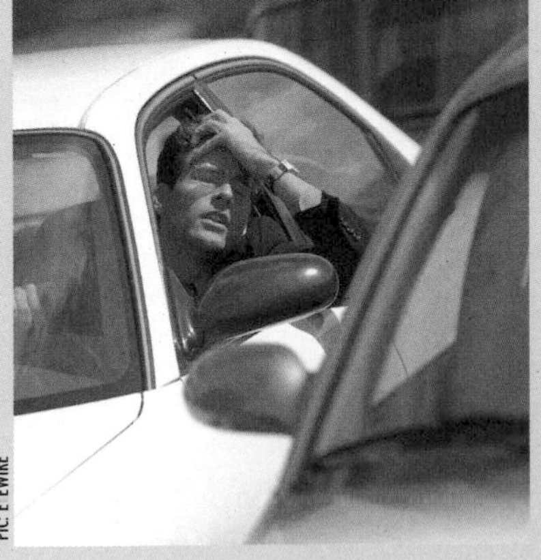

PIC: E'EWIRE

Standing patiently in line has become such a phenomenon that there are 'queueing theorists' at work in American universities, making mathematical studies and devising theoretical models of behaviour.

We Brits might grumble at time wasted standing in queues, but at least we recognise the fairness of this first-come-first-served method, when compared to the continental, every-man-for-himself approach.

And if we're being honest, perhaps, we'd have to admit that, deep down, we quite enjoy a good queue. Just witness the remarkable scenes at the funeral of the Queen Mother last year. That occasion combined all the very best elements of a British day out – the pomp and ceremony combined with a very, very long queue. Strangers, forced together for hours on end, struck up conversations, swapped memories and shared packed lunches.

All in all, perhaps the most relaxing way to spend a Bank Holiday must be to get out your deckchair, settle down with your copy of YOURS and a cup of tea and enjoy the garden, smug in the knowledge that you have avoided the usual Bank Holiday madness.

COSMETICS TO DIE FOR

Today, with a dab of powder and a lick of lipstick we're ready to face the world and confident our make-up has no harmful ingredients. But go back 500 years and women literally put their lives at risk in the pursuit of beauty.

Queen Elizabeth I was a fashion icon and her style was copied by the well off. She plucked her hairline back over an inch to produce a high forehead and wore her hair a mass of red curls. The red hair dye was made from a mixture of lead, sulphur and quicklime: All irritants to eyes, skin and lungs. These chemicals are today used in industrial processes such as glass-making or photo-processing where they are treated with caution.

Elizabethan women believed pale, translucent skin was a sign of nobility and delicacy, and even went to the extent of tracing blue lines on their foreheads to mimic veins. Skin whiteners were used from the 1500s. Most common was ceruse, a combination of white lead powder and vinegar. It was applied in thick layers to the face, neck and bosom and never washed off and, as well as an off-putting smell, it had serious side effects. Lead is a poison that accumulates in the bones and tissues, attacking the central nervous system. Prolonged exposure damages internal organs and the brain.

Lead powder went out of fashion because it made skin grey and shrivelled but sadly, the replacements were no less toxic. Alum and tin ash mixed with egg white were used, both caustic chemicals causing irritation to the skin, eyes and breathing.

Eyes were highlighted using powdered antimony to darken the lashes – repeated use of this caused blindness.

PIC MARY EVANS PICTURE LIBRARY

Belladonna, a poison and a sedative, was used to dilate the pupils and make eyes sparkle. Modern drugs derived from belladonna are only available on prescription and used to treat ulcers, as a poison antidote or as a pre-anaesthetic.

The lips were reddened by fucus red, more accurately known as red mercuric sulphide. Mercury is poisonous with exposure leading to personality changes, trembling and dementia. The Mad Hatter in Alice in Wonderland was no work of fiction – mercury was used extensively in the 19th century as a cloth preservative in the hat-making industry. In towns like Luton these trembling, strange-looking people were a common sight.

Mercury was also used as a facial peel to literally strip away the top layer of skin in an effort to rejuvenate it and this is possibly the only cleansing the skin had. The common belief was that frequent washing opened the pores and allowed illness to enter the body. This combined with the ravages of smallpox lead to a blemished complexion. Spots, sores and freckles were treated with dubious preparations of lemon juice, mercury, honey and alum, and scars disguised with stuck-on black patches.

Fashions changed after the death of Elizabeth and elaborate, high hairstyles became popular by the 18th century. These could take a whole day to arrange and, once done, would stay untouched for weeks. Lard was used as a setting gel with a dusting of white lead powder to counteract the greasiness. The arrangement might even include a live bird or small animal. The entire effect was so rancid the wearer was forced to sleep with her head in a cage to keep away rats!

Apart from a cage over their heads they were also urged to sleep with their mouths open. The rich ate far too many sweets so their teeth decayed and fell out. The theory was, if they slept with their mouths open, the circulating air would keep their teeth healthy.

Cosmetic use reached its peak in 18th-century Europe, with both sexes wearing heavy powders and paint. The French Revolution ended the industry but France revived it by leading the way in the scientific manufacture of beauty aids in the early 1900s. By this time the ingredients of products was regulated. Today, all cosmetics are strictly tested before they reach the shop shelves.

While the old portraits give an illusion of romantic living, nothing was further from the truth. People were unhealthy, dirty and infested with lice. They neither bathed nor changed their clothes but hid their bodily smells with heavy perfumes.The cosmetics of the day, liberally applied and never removed were absorbed into the body causing discomfort, disability and even death.

Maybe, these ladies were the first true fashion victims.

– Elaine Saunders

September 2003

HIGH DAYS AND HOLIDAYS...

PIC: HULTON ARCHIVE

Braemar Highland Gathering
Although many Highland clans had long held annual gatherings, the increasing popularity of the Highland Games dates back from Queen Victoria's patronage of them. The most famous of these is held at Braemar in Aberdeenshire during early September. The athletic events include putting the stone, throwing the hammer and tossing the 19 feet, 1201b caber (the latter must complete a perfect semi-circle in the air).

Old Uncle Tom Cobbley and all...
Widdecombe Fair is held on the second Tuesday of the month. Its only real claim to fame is the famous song and the subsequent death of the poor mare and its haunting of the Dartmoor roads are probably the best-known chunk of Devonshire folklore. Widdecome Fair is now rich in rides and jugglers but is still in part an agricultural event.

Michaelmas (September 29)
Michael does not fit the usual saints' profiles. He is not a mortal but an angel who evicted Lucifer from heaven. Michaelmas was the end of harvest, often the end of the farming year – so that meant dozens of fairs, hence, 'Now Michaelmas is coming, boys, what pleasure we shall find. We'll make the gold and silver fly like chaff before the wind'.

MONDAY	1
TUESDAY	2
WEDNESDAY	3
THURSDAY	4
FRIDAY	5
SATURDAY	6
SUNDAY	7
MONDAY	8
TUESDAY	9 YOURS Autumn Special on sale
WEDNESDAY	10
THURSDAY	11
FRIDAY	12 Southampton International Boat Show starts
SATURDAY	13 Last night of the Proms
SUNDAY	14
MONDAY	15
TUESDAY	16
WEDNESDAY	17
THURSDAY	18

FRIDAY	19
SATURDAY	20 Southampton International Boat Show ends
SUNDAY	21
MONDAY	22
TUESDAY	23
WEDNESDAY	24
THURSDAY	25
FRIDAY	26
SATURDAY	27
SUNDAY	28
MONDAY	29 October YOURS on sale
TUESDAY	30

This month don't forget to...

- Make inquiries at your local surgery or medical centre about having a 'flu jab.
- Give some thought to getting the garden ready for the colder months ahead.
- Blanch and freeze chopped apples – for pies and apple sauce in the winter months
- Challenge your grandchildren to a game of conkers!

Bill Cosby

PIC: REX

It happened in September...

September 30, 1947: Women were urged to wear shorter skirts by the Government to save on cloth.

September 26, 1952: Sugar rationing was over after nearly 14 years.

September 15, 1978: Georgi Markov, a Bulgarian defector, was fatally stabbed in the thigh with a poisoned umbrella tip at a bus stop on London's Waterloo Bridge.

September 14, 1992: Bill Cosby was named America's highest-paid entertainer, earning $98 million during 1991-2.

September 1-7

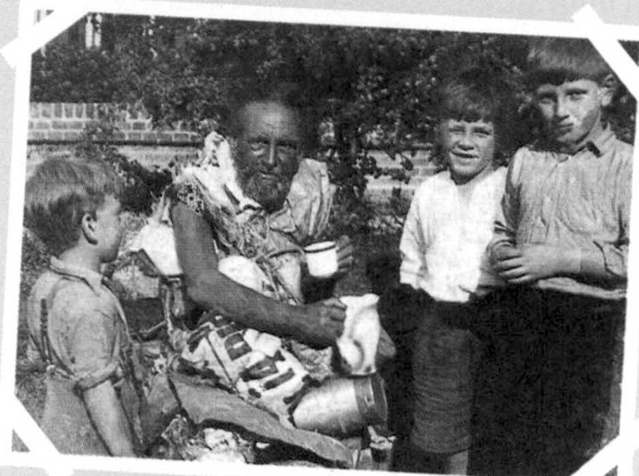

Treasured Photo

This photo shows Paper Jack, a well-known character in the Wallington and Croydon area of Surrey in the late '20s and '30s. Mr G M King of Reading is one of three brothers pictured with him outside their house: 'My mother had just made him a jug of tea,' writes Mr King, 'but he always supplied his own tea in a screw of paper. I'm on the right in the picture, taken around 1929. Paper Jack was very fond of children and was a well-educated man who had obtained a degree as a surveyor. I understand he took to the road when the lady he was engaged to jilted him. Sadly, he was killed in a road accident in the blackout during the war.'

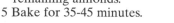

Pause for thought

'I wrote these lines after being deeply moved by an article in YOURS magazine, Losing the one you love,' writes A I White of Shifnal, Shropshire. 'My husband and I married in 1942 and reading of those people who have lost their partners makes us realise how lucky we are.'

When I have gone from you
And you are alone
Please don't grieve.
Think of all the happiness we have known.

Parting I know is hard to bear
So think only of the happiness
We were able to share.

Memories I know can
Reduce you to tears.
So dwell only on the happy ones
We made over the years.

Remember me sometimes
But don't be sad.
Think of all those happy times
And be glad.

I wish I'd said that...

"The whining schoolboy, with his satchel,
And shining morning face, creeping like snail
Unwillingly to school."
– William Shakespeare, As You Like It

Tea-time treats

Harvest Slices

Serves 6-8

- 12 oz/350 g puff pastry, thawed
- 4 oz/100 g chocolate cake crumbs
- 2 oz/50 g ground almonds
- 5 oz/150 g flaked almonds
- 2 oz/50 glacé cherries, chopped
- 8 Cadbury's Flakes (a 99 pack), crumbled
- 2 eggs
- 1 teaspoon almond essence
- 3 tablespoons clear honey

1 Preheat oven to 180°C/350°F/Gas Mark 4.
2 Roll out pastry and use to line a lightly greased 10 x 12in/25 x 30 cm baking tray.
3 Mix cake crumbs and ground almonds with 3/4 of the flaked almonds and all the cherries and chocolate flakes.
3 Beat eggs with almond essence and 2 tablespoons of honey and mix into the dry ingredients.
4 Spread filling over pastry, brush edge with water, fold over, sealing the edges and ends. Place on baking tray with the fold underneath. Warm remaining honey and brush over pastry. Sprinkle over remaining almonds.
5 Bake for 35-45 minutes.

Well, fancy that!

A blue whale eats up to four tonnes of krill every day – the equivalent of a fully grown African elephant! The blue whale can also 'blow' a spout of water nearly 40 feet high.

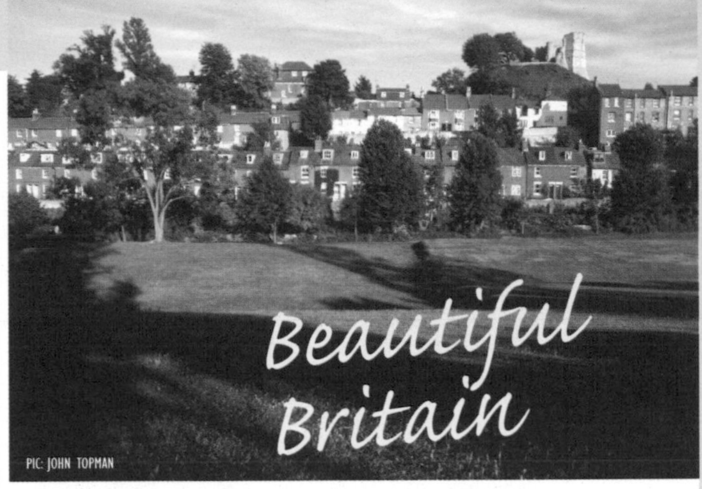

PIC: JOHN TOPMAN

LEWES, EAST SUSSEX

Lewes, a town of narrow, twisting streets, ancient passageways (known as 'twittens') and historical treasures, is set on a hill on the South Downs, looking down towards the chalk cliffs and the south coast. It was originally developed by the Saxons, who called it 'Hlaew', meaning 'small hill'.

Not far from here is Pevensey, where William the Conqueror landed in 1066 to claim England. He soon recognised the advantage of Lewes's high position, and gave the town to William de Warenne, who built Lewes Castle on the site of the old Saxon fort. William de Warenne also built the Cluiac Priory nearby, which at the time grew to be larger than London's Westminster Abbey.

Lewes has had its share of grim events and, in the 16th century, 17 Protestant martyrs were burned to death in the High Street after the Catholic Queen Mary restored papal supremacy in England.

These days it is the county town of East Sussex and is popular with visitors who enjoy wandering around the picturesque streets, taking in the lovely views across the South Downs and shopping for antiques.

"You Must be joking"

A man ran into a pub in an agitated state. "Has anyone here got a large black cat with a white collar?" he asked. Nobody answered so he tried again. "Does anybody have a large black cat with a white collar?" But still no one answered. "Oh dear," he murmured, "I must've run over the vicar."

Letter of my life

Mr H J Arnold, Birchington, Kent

In September 1944 I was a POW in Austria, in a working party at a village named Neudorf. By then I had been a POW for more than three years, having been captured in Greece in April 1941. As you can imagine, I was in low spirits, often wondering if I would ever get back home.

Then on September 5 I received the 'letter of my life'. It was from my brother, dated July 21, 1944. After reading it my spirits soared and I began to believe that I would be going home again. It described the recent Allied successes on all fronts and predicted that the war would be over within months. I eagerly showed the letter to my fellow POWs and we all gave a loud cheer, had a brew-up and toasted the good news. In previous letters any mention of Allied success had been blacked out by the German censors so this one must have been let through because the censor's stamp is clearly shown on it.

As the Russians approached the Austrian border we were transported in cattle trucks to a camp in the Austrian Alps, where we were eventually released by the American Army, in May 1945.

After four years of incarceration I arrived back in this country on what used to be Empire Day, May 24.

TIP TIME

To clean tannin and coffee stains from cups, rub on a half-and-half mixture of bicarbonate of soda and salt, then wash in as usual.

Mrs M D Moore, Shrewsbury

HEALTHY LIVING

A little of what you fancy…

Great reasons to eat chips!

- ❑ A 100g helping of oven chips contains 12mg of vitamin C.
- ❑ Chips contain carbohydrate, which gives you energy.
- ❑ A 100g portion of oven chips contains just 4.2g of fat and 273 calories.
- ❑ If you're making your own chips, cut them thickly and keep the oil very hot – your chips will absorb less fat.

September 8-14

Healthy Living

Eastern promise

The ancient Chinese art of T'ai Chi trains both mind and body in balance, control and coordination. The graceful movements or poses are performed slowly and deliberately and because they are so gentle, it's perfect for people of any age. It is excellent for strength, coordination, balance, flexibility and breathing – and it's wonderful for stress relief. Practitioners also report feelings of harmony and wellbeing – such as might be achieved by yoga and meditation. You will need an expert teacher to learn T'ai Chi. Ask at your local library for details of classes near you.

Tea-time Treats

Marzipan Fingers

Makes 12-15

- 8 oz/225 g marzipan
- ¾ cup digestive biscuit crumbs
- ½ cup desiccated coconut
- ½ cup mixed dried fruit, chopped
- ¼ cup chopped nuts
- ¼ cup raspberry jam
- 1 tablespoon icing sugar
- 1 dessertspoon cocoa
- 1 to 2 tablespoons sherry
- 6 oz/175 g plain cooking chocolate

1 Divide marzipan in half. Roll out each piece to measure 9 in/23 cm square and use one piece to line a tin of the same size.

2 Mix remaining ingredients, except the plain chocolate, and spread over marzipan base. Place other piece of marzipan on top.

4 Melt chocolate in a bowl over a pan of simmering water. Spread chocolate over the marzipan and leave until cold. Cut into fingers.

TIP TIME

Use a potato peeler to slice cheese for salads and sandwiches.

Mrs S Kay, Blackpool

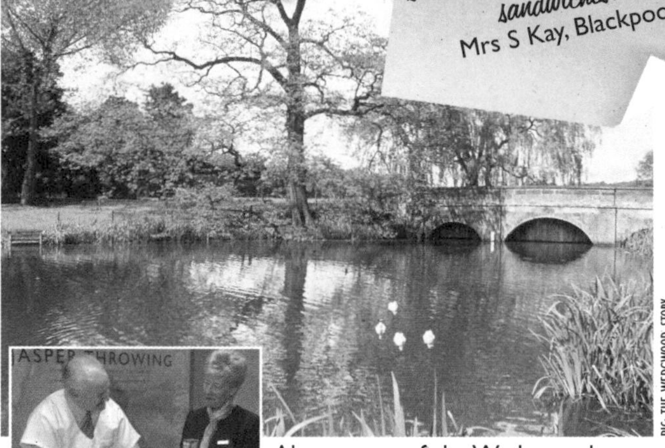

PIC: THE WEDGWOOD STORY

Above: part of the Wedgwood Estate and, left, a demonstration at The Wedgwood Story

Well, fancy that!

The combination 'ough' can be pronounced in nine different ways. The following sentence contains them all: A roughly-shaved, dough-faced, thoughtful policeman strode through the streets of Scarborough. After falling into a slough, he coughed and then had a fit of the hiccoughs.

Staffordshire Potteries

This area has its heart in Stoke-on-Trent and is the home of some of Britain's most famous china, such as Royal Doulton, Wedgwood and Spode. But did you know that the man who became the most famous potter in this area, Josiah Wedgwood, began working in the family business when he was only nine years old?

Josiah Wedgwood was born in 1730, the 12th child of parents who were potters themselves. As he grew older, he began to experiment with techniques that eventually led to his distinctive blue and white designs, among others.

Wedgwood was a member of the Society of Friends (Quakers) and he had a keen interest in social welfare. In 1769, when he opened his new factory, he also built a village for his workers and he was a keen supporter of the anti slave trade movement.

Treasured Photos

Mr B Allen of Builth Wells writes:

'In September 1939, when I was eight, I was evacuated from Birmingham to Builth Wells – a big difference from the city I was used to. I soon learned the country ways, wandering over the fields, climbing the hills and milking the cows. The photo was taken on market day (*I'm the scruffy one on the right*). It wasn't all play. One of my jobs was to collect wood for the fire in a small truck, or take it to the nearest farm and fill it with manure for the allotment. I made many friends in Builth. When I returned to Birmingham in 1942 I was called Taffy, but soon lost my Welsh accent. Over the years I returned to Builth Wells many times, even taking my new wife there on honeymoon. When we retired we decided to move away from the city – where else but to Builth? We love it here. I'm still known as the evacuee who came back.'

I wish I'd said that...

"Thank heavens, the sun has gone in and I don't have to go out and enjoy it.
– Logan Pearsall Smith, British writer"

Letter of my life

Mrs E D Clapton, Saltney, Chester

Aged 81, I still vividly recall an unexpected letter which arrived when I was 11 years old, my father having been ill with heart trouble for the past year.

Preparing for my first term at secondary school, my mother was worried about the purchase of a new school uniform.

One afternoon during the summer holidays, there was a knock on the door and my mother was confronted by a man holding a letter who handed it to her, saying 'There is no answer'. The letter was addressed to my father. Opening it together, they read, 'This letter is an apology. Duties have prevented me from visiting you during your illness. Will you please forgive me and accept the enclosed note to provide something which I hope will bring you pleasure'. It was signed by my father's employer.

With my father's express wish, my mother sped on her bicycle to our local town and returned with a brand new school uniform. When I came in from play my mother, eyes shining, showed me the purchase as she explained what had happened.

Although my gratitude could in no way match that of my parents, the memory of that letter which changed a course of events then has given me optimism in many adverse circumstances during my lifetime.

Pause for thought

On the second anniversary of the terrorist attack on New York's Twin Towers, Margaret Davies from Croydon in Surrey offers this poignant memory of that terrible day:

When a City lost its Breath

A city lost its heart, a city lost its breath
One sunny day when the world was at rest.
Two strikes of the iron bird in the sky
Into twin towers standing so straight, so high.

These twins were the country's backbone of life
But now they have crumbled amid cruel strife.
Fire engines' sirens are blasting away,
So many lives lost on this fatal day.

But this country's flag has never lost its will to fly
Although many people had seen loved ones die.
We live in a world hurting with pain
Please God, I pray it will never happen again.

"You must be joking"

Letter from 'Costa Packet' Holiday Company:

'Dear Sir,

With reference to your letter re Majorca tour, the flight you mention is completely booked, but we will inform you immediately if someone falls out, as usually happens.'

September 15-21

Treasured Photos

Mrs P Bevan, writing from the Isle of Man, has childhood memories of Peterborough:

'We lived in Churchfield Road. I remember when I was about four walking to the duck pond at the end of the road, which was out of bounds because of the busy road. The boy next door was school age but at weekends I was allowed to play with his car and tricycle. His father was a racing driver and the boy had many toys. I loved these times, especially when the father brought his racing car round. It was the shape of the day, long and bullet-like, in racing green. His name was Jack West. The photo is of my mother and me outside our house.'

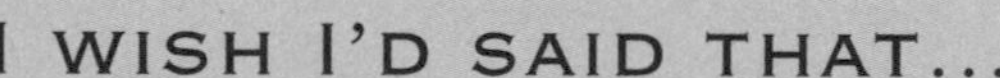

I wish I'd said that...

"I make mistakes: I'll be the second to admit it. – Jean Kerr, American playwright"

Well, fancy that!

Your mouth produces 1.8 pints of saliva a day!

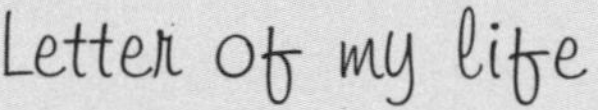

Letter of my life

Not a letter, but a telegram that meant the world to me.

Jeannie Wilson, Caerphilly, Mid Glamorgan

In September 1943 I was in a maternity home waiting for my baby to be born. My husband, Mick, was a pilot with 129 Spitfire Squadron, stationed on the south coast. We wrote to each other every day, but for three days – from September 15 – I had not had a letter. I was living on my nerves from day to day, not knowing why Mick's letters had stopped coming and fearing the worst.

Unbeknown to me then, his plane had been shot down over the English Channel. He baled out into the sea and, fortunately, one of his squadron had seen him go down. He was picked up by a rescue boat and taken to the RAF sick quarters at Marston. His Commanding Officer had notified my home address, not knowing I wasn't there.

On the morning of September 18 my lovely daughter was born – my sister wired the news to Mick's squadron address and, later that day, I received my joyous telegram – still unaware of the dramatic happenings of the previous day. It read 'CONGRATULATIONS DARLING I THINK YOU'RE WONDERFUL ALL LOVE MICK'.

Tip Time

Smells can be removed from a microwave oven if a bowl of water with 15 ml of lemon juice is placed inside for one minute at high power. Remove the bowl and wipe the oven clean using the condensation that has formed.

Sylvia Stilts, North London

Tea-time treats

Lamingtons

Makes 15-20

- 2 oz/50 g butter
- 2 oz/50 g cocoa powder
- 6 tablespoons boiled water
- Vanilla extract
- 12 oz/350 g icing sugar, sifted
- Plain sponge, cut into small rectangles
- 7 oz/200 g desiccated coconut

1. Gently heat butter in a pan until just melted. Dissolve cocoa in the boiled water and add to the butter with the vanilla extract.
2. Gradually stir in icing sugar and beat to a fairly runny consistency.
3. Coat the sponge pieces with the icing by putting the sponge on a fork and dipping it carefully into the icing bowl.
4. Roll each piece in coconut to coat. Leave to dry on a wire rack.

PIC: JERRY HARPUR/HATFIELD HOUSE

Hatfield House, Hertfordshire

This is a Jacobean house, built in the early 17th century and modelled on an earlier Tudor palace where Elizabeth I spent a lot of time as a child. Her sister, Mary Tudor, kept her at Hatfield, under house arrest, and she was still here when she heard that she was to become queen. Part of the oak tree where she was sitting when she was given the news is still on display today.

Inside, at the head of the carved oak Grand Staircase, there is a newel post carved with the figure of John Tradescant, the botanist who set out the gardens of the house.

Most of the old house that Elizabeth knew was demolished in 1608 when Robert Cecil, chief minister to James I, built the current house, using many of the bricks from the original palace. This is the house that stands today, and it contains many historical treasures, including some hats, gloves and stockings that may have belonged to Elizabeth and the draft of the execution order for Mary Queen of Scots.

The gardens have been created fairly recently, but the aim has been to recreate, as far as possible, the garden style of the early 17th century, in keeping with the house.

Pause for thought

'I wrote this poem after the birth of my grandson,' writes Edward Bennett, Radstock, Bath

A Granddad's Thoughts

I've just become a Granddad
To a bonny little chap.
He was but a few days old
When first I held him in my lap.

I gazed at him in wonder
For a miracle it is
To see a new-born baby
When there's nothing gone amiss.

He looks so helpless lying there
A-wriggling of his toes,
I reckon he looks a bit like me
But then, I'm biased I suppose.

I feel him warm and vital,
His life has just begun,
I'm thrilled: There's a bit of me in him,
For he's my handsome grandson.

He doesn't know his Granddad yet,
It's perhaps a little soon,
But the love I have for him, I think,
Is better than a silver spoon.

I'm getting on a bit, you know,
I'm in my seventh age,
But he has given me new life,
I'm just turning o'er a page.

I hope that when he comes of age
If perhaps I can't be there
He'll not forget just now and then
To say for me a prayer.

I wish him a good and Christian life
And a goodly share of joy,
Not too hard, but not too soft.
What better wish for the boy?

Healthy Living

Stepping out

Walking is a wonderful form of exercise. Here are a few tips to get you started:

- ❑ Warm up by walking on the spot. Start slowly and increase your pace gradually.
- ❑ If you develop a stitch, slow down or stop until it passes.
- ❑ Don't overdo it – the ideal pace is when your heart rate is increased, but you should still be able to hold a conversation without being breathless.

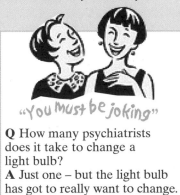

"You must be joking"

Q How many psychiatrists does it take to change a light bulb?
A Just one – but the light bulb has got to really want to change.

September 22-28

I WISH I'D SAID THAT...

"Calling a spade a spade never made the spade interesting yet. Take my advice, leave spades alone. – Edith Sitwell, English poet, in a letter"

"You must be joking"

"Waiter, how long will my sausages be?" asked the disgruntled diner.

"I don't know, sir, we never measure them."

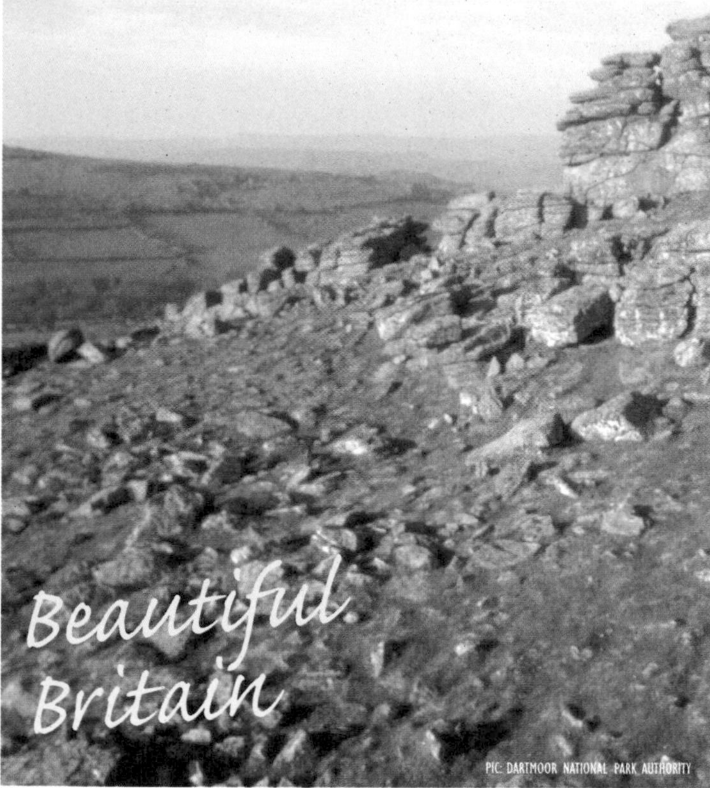
Beautiful Britain

PIC: DARTMOOR NATIONAL PARK AUTHORITY

DARTMOOR, DEVON

Covering 365 square miles, Dartmoor is named after the river Dart and is famous for its wild terrain, ponies and tors – rocky formations that are remains of the volcanic activity that created the area. One of these is Hound Tor, and legend has it that the rocks are the remains of a bowman's dog, which, along with its master, was turned to stone by witches.

Nearby is the grave of Mary Jay, known as Jay's Grave or Jay's Cross. The story goes that Mary Jay was a poor, young farm worker who became pregnant by the farmer's son and hanged herself as the shame was too much for her to bear. Mysteriously, to this day, her grave always has fresh flowers on it – and it has never been discovered who puts them there, leading to speculation that it could be kindly spirits, ghosts or pixies.

Pause for thought

Sandwiches

His mam's
tomato sandwiches
always tasted super
on Ronnie Thompson's
butter-bright doorstep.
Soaking cosy in the sun
waiting for him to come
out to play.

And the purring cat
so friendly
with milky saucer.

At home
my mum knocked up a round
of tomato sandwiches
for our doorstep.
Not the same.

The grass is always greener
the doorstep is always brighter
on the other side of the street

But maybe it was the cat.

Harold Hyatt, Leeds

TIP TIME

To clean a burned iron, sprinkle salt on the ironing board and run the iron over it.

Maureen Thayre, Kirriemuir

PERFECT PUDDINGS

Ginger Quickie

This easy recipe comes from Marian Cunliffe of Farsley, West Yorkshire who advises being generous with the jam!

- 1 packet ginger biscuits
- Pineapple jam
- ½ pint/275 ml double cream, whipped

1 Spread each biscuit with pineapple jam.
2 Put a layer in a glass dish, then a layer of cream, then another layer of biscuits and so on. End with a layer of cream.
3 Cover and chill the dessert overnight in the refrigerator. Serve the next day, when all will be amalgamated and delicious!

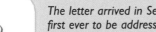

Letter of my life

The letter arrived in September 1946, my 14th birthday, and was the first ever to be addressed to me personally. Inside the envelope was a £1 note and a wedding photograph. I can remember thinking that the lady in the picture, in her lovely hat, looked like a film star. The bridegroom looked equally distinguished.

The letter explained that the beautiful lady was my mother, and the man was to be my stepfather. The £1 was to pay for my train ticket from Bath to London, where I would be met by my 'parents' and taken to live in Folkestone with my four sisters, two of whom I knew nothing about.

I did know that, from the age of two, I had been placed in the care of the Church of England Society together with two of my sisters. We are in the photo, with me on the left. But I could remember nothing of my mother or father.

After 12 years, our family was to be reunited – all thanks to that astonishing letter.

Frances A Ranford,
Lyminge, Folkestone

HEALTHY LIVING

Take the pain out of dieting

- ❑ Give up sweetening your tea and coffee – after a day or two, you won't miss it.
- ❑ Recognise your danger times – mid-morning, mid-afternoon, or late in the evening, and have a ready supply of healthy snacks available for when you get 'the munchies'.
- ❑ Fill up on carbohydrates (potatoes, pasta, rice, bread) and protein (lean meats, fish and dairy products), which have half the calories of fat.

TREASURED PHOTOS

When she was 11 Mrs A Ansell of Stevenage took part in the annual Hitchin Hospital Procession, wearing fancy dress:

'My father concocted and assembled the idea, my mother made the clothes. I was delighted to win First Prize in my class, 10 shillings. It was a small fortune in those days.'

Well, fancy that!

The average person speaks 5,000 words a day – 80 per cent used in talking to oneself.

DO YOU REMEMBER...

PIC: HULTON ARCHIVE

...Rubik's Cube?

THE Rubik's Cube was quite the most irritating little toy of the 1970s. But it was more than just a toy – it was a teaching tool, a challenge for the mathematically gifted and an international craze.

It was invented by a Hungarian inventor, Ernö Rubik and looked simple enough; a six-sided cube, each side a different colour. Sides could be rotated on any axis to create different colours on every side.

The trick was then to restore cubic harmony by getting each side back to a solid colour – easier said than done! While we mortals fiddled and twiddled for hours, cube prodigies raced to complete the cube in a matter of seconds.

By 1983 an estimated one hundred million Rubik's Cubes had been sold across the world.

...Green Shield stamps?

TRADING stamps had been around since the beginning of the 20th century in America but the phenomenon had yet to take off in the UK. In 1957 the Green Shield Trading Company was registered and business began the following year. The major outlets were sceptical, so the concept was sold to corner shops. By 1962, Green Shield stamps were available in smaller shops throughout the UK.

Big supermarkets eventually made their move and the age of the Green Shield stamp had arrived. Hysteria reigned and it was reported that Tesco in Leicester was beseiged by grappling housewives.

What a triumph to acquire bathroom scales, vacuum cleaners and hair dryers just by collecting books of stamps! But by the mid 1970s, trading stamps were on the way out. Green Shield joined forces with Argos in 1978 and stamps finally ended in 1980.

Brits for all seasons

A LITTLE OF WHAT YOU FANCY

AT last children have gone back to school and life is more peaceful. You can reclaim your favourite park bench, travel in comfort on the buses (if you avoid the school run) and enjoy a browse around the shops or library without excitable kids dashing about. Children make life more fun for the most part, but the school summer holidays give us an overdose, and it's a relief when things return to normal.

If you've spent summer snacking on salads and light meals, you might fancy something heartier, now the days are chillier.

PIC: FOTODISC

Fry-ups are what we Brits do best, from a full English breakfast, to egg and chips. Your doctor might not advise too many fry-ups, but a little of what you fancy does you good.

A good breakfast sets you up for the day, and you can't beat a plate of eggs, bacon, sausage, mushrooms, tomatoes and fried bread now and again – washed down with a mug of tea.

When it comes to bacon, Britons are the biggest consumers in Europe, spending more than £430 million on prepacked rashers alone!

A good Sunday roast could be back on the menu, too. Roast beef and Yorkshire pud, lamb with mint sauce, pork with apple sauce or the roast chicken are all very popular – and all equally likely to be followed by forty winks in an armchair!

Chip pans have gone out of fashion but the occasional portion of nice, home-cooked chips is a treat, served with salt and vinegar, ketchup, brown sauce, ketchup or mayonnaise. Our European neighbours, with their skinny French fries, don't know what they're missing!

Missing links

The three words in each clue have a fourth word in common – and that's your answer. For instance, clue 5 Down gives you the answer ASH (mountain ash, ash-tray, Ash Wednesday).

ACROSS
1 Hit, Sleeve, World (6)
4 Baked, Better, Hearted (4)
8 Stop, Toothed, Watford (3)
9 Boa, Tail, Weight (7)
10 Book, Fight, Role (5)
11 Keeper, Masonic, Porter's (5)
13 Charles, Mountains, Road (5)
15 Button, Don't, Stations (5)
17 Lichfield, Moore, Saint (7)
19 Cream, Skate, Thin (3)
20 Break, Keel, Tempered (4)
21 Fly, Komodo, Snap (6)

DOWN
1 Angle, Birth, Handed (5)
2 Gains, Letter, State (7)
3 Air, Assault, Range (5)
5 Mountain, Tray, Wednesday (3)
6 Meat, Police, Storm (5)
7 Boy, Story, Walk (4)
12 Ballroom, Bear, Morris (7)
13 Crab, Pie, Toffee (5)
14 Doctor, Drier, Top (4)
15 Faced, Player, Red-hot (5)
16 Come, Spring, Sweep (5)
18 Bow, Neck, Pin (3)

1		2		3		■	4	5 A		6
	■		■		■	7	■	S	■	
8			■	9				H		
	■		■		■		■	■	■	
10					■	11		12		
■	■		■	■	■	■	■		■	■
13				14	■	15				16
	■	■	■		■		■		■	
17		18					■	19		
	■		■		■		■		■	
20				■	21					

Solution on Page 159

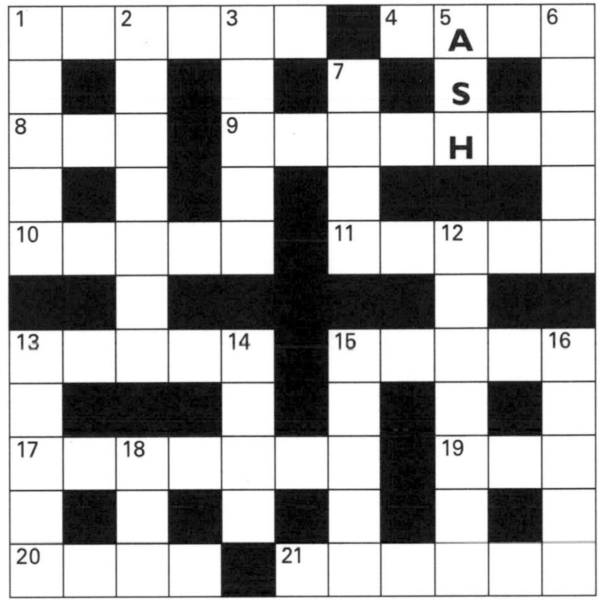
PIC: MIRROR

Cryptograms

In a cryptogram, each letter of the alphabet is substituted by another. Can you crack these coded sentences to reveal two quotes by the pictured Hollywood star? Each sentence is in a different code and, to help you, the word 'THE' is in both.

1 J OHZHC NA ALX LOKHPP J KAAW KJWH RASO GCSEBACT XVH UAZJH PXSC. JB FAL ESOX XA PHH XVH NJCK OHMX TAAC, NA OHMX TAAC.

A	B	C	D	E	F	G	H	I	J	K	L	M	N	O	P	Q	R	S	T	U	V	W	X	Y	Z

2 JPR FCZJ KFSCMJQLJ JPKLA Q UCFQL OQL PQHR, LRGJ JC PRM JQTRLJ, CE OCXMZR, KZ PRM PQKMYMRZZRM.

A	B	C	D	E	F	G	H	I	J	K	L	M	N	O	P	Q	R	S	T	U	V	W	X	Y	Z

Solution on Page 159

TOMMY

By L J Reeves.

An evening at the theatre gets more and more unlikely when an unexpected visitor arrives on Jane's doorstep

"I'm like the white rabbit in Alice in Wonderland, always late," Jane muttered, slamming the door on the ringing telephone. It could be something urgent; even be David ringing from Canada. 'No, he's never going to phone again, not after that email I sent him'. Technology was fine, but it didn't allow for reflection.

She hurried down the path, already late for the theatre after a hectic day at work. It was then she noticed a dark lump huddled on the verge.

She looked at the object, nudging it with her shoe. She could see in the half light that it was a creature of some sort, so she ran to her car and scrabbled about in the glove compartment for the torch she always carried (and could never find) and dashed back to shine it on the object. It was a tortoise!

Now Jane knew nothing about tortoises but thought it was hibernating – at the wrong time of year. In fact, it looked rather dead to her.

"It's no good, I'll have to do something with it," she grumbled. Her eyes alighted on a battered piece of cardboard and, putting on her gloves, she began to slide the cardboard underneath. 'If it starts to move while I'm doing this, I'll scream', she thought. She managed to pick it up, then she stopped in her tracks. What now? She looked around, waiting in vain for a tortoise lover to come to the rescue! Oh well, she'd have to take it into town with her and drop it off at the vet's.

Five minutes later, she was finally on her way, her unwelcome passenger sitting beside her on the front seat, still on the cardboard tray.

She pulled into a lay-by and used her mobile phone to ring her friend, Sally, to warn her she was running late. After what seemed like an eternity, she heard Sally's muffled voice speaking as if from a great distance: "There you are, I've been trying to get you for ages." Jane guiltily remembered the ringing telephone. Sally continued: "I'm afraid I can't come tonight – I've got an awful cold. Perhaps you can get someone else to go with you." With that, the phone went dead, just as Jane was about to relate her tortoise crisis. What a lovely evening this was turning out to be – all dressed up, missing out on the theatre with a nice natter afterwards, and this, this... crustacean still to deal with.

She looked around, waiting in vain for a tortoise lover to come to the rescue!

Sighing, she forced the car into gear and set off for the town centre, but her heart sank as she approached the vet's – a large, white building on the corner of the precinct – as there was no sign of life. Why couldn't they stay open all night like supermarkets and chemists? And to make things worse, it had started to drizzle!

She was about to turn away when she noticed a side door with a tarnished plaque proclaiming — Jonathan Wellcome, Veterinary Practitioner (and then about a yard of impressive letters) but it was the last part that interested her – Flat 1. Glancing up, she saw there was a flat above the premises. In fact, she could just make out a chink of light through what passed for lace curtains. Jane pressed the buzzer and then jumped as a disembodied voice boomed at her: 'Who is it?" Flustered and a little embarrassed, Jane started to explain about the tortoise, but was rudely interrupted by an irritable: "Oh, I'll come down", and a click.

The door opened to reveal a tall man in his thirties, with an expression that matched his tone, demanding: "What do you want at this time of night?" Jane was tempted to point out that it was only 6.45 but thought better of it – after all, she needed his help. He listened impatiently to her, then without a word, strode past her to the car and lifted out the tortoise, saying: "Come on up and I'll look at it."

Jane locked her car and followed him, catching a glimpse of herself in the mirror at the top of the stairs – what a sight she looked, her hair flattened to her head and her make-up starting to run!

"In here!"She found him cradling the tortoise in surprisingly gentle hands. As he took no further notice of her, she gazed around the room, wrinkling her nose at a strange smell coming, she concluded, from a large Labrador curled up on an ancient sofa. It barked once, then went back to sleep.

"Well, there's nothing wrong with it, it was just resting – no need to panic," the vet said.

Jane replied huffily: "I hope you don't think I'm the sort of person who bothers people unnecessarily? Will you be able to find him a good home?"

He stared at her, like an irritated lecturer being asked a question by a dim student. Jane hastily added: "How much do I owe you?"

"There's no charge but most people give a small donation towards food and drink – for the animals, I mean," he said with a grin.

'Well, he's not without some humour', Jane thought, fumbling in her handbag. He added: "Shall we say £25?"

Escorting her down the stairs, she was conscious of his presence watching her. "Goodnight," he said and thrust a crumpled business card into her hand, then closed the door firmly.

Annoyed at being treated so offhandedly, Jane drove off, thinking 'I could put the creature through university for that price'. But gradually she began to thaw – after all, she'd done her bit for animal-kind and had left the tortoise in safe hands. She wondered whether all vets were as abrupt as this Jonathan Wellcome, but had to admit there was an attractiveness about him – in a casual, crumpled sort of way. He did have rather nice blue eyes and long eyelashes and a strong, square chin and… 'For goodness sake, pull yourself together…' she told herself.

By the time she reached home she was in a much better mood. She picked up the business card from the passenger seat, and turning it over, saw a scribbled note which said: "Like my dog, my bark's worse than my bite!" She smiled at this, thinking, 'Well, it wouldn't hurt to phone in a couple of days, to see how my tortoise is getting on, would it?' Absorbed in her thoughts, she almost tripped over a box near the garage door that she hadn't noticed before, with an envelope lying near it.

She read, 'Dear Jane, Sorry you were out. Must run – going away for the weekend. Can you look after Tommy for me? I've left him in his box by the garage, love Auntie Vi. PS: He's bound to feel a bit lost, so be sure to give him lots of TLC!'

October 2003

HIGH DAYS AND HOLIDAYS...

Conkers at the ready
Head to Ashton in Northamptonshire this month, for the World Conker Championships. The traditional cries of 'Hobily, hobily honker, my first conker' will be echoing around the village green, as contestents try to outcrack each other before 5,000 spectators.

PIC: HULTON ARCHIVE

St Osyth's Day (October 7)
By invoking St Osyth, hearth and homes can be kept free of calamity in the year ahead. Last thing before bed, rake the ashes in the grate and mark them with a cross. A prayer should then be offered to the saint to protect the house from 'fire, water and all other calamities'.

Lion Sermon (October 16)
Today at the church of St Katherine Cree in London, the Lion Sermon takes place. It celebrates the exploits of the 1646-7 Mayor of London, Sir John Gayer. Saved from a lion when he was in Syria, he was so happy he left a sizeable gift of £200 in his will for the poor on condition that his story be told every year in the Lion Sermon.

Civil War showdown (October 23)
This day in 1642 the Battle of Edgehill was fought. A monument near Kineton in Warwickshire commemorates the battle and a local thoroughfare Red Road is named after the stream of blood that ran afterwards.

WEDNESDAY	1
THURSDAY	2
FRIDAY	3
SATURDAY	4
SUNDAY	5
MONDAY	6
TUESDAY	7
WEDNESDAY	8
THURSDAY	9
FRIDAY	10
SATURDAY	11
SUNDAY	12
MONDAY	13
TUESDAY	14
WEDNESDAY	15
THURSDAY	16
FRIDAY	17
SATURDAY	18

SUNDAY	19
MONDAY	20
TUESDAY	21
WEDNESDAY	22
THURSDAY	23
FRIDAY	24
SATURDAY	25
SUNDAY	26 British Summer Time ends
MONDAY	27
TUESDAY	28
WEDNESDAY	29
THURSDAY	30 November YOURS on sale
FRIDAY	31 Hallowe'en

This month don't forget to...

- Look in the local paper to find out where your nearest organised firework display is.
- Make your Christmas pudding and Christmas cake – they will have matured nicely by Christmas, especially if you 'feed' the cake with brandy at regular intervals!
- Put the clocks back one hour the night before October 26.
- Change your summer hanging baskets and window boxes to autumn/winter displays.

Yul Brynner

It happened in October...

October 23, 1917: The Commons voted in favour of allowing women to become MPs.

October 4, 1949: Three generations of the Bowler family attended celebrations marking the centenary of the bowler hat.

October 31, 1951: Zebra crossings were introduced.

October 16, 1985: Yul Brynner died of lung cancer and left behind a short film begging all smokers to give up cigarettes.

September 29-October 5

Treasured Photo

Audrey Hughes of Wilmslow, Cheshire, sent us this photo: 'These are members of the Ladies Cycling Club in Burton-on-Trent taken about 100 years ago, I think. My great-aunt Nellie is second from the left.'

Well, fancy that!

English soldiers were called Tommies, because the name Thomas Atkins was the example name used on the forms soldiers had to fill in.

TIP TIME

Stand your mixing bowl on a damp dishcloth to keep it steady.

Pause for thought

'My late mother-in-law kept these lines in her Prayer Book,' writes Cecily Thomlinson, of Thame, Oxfordshire. 'Three of her sons, including my then boyfriend, aged only 18, were prisoners of war. We were eventually married on the day Japan surrendered. Sadly my husband died in 1994. My family and I still miss him dreadfully and always will.'

Petition

Before I slip into my bed's delight
I say a little prayer for you each night.
I pray the mighty miracle of sleep
May fold your tiredness in slumber deep.
If you are sad or lonely for a while,
I ask that something causes you to smile;
But most of all that God, who understands,
Will gently hold your soul between His hands.

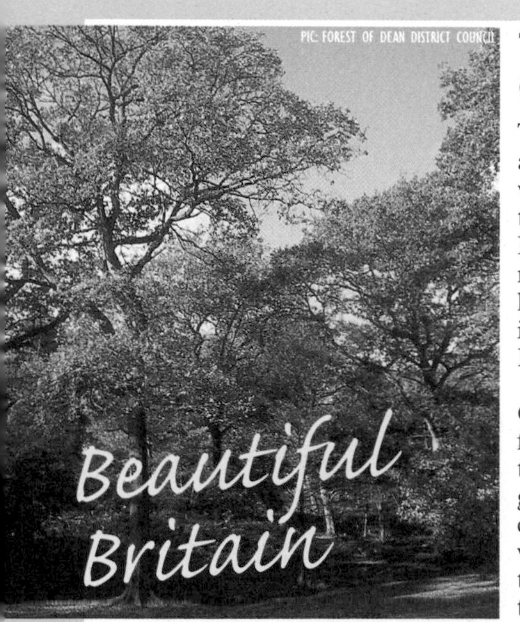

PIC: FOREST OF DEAN DISTRICT COUNCIL

The Forest of Dean, Gloucestershire

The Forest of Dean covers an area of 42 square miles (28 of which are woodland) and used to be a royal hunting ground. However, its history goes back much further than this, as it has been a source of wood, iron and stone since before Roman times.

Clearwell Caves, near Coleford, have been mined for iron ore from Celtic times, 2,700 years ago. They got their name from the crystal-clear pools, overhung with stalactites, which used to be the drinking water for the local people. Today, the caves are open to visitors and it is possible to see the marks from the miners' picks on the walls.

This area is also coal mining country – there is a huge coal seam running underneath the forest. For the past 700 years, a group of locals have retained the right to mine anywhere in the forest, after their ancestors won this right as a reward for their tunnelling skills. They are known as 'free miners' and can lay claim to this right after working for a year and a day underground.

I WISH I'D SAID THAT...

"No spring nor summer beauty hath such grace, As I have seen in one autumnal face."
– John Donne, English poet

Letter of my life

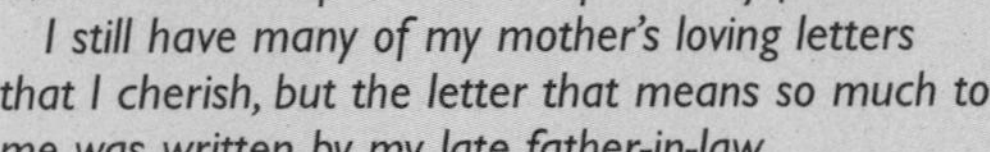

Marcia Walters, Wrexham

My mother had four sons before me and I was often told of my father's great delight upon having a daughter at last. Sadly, I didn't have an opportunity to know him because he died very soon after his return from active service in the war. I felt I had missed something special in my life by not having had a chance to build up a relationship with my father.

I still have many of my mother's loving letters that I cherish, but the letter that means so much to me was written by my late father-in-law.

When my husband, David, and I became engaged in 1960, I asked my future father-in-law if he would object to my calling him 'Dad' after my marriage. His reply was that he would object if I were to call him anything other, because he looked on me as another daughter. But he was not a great one for expressing his feelings. So it was a surprise to me to receive a letter from him following the birth of our son in 1963.

Following a difficult labour and birth, Alex arrived tired and battle-weary. His skull was fractured and we were deeply worried, especially when he was baptised before an operation to correct his skull damage at only eight days old. I was moved to receive the letter from my father-in-law, telling me how pleased he was to have a grandson. His light-hearted, considerate touch lifted my spirits at a time when we needed support and encouragement. I was further touched, not only because his eyesight was failing, but because he had not put pen to paper for years. I read and re-read the letter. It was a comfort during those anxious days and months until we knew our son was all right and had suffered no lasting damage. So I treasure his letter, not just because of the time and occasion but because it was the only letter I'd ever had that was signed, 'Love, Dad'.

"You must be joking"

Signs seen in shops:
Wine shop: *Thirst come, thirst served*
Maternity shop: *You should have danced all night*
Travel agent: *Why don't you go away?*
Undertaker's: *Drive carefully – we can wait.*

HEALTHY LIVING

Use it or lose it!

Keep your brain cells busy:

- ❑ Take up a new interest. It doesn't have to be academic – dance classes, a new language, or dress-making are all ideal.
- ❑ Playing cards, doing crosswords and puzzles are great workouts for the old grey matter.
- ❑ Don't be scared of new technology. It may seem tricky at first but you'll get there in the end.

TEA-TIME TREATS

Orange and Sultana Scones

Makes 10

- 8 oz/225 g self-raising flour
- 1 teaspoon baking powder
- 2 oz/50 g butter or hard margarine, cut into small pieces
- 1 oz/25 g caster sugar
- 2 oz/50 g sultanas
- Grated rind 1 orange
- 1 medium egg
- 3 fl oz/75 ml milk, plus extra to glaze.

1 Preheat oven to 220°C/425°F/Gas Mark 7.
2 Sieve flour and baking powder into a bowl. Rub in butter or margarine until mixture resembles fine breadcrumbs. Stir in sugar, sultanas and orange rind.
3 Beat egg with the milk and add to the bowl, stirring to make a soft dough. Turn on to a floured surface and knead dough lightly until smooth.
4 Roll out lightly about ¾ in/2 cm thick or pat it with your hand. Cut into 10 rounds with a 2 in/5 cm cutter. Put scones on a baking sheet and brush tops with milk. Bake for 12-15 minutes or until well risen. Transfer to wire rack to cool.

PIC: TATE & LYLE SUGARS

October 6-12

Perfect Puddings

Spiced Bread Pudding

Serves 6

- 8 oz/225 g stale wholemeal bread
- ½ pt/275 ml milk, plus an extra 4 tablespoons in a separate bowl
- 4 oz/100 g mixed dried fruit of your choice
- 2 oz/50 g butter or margarine
- 4 oz/100 g dark brown sugar
- Ground mixed spice, to taste
- 1 egg
- 4 tablespoons milk
- Pinch ground nutmeg

1 Preheat oven to 180°C/350°F/Gas Mark 4 and grease a shallow ovenproof dish.
2 Roughly break up bread and put in a bowl with the first quantity of milk. Leave to soak.
3 Add dried fruit, butter, sugar and mixed spice. Beat well. Whisk together the egg and remaining milk. Add to the bread mixture.
4 Turn into prepared dish and sprinkle with ground nutmeg. Bake in the oven for 45 minutes until set.

Healthy Living

Get a good night's sleep

- ❑ Avoid drinks containing caffeine, late in the evening.
- ❑ Relax in a warm bath and wind down before bed.
- ❑ Lie back and listen to soothing music.
- ❑ Read a few pages of a book.
- ❑ Try to go to bed and get up at the same time daily.
- ❑ Try a few drops of lavender oil on your pillow.

PIC: BY GRACIOUS PERMISSION OF H.M. THE QUEEN

Pause for thought

A Meditation

What happened to the world we knew?
When we were young, and as we grew
We lived our lives in simple ways
And tried our best through all those days.
Our homes were blessed with loving care,
All we possessed with friends we'd share.
No thoughts of riches we conceived,
Our families close, and we believed
Their caring love was always there,
Without this warmth our lives are bare.
By reaching out to one another
So much from each we might discover.
Contentment then would live again,
Show that you care, 'twill not be in vain.

Florence Homer, East Preston, West Sussex

Treasured Photo

Mrs Joan Maxtone writes: 'My twin sister Kathleen and I decided to send you this photo of ourselves in our lovely pram, taken in 1936. We used to live in Market Rasen, Lincolnshire, but are now living just two miles apart in beautiful Perthshire, Scotland.'

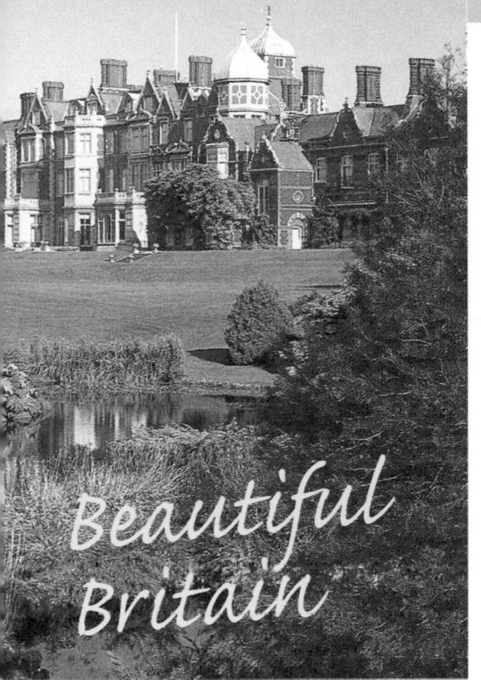

Sandringham, Norfolk

This 20,000-acre royal estate has been home to the Royal Family since it was bought for Edward, Prince of Wales (who was crowned Edward VII in 1902) by his father for £220,000.

Edward was very keen on punctuality and enjoyed shooting so much he didn't want to waste any time that could be spent in the open air. To ensure everyone around him was punctual too he adopted a system that became known as 'Sandringham time', which meant keeping all the clocks at Sandringham forward by 30 minutes. This system remained in place until the reign of Edward VIII.

It's possible to visit the house from April to September, when the Royal Family is not at home. They spend three weeks here in the summer, during July and August.

Sandringham houses a museum that contains a collection of vintage cars and various other items of interest connected with the Royal Family.

TIP TIME

For a quick ice and a slice with your gin and tonic slice one lemon and quarter each piece. Place a piece of lemon with water in each icecube container and freeze.

Letter of my life

In the 1950s, I was a student in Edinburgh where I met and fell in love with a young student nurse from the Hospital for Sick Children.

Although she transferred her studies to Leeds before I graduated we kept in touch and eventually became engaged.

Two years of National Service followed, so our courtship was by letters and the occasional weekend leave until the summer of 1958, when we went on holiday to North Wales with her parents.

It was there that Janet broke off our engagement, telling me that while there was no-one else, she didn't love me enough to marry me. Sadly, I accepted her decision and promised I would make no further attempt to contact her. Four months later I returned to Edinburgh.

Two years later, I received a letter from a stranger who told me she was a friend of Janet's, who had confided in her that she loved me still and regretted ending our relationship. I was full of joy and I wrote a long letter pouring out my love for her. But then, as I paused to seal it, I reasoned that if she had had a change of heart surely she would have contacted me herself. As she hadn't done so, then I could only assume that she hadn't changed her mind. So how could I break my earlier promise to her and risk the pain and humiliation of further rejection? So I put the letter, together with her photograph, in my box of private belongings – where they remain to this day.

That letter was a pivotal point in my life and I often think how very different my life might have been had I had the courage to post it.

Mr G H Thomas, Kirkland, Cumbria

"You must be joking"

Having just had her first baby, a young mum was returned to the ward. The woman in the next bed, who had just given birth to her eighth child, was just finishing her supper. "What did you have?" asked the young mum excitedly. "Chicken," said her neighbour.

Well, fancy that!

About 27 per cent of food in developed countries is wasted. It's simply thrown away.

I wish I'd said that...

The human mind is like an umbrella – it functions best when open.– Walter Gropius (1883-1969), German architect

October 13-19

HEALTHY LIVING

Burn it off!

Here's a quick guide to the number of calories you burn per hour:

- ❑ Sleeping – 70
- ❑ Standing – 108
- ❑ Vacuuming – 250
- ❑ Cleaning the windows – 300
- ❑ Walking at 3mph – 300
- ❑ Ballroom dancing – 360
- ❑ Swimming – 380

TEA-TIME TREATS

Carrot Cake

- 2 eggs
- 2 oz/50 g soft dark brown sugar
- 3 fl oz/75 ml vegetable oil
- 7 oz/200 g finely grated carrots
- 1 oz/ 25 g desiccated coconut
- 2 oz/50 g black treacle
- 4 oz/100 g wholemeal self-raising flour
- 1 ½ ground cinnamon
- 2 oz/50 g raisins
- 1 oz/ 25 g chopped nuts

For the icing:

- 1½ oz/40 g margarine or butter
- 3 oz/75 g icing sugar
- 1 tablespoon lemon juice and a little grated rind

1. Grease and line a rectangular cake tin. Preheat oven to 190°C/375°F/Gas Mark 5.
2. Whisk eggs and sugar until thick and creamy. Slowly whisk in the oil. Add the remaining ingredients and combine.
3. Spoon mixture into tin and level surface. Bake for 40 minutes. Cool on a wire rack.
4. When cake is cold, mix together icing ingredients and spread over cake.

Letter of my life

Mr R E Fawcett, Llandudno

More than 30 years ago I received a letter from a couple I met in Rotterdam in 1945. They were Marjorie and Oscar Eberle-Getlieb. Marjorie was Jewish and had suffered many privations during the war, including the loss of both her parents in a gas chamber. Oscar, although he wasn't Jewish, had also suffered at the hands of the German army at that time. Here is part of their letter:

'...When I look out of the window at the harbour in front of our house and realise the freedom Oscar and I enjoy together with our friends, and the rest of our 12 million Dutch citizens. I do realise that you are one brick in the chain of men who gave all they had to give, namely their life, to make us free. And though we cannot repay your willingness, Oscar and I wanted to commemorate this happy occasion by planting a tree in the land that is most dear to us, Israel. Enclosed you find the certificate of the planting. Maybe it means something to you that, somewhere in the hills of Jerusalem, a little tree keeps your name alive as a token of our gratitude.'

I greatly treasure this letter as to my mind the Dutch people were the most appreciative of the European countries that were liberated, and they give expression to this even today. In particular, the schoolchildren annually place flowers on the graves of the men who died fighting for their parents' liberation.

Pause for thought

In the Golden Weather

Head for the Downs,
In the golden weather,
Past fields quilted amber and brown.

Stroll through the woods,
Where warm autumn breezes
Bring weary leaves tumbling down.

Study the birds,
In the golden weather,
Assembling to say sad goodbyes.

Sigh as they soar,
Through the cool, misty morn,
To roost beneath warm, southern skies.

Glean as you go,
A rich harvest of memories,
Leaving your worries in town.

Head for the Downs,
In the golden weather.
Past fields quilted amber and brown.

Eirlys Jones, Cranleigh, Surrey

TIP TIME

To open lids on jars, simply tap around the rim of the lid with the handle of a knife. It works every time.
Joan Charles, Guildford

Well, fancy that!

Winston Churchill was a stutterer. One school report advised: 'Because of his stuttering, he should be discouraged from following in his father's political footsteps.'

TREASURED PHOTO

Joyce Earle, Membership Secretary of the Dagenham Girl Pipers Veterans Association, sent us this photo of herself and her friend Kathleen Howell: 'We both joined the band in 1946 and this photo in uniform was taken at the Edinburgh Festival in 1950. We hadn't seen each other for nearly 50 years when we met again at the band's 70th birthday celebrations in 2000 and renewed our friendship. It was a really lovely day.'

PICS: SCARBOROUGH BOROUGH COUNCIL

WHITBY, NORTH YORKSHIRE

Whitby is a town along a part of coastline that includes cliffs, coves and beaches. This area has a history of smuggling and along the coast, at Robin Hood's Bay, it is said that the maze of tunnels and passageways connecting the houses is such that a ball of silk could be passed from the bottom to the top of the village without seeing daylight.

Whitby itself is set in a ravine at the mouth of the river Esk and is dominated by the ruins of Whitby Abbey on the clifftop. It is a town of tiny alleys and streets, clambering up from the busy port, and its Anglo-Saxon Church of St Mary is of particular interest, featuring as it does carved pews made by ships' carpenters from the whaling fleet that used to be very successful here. Also of interest to those who love a scary story is St Mary's churchyard, which was the inspiration for Bram Stoker's classic novel, Dracula.

Whitby's most famous inhabitant was Captain Cook, who sailed from here straight into the history books, and his former home is now a museum.

"You must be joking"

"I say, I say, I say, there's something in the fruit bowl shouting for help."

"Don't worry, it's only a damson in distress."

I WISH I'D SAID THAT...

"What of October, that ambiguous month, the month of tension, the unendurable month?"
– Doris Lessing, English writer

October 20-26

Pause for thought

'I came across this prayer 25 years ago,' writes Alice Weaver, from Winchcombe in Gloucestershire. 'I don't know who wrote it, but I have given it to many friends and found it most helpful.'

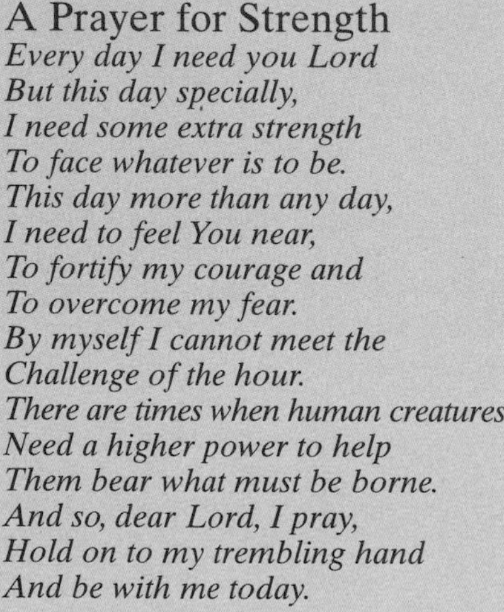

A Prayer for Strength

Every day I need you Lord
But this day specially,
I need some extra strength
To face whatever is to be.
This day more than any day,
I need to feel You near,
To fortify my courage and
To overcome my fear.
By myself I cannot meet the
Challenge of the hour.
There are times when human creatures
Need a higher power to help
Them bear what must be borne.
And so, dear Lord, I pray,
Hold on to my trembling hand
And be with me today.

TIP TIME

Use a dab of glue instead of Sellotape when wrapping presents for children. They'll find it much easier to unwrap their gifts.

HEALTHY LIVING

Healthy hair

Keep your hair in good condition to boost your confidence.

- ❑ To ensure the hair forming beneath your scalp is healthy avoid eating too many sweets, chocolate and cakes. Replace with fresh fruit and veg.
- ❑ Boost the shine of your hair after washing by sealing the cuticles with a blast of cool air once the hair is dry.
- ❑ Banish dandruff by massaging vinegar into the scalp and then rinse out.

"You must be joking"

A vicar called at one of his parishioner's homes and a girl answered the door. "Is your sister in?" "No, she ain't."

"Is your dad in?" "No, he ain't."

"Where's your grammar, my child?" the vicar remonstrated.

"She's asleep in front of the fire!" the child beamed.

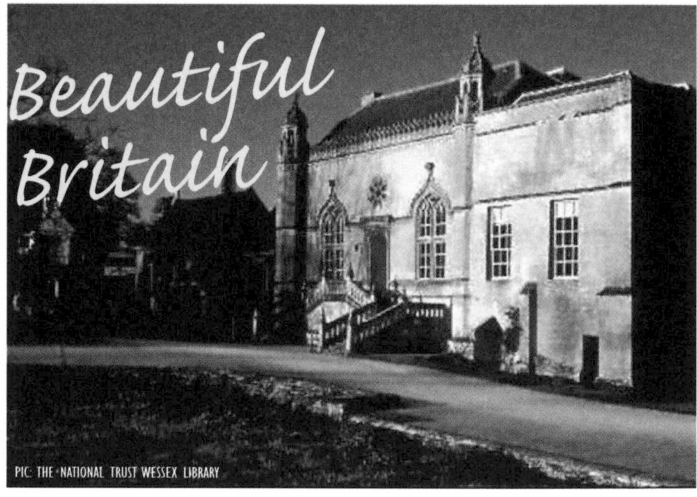

PIC: THE NATIONAL TRUST WESSEX LIBRARY

LACOCK, WILTSHIRE

This beautiful village dates back to Saxon times, and while there are many medieval buildings, there are very few that were built later than the 18th century.

Lacock is thought to be the birthplace of photography, and the Fox Talbot Museum of Photography, inside Lacock Abbey gates, details Fox Talbot's pioneering work which included the invention of the photographic negative which meant, for the first time, more than one print could be made of a picture.

The abbey itself dates back to 1232, when it was built as a convent. It was then sold by Henry VIII to Sir William Sharington in the 16th century, who turned it into a family home – and added a brewery, although he did retain some of its medieval features.

Lacock is also a popular television location, being the setting for the BBC's adaptations of Jane Austen's Emma and Pride & Prejudice.

Letter of my life

In the closing stages of the war, censorship having been lifted, a women's magazine offered to put readers in contact with Australian penfriends. I took up the offer and was put in touch with a teenager from Melbourne called Nola (above). As I was married (right) and Nola a teenager, it seemed unlikely correspondence would continue but, as we exchanged letters, a friendship developed.

In the course of time Nola married and had five children; she is now the proud gran of nine.

Never in my wildest dreams did I expect to meet my penfriend in the flesh but, in 1989 (43 years after our first introductory letter) my husband and I made the trip of a lifetime and we finally met, in Melbourne. It was a joyful occasion. Nola and I were compatible – and so were our husbands! We stayed in their home and were taken to places that had been to us just names in an atlas. Letter writing has become much easier as a result of meeting Nola and her family in their home setting.

Since then we have celebrated our Golden Weddings, still correspond regularly, and have become as close as sisters. Sometimes, when I'm in a reflective mood, I'm amazed by the fact that a lifetime friendship resulted from merely chancing on a small item somewhere in the pages of a women's magazine.

Kathleen Maudsley, Rock Ferry, Cheshire

I WISH I'D SAID THAT...

"Time is the ultimate commodity and you are born with only so much to spend; and nobody ever knows the exact amount." –Tom Clancy, American author

Well, fancy that!

In 1927, Walt Disney created an animated character called Mortimer Mouse. His wife Lillian persuaded him to change the name to Mickey.

TREASURED PHOTO

Mrs D Haslam of Padgate near Warrington writes:

'This is a picture of me in my servant's uniform when I was 17 years old. I feel that I was one of the last young ladies to go into service in my area. It was wartime and I had a nice situation with Group Captain Insall. I lived in, had my own bedroom and bathroom, and was treated very kindly. I earned twelve shillings and sixpence weekly, and all my keep and uniforms. In the photo, taken by the cook, I am in my afternoon apron, but took my cap off for the camera. I even went on holiday with the family, to the Countess of Stowe's estate near Shepton Mallet. It was my first holiday ever.'

PERFECT PUDDINGS

Chocolate and Walnut Tarts

Makes 8

- 1 lb/450 g shortcrust pastry
- 6 fl oz/175 ml golden syrup
- 4 oz/100 g soft dark brown sugar
- 3 eggs
- 3 oz/75 g butter, melted
- 1 oz/25 g plain flour
- 1 teaspoon vanilla essence
- 1 oz/25 g cocoa powder
- 5 oz/150 g walnut pieces

1 Preheat oven to 180°C/350°F/Gas Mark 4.
2 Roll out pastry and use to line eight 4 in/10 cm flan tins. Prick bases with fork and bake blind in oven for 15 minutes until golden. Lower oven temp to 170°C/325°F/Gas Mark 3.
2 Heat the syrup and sugar in a pan until melted. Allow to cool, then beat in the eggs. Stir in the melted butter, flour, essence and cocoa.
3 Pour half the syrup mixture into the pastry case, add the walnut pieces and spoon over the rest of syrup mixture.
4 Bake for 15 minutes or until set. Serve warm with cream.

October 27-November 2

TREASURED PHOTO

We were struck by these 'then' and 'now' photos. Mrs M Cunliffe of Pudsey explains how important they are to her:

'I was born in 1922 in a house named Bonscale, near Ullswater.

I had no thoughts of finding the place of my birth until eight years ago when I had a holiday with my son and has family in Glenridding. I had a sudden longing to find Bonscale. I had seen an old photo of the house, and one of my parents sitting on an old stone seat.

We set off on a beautiful day, looking for my old home. My son, studying a map, felt a house below us should be Bonscale. I couldn't be sure, and there was no reply to our knock at the door. Disappointed, I walked down the bank towards the lake. Suddenly, I found the stone seat where my parents had been photographed so many years before! It was a moment of rare emotion. I was photographed on the seat with my granddaughter.'

I WISH I'D SAID THAT...

"The last red leaf is whirled away,
The rooks are blown about the skies."
– Alfred Lord Tennyson, English poet

Letter of my life

I left school not really knowing what I wanted to do with my life. I took a job in a local accountant's office, but soon grew bored with adding up other people's money. But jobs were thin on the ground and my nose remained firmly to the grindstone.

I dreamed of escape by becoming a writer. I saved up and bought a typewriter and bombarded local and national newspapers and magazines with ideas and articles. I collected an impressive array of rejection slips.

Life went on like this for several years until one day I saw a letter appealing for people to join an expedition to work in the French grape harvest. It wasn't addressed to me personally but the letter's effect on my, by now almost moribund imagination was such that it might have been.

I gave up my job, joined the expedition and spent several months roaming southern France, laying down some of the vintage that has since been enjoyed by subsequent generations of travellers to France.

It was no idyll – it was hard, unrelenting work – but as an experience it was invaluable.

After returning home and allowing the episode to marinate for a while, I wrote a piece about it that was accepted by a national magazine. The editor's letter of acceptance was a milestone in my life only marginally less important than the one which acted as the original spur.

Soon after I was offered a job on a weekly newspaper and have since enjoyed a career in journalism.

Wynford Perry, Warrington, Cheshire

TEA-TIME TREATS

Cinnamon Spread

- 2 oz/50 g butter or butter substitute
- 2 oz/50 g soft brown sugar
- ½ teaspoon ground cinnamon

1. Put butter into a bowl and beat until softened. Add the brown sugar and beat until smooth and well blended. Beat in the ground cinnamon.
2. Turn into a small pot and refrigerate until ready to serve. Delicious spread on scones and toast.

Pendle, Lancashire

Famous for the Pendle witches, Pendle is named after nearby Pendle Hill, which, to this day, is inundated by around 5,000 people bearing lanterns and torches each Halloween, because of its association with stories of witchcraft.

The story starts in the early 17th century, when 'wicca', the ancient pagan religion, still survived in remote villages, while the church presented witchcraft as devil worship.

One spring day in 1612 a young girl was begging locally, when she appeared to paralyse a pedlar with a curse. Accused of witchcraft, she confessed, but in turn made accusations against other women from the town.

More confessions followed, and more incriminating 'evidence', including human bones found near one of the women's homes, and they were imprisoned in Lancaster Castle. Despite a plot to free them, they were tried as witches, found guilty and hanged in front of huge crowds.

By the time the last witchcraft trial in England in 1712 took place, around 1,000 people had been executed as witches.

Newchurch, in Pendle, is home to St Mary's Church, which is known for its 'Eye of God' tower, thought to watch over parishioners and protect them from witchcraft. It is said that it was from this churchyard that the Pendle witches stole bones to use in their spells.

Well, fancy that!

Riddle: What is often returned but never borrowed?
Answer: Silence.

"You must be joking"

"I say, I say, I say, today I fought off the powers of darkness."
"How did you do that?"
"I paid my electricity bill."

Pause for thought

Hope

Hope is a happiness held in the heart,
When happiness seems to be gone.
Hope is a quiet joy deep within,
Encouraging us to go on.
Hope is a light that burns in the night,
In a place where a miracle starts,
And every good thing
will come in its time
As long as there's hope in our hearts.

Mrs M L Georgeson,
Monifieth, Angus

Healthy Living

Tips on reducing varicose veins

- Regular exercise – walking, cycling, swimming – will keep blood vessels healthy.
- Avoid tight fitting clothes or underwear that will restrict the blood flow.
- Don't leave legs crossed for long periods.
- Stick to a high-fibre, low-salt diet.
- Kick off those high heels.
- Rest legs on pillows while sleeping.
- If you smoke – give it up.

Tip Time

Don't know what to do with those fireplace ashes? Save them for spring and use them to keep slugs out of the garden. Slugs don't like ashes.

DO YOU REMEMBER...

...Barry Bucknell?

BARRY was British TV's original DIY expert in the 1950s and '60s. His first programme was Barry Bucknell's Do It Yourself, which was later followed by Bucknell's House.

The programmes were transmitted live, often with disastrous results – they always kept you on the edge of your seat waiting for the shelf to fall down or the next nail to be bent!

Apparently Barry used to rehearse a lot at home, with his wife timing him with a stopwatch. But even with all the rehearsing, there were still hiccups, such as the time he oversoaked some ceiling paper and it dropped down on him. Not the way to do it, but the audience loved it!

Barry designed the Mirror, a family sailing dinghy which has sold more than 89,000 models, plus a special two-man canoe for the Royal National Lifeboat Institution.

...Hula-Hoops?

HULA-Hoops – made from polyethylene – were first introduced to this country in 1958 and soon the whole nation was Hula-Hooping,

PIC: HULTON ARCHIVE

with Hula-Hoopers able to perform tricks while keeping the hoop going. Some could even Hula-Hoop round wrists and ankles, or bend down and tie their shoelaces.

Countrywide competitions were staged and many women used it as part of a keep-fit campaign. Good for trimming the waist!

Brits for all seasons

A TIPPLE OR A TANGO

ON a crisp autumn day, there's nothing like a quiet drink in your favourite local, or a drive out to a country pub for a bite to eat. All across Europe you'll find bistros and bars, but in Britain, old-fashioned pubs reign supreme – there are more than 60,000 in the UK alone.

Many pubs have been taken over by restaurant chains and have lost their identity, but independent pubs still remain, where you know the landlord, can find a favourite corner by the fire and order a simple meal with your tipple. In these days of metric measures, happily we can still order a pint of beer.

PIC: CORBIS STOCKMARKET

The great and the good have frequented pubs for centuries. In Dickensian times, when water wasn't fit to drink, vast quantities of ale were consumed, even by small children. These days, the local pub is still the hub of many towns and villages, and British brewers do a roaring trade, brewing nearly 27 million pints a day.

Non-pubgoers may prefer the genteel atmosphere of a tea dance – another very British tradition.

You don't need your own partner to enjoy a dance; a large percentage of dancing pairs are two women. Classic foxtrots and waltzs, are performed to old-time music and there's plenty of tea.

So get out your dancing shoes and let's tango!

● **For a special treat, London's Waldorf Hotel holds traditional tea dances on the last Sunday of every month from 3-6pm. For details call 0870 4008484 .**

Letter set

We've given you all the letters you need to make the answers for each row and column of this crossword. Cross-referencing coupled with anagram skills will help you to complete the puzzle.

ACROSS
1 HGMOSTUY
2 EINORTUY
3 AEGILLS
4 AAEELLRT
5 DILMT
6 ADFHLNPU
7 AAEILOR
8 EEELOOPR
9 DDEEEKNY

DOWN
1 AEEGHHRU
2 AELNNOOT
3 DEEGILLN
4 ADDET
5 DEFIIMSTY
6 ELMUU
7 AKLOOORS
8 AAEILPRT
9 EELLPRYY

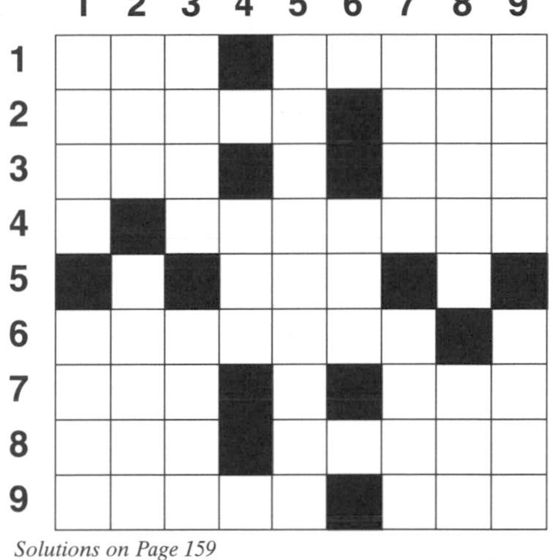

Solutions on Page 159

Hallowe'en quiz

Here's a creepy collection of quiz questions on things that go bump in the night.

1 Which monster of verse has 'jaws that bite' and 'claws that catch'?

2 Which former Bond villain played psychiatrist Dr Loomis in the Hallowe'en horror films of the 1970s, '80s and '90s?

3 Who wrote the macabre stories The Fall of the House of Usher, The Tell-Tale Heart and The Pit and the Pendulum?

4 Who played the vampire in the 1922 German film Nosferatu?

5 According to Scottish tradition, what gift is possessed by those born on Hallowe'en?

6 Which actor, famed for playing all the best-known screen monsters, called his 1977 autobiography Tall, Dark and Gruesome?

7 What is the name of the piece by composer Modest Mussorgsky which was inspired by a witches' sabbath in a story by Gogol?

8 Which wisecracking actor starred in the 1939 spooky comedy film The Cat and the Canary?

9 What is the name of the hero who slays the monster Grendel in an Old English epic poem?

10 Which Japanese dinosaur-like film monster made its screen debut in 1955?

11 Which monster of Greek mythology inhabited the Labyrinth in Crete and was destroyed by Theseus?

12 Which classic horror story by Mary Shelley is subtitled ...or the Modern Prometheus?

13 Which fabled fire-breathing beast has the head of a lion, the body of a goat and the tail of a serpent?

14 Which screen monster, an 18-inch model animated by Willis O'Brien, saved the RKO studio from bankruptcy during the Great Depression?

15 Which comedy duo had screen encounters with Frankenstein, The Killer, The Invisible Man, Dr Jekyll and Mr Hyde and The Mummy?

16 Where and when did the notorious witch hunts take place during which Arthur Miller's play The Crucible is set?

17 Which ruined English abbey is featured in Bram Stoker's vampire novel Dracula?

18 Which British actor (*pictured*) said, 'When I was nine I played the demon king in Cinderella and it launched me on a long and happy life of being a monster'?

PIC: MIRROR

19 Who wrote the 1886 novel The Strange Case of Dr Jekyll and Mr Hyde?

20 The 2001 film, Shrek, winner of the first Academy Award for Best Animated Feature Film is about what type of monster?

DAYS IN THE DIGS FROM HELL

Landladies themselves could be more than a touch theatrical in the heyday of touring live shows, as many a young dancer found out to her cost By Trixie Davenport

When televisions began to dominate our living rooms and bingo took over so many of our lovely theatres, they brought about the slow decline of variety shows and revues.

All the dancers, jugglers and acrobats, and the comics, the duos, the big-name artistes who topped the bill, had to find new venues and new ways to show off their talents.

But whatever happened to all those wonderful and eccentric landladies who were such an important part of showbusiness life?

As a professional dancer in the '30s and throughout the '40s, the landlady was a vital part of my life. Every town had at least two theatres in those days. The resident theatre manager would have a list of digs, all within easy reach of the theatre. If you knew of a good address from a previous visit, it was a bonus – otherwise you took pot luck.

Depending on the type of show it would probably be for a week, maybe two – although pantomime could last from four to eight weeks – and occasionally you might find yourself in the digs from Hell.

Most of the landladies did their best to make it a home-from-home for us all, from the stars at the top of the bill down to the chorus line.

These ladies understood our hours of working – band call on Monday morning, two evening performances, with a matinée on Wednesday and Saturday. They would provide a substantial breakfast to sustain us through the day, accepting it as normal to make our main meal after the last show each night.

One landlady's idea of a varied menu consisted of giving us a different jar of meat paste every night. And just to add insult to injury, she expected three of us to share this magnificent feast!

I started my career with two friends from my dancing-school days. This friendship lasted many years, and saw us through the excitement of touring and coping with air raids and doodlebugs through the war years.

I remember we played Wood Green Empire in the middle of a really bad winter. The nearby house we had booked into was absolutely perishing. When one of us took a bath, there was no room for false modesty because the other two stood in the bathroom waiting their turn and sharing the warmth of the steamy atmosphere.

It was often expected that the three of us would share a bed – it wasn't considered odd in those days. Arriving at new digs in Grimsby, I was delighted to see a double and a single bed, so I threw myself down on the single, shouting 'I claim this'. After supper that night, we climbed the stairs to our room. The door leading to the bathroom was alongside my bed, with a step down to it, so I opened the door and leaned around feeling for the light switch before stepping in. As I blinked at the light flooding the room, I was horrified to see the entire floor was a heaving mass of cockroaches. I spent a very miserable night pleading with my friends to make room for me in their bed.

Every theatre gave us complimentary tickets for the show and we usually handed a couple to our landlady. In Swansea, the landlady was escorted by her son and for the rest of our stay he joined us at mealtimes and followed me about, insisting he was going to marry me. He was all of 12 years old.

There were several towns we always looked forward to playing. In Salford, for instance, we stayed with Aunt Kate, as everyone called her.

A little dumpling of a woman, she was as wide as she was tall. She was a wonderful cook and after an excellent dinner she would have us in stitches, telling stories of the folk she had met as a variety artiste herself, and then as a landlady.

One of the most frightening experiences of our young lives was in... well, perhaps, I'd better not give the location, but I shall never forget it.

It was a wet and gloomy winter's day when we arrived at the big, eerie-looking house. As we entered the dismal hall I felt a shiver run down my back. We were shown the sitting/dining room, then the owner took us up to the second floor along a dark, narrow passage to a large bedroom with two double and two single beds.

Later, ready to go to work and making our way back along the passageway lit by a very dim light bulb, we saw figures coming towards us out of the darkness. You can imagine the scene as three girls tried to get down the stairs at once. We hadn't noticed on arrival that there was a huge mirror at the far end of the hall, and what we were seeing was probably our own reflection.

Making our way back along the passage to bed some hours afterwards we noted the door next to ours was padlocked, yet we could see a light from the window above the door. After a mad scramble into the bedroom and with all those beds to choose from, no-one wanted to sleep nearest the door. We eventually all climbed into one of the double beds on the far side of the room.

The next morning, as our landlady served breakfast, she casually mentioned that she and her family lived in the house next door and we were her only boarders. Our first thought was, 'Well who's in the room next to ours?' That night we jammed a chair under the door handle.

Throughout the week the journey up and down stairs became more frantic as we tried desperately to stay glued together. Our nerves in tatters and, with vivid imaginations working overtime, we even convinced ourselves that we heard groaning coming from the locked room. At the end of the week we were glad to move on.

Some months later, a double act, The Yale Bros, wanted a dance troupe as part of a show for USO (United Service Organisation) – this was a similar set-up to ENSA, but touring the American air bases in the UK.

Off we went to Bury St Edmunds to a hostel. It was very nice – four to six in a bedroom, plenty of showers and bathrooms.

We were very well looked after, the only drawback being the formidable lady in charge of the hostel. She made it plain straightaway that she didn't like Limeys, as the Yanks called the English, and she promptly laid down the rules. Doors would be locked at 11.30pm – definitely no male visitors at any time. Yet the American girls staying there did as they pleased.

As we expected to be there for some time, we accepted her conditions and, apart from a couple of small disagreements, things appeared to go along pretty well. Until one night...

Sitting around chatting before going to bed, we heard the sound of pebbles tapping against the window. Looking out, there was one of our girls making frantic signs that the front door was locked. Sending signals back not to worry, one of us would creep down and open the door. Easy we thought, only to discover our 'jailer' was prowling around downstairs.

We needed another plan, but our biggest problem was we were on the first floor. Then one of the girls noticed the flagpole outside the window. After further gestures and whispering, the culprit understood she was to climb up the drainpipe to reach the pole so that we could haul her through the window.

After several heart-stopping efforts she began the journey up the drainpipe.

We held our breath as she reached towards the pole. This was where all her training in those high-kick routines would come to the fore. Missing the target the first couple of times, with a final supreme lunge she flung her leg over the pole and began to come slowly towards our outstretched hands, with a look of sheer terror on her face. We were able to grab hold and drag her through the window head first. We all landed on a bed gasping.

Then the giggles started, building into such hysterical laughter that we had to stuff pillows into our mouths to prevent the housekeeper hearing us.

Surprisingly, as the months passed, our landlady seemed to grow fond of us. When I think about it now, I realise it was no easy task having so many young girls under one roof... and these wonderful ladies have become part of my memories of a wonderful period in my life.

November 2003

HIGH DAYS AND HOLIDAYS...

All Saints' Day (November 1)
Today – All Saints' or All Hallows' – is a celebration of the redeemed but many of today's antics were not devout. It was a day for pranks, hiding ploughs, throwing things at doors or losing animals.

Bonfire Night (November 5)

PIC: HULTON ARCHIVE

Guy Fawkes' night, with its tradition of burning a guy or an effigy, dates back to the 17th century, but there are older bonfire festivals that were an essential part of the Hallowe'en celebrations. Burning effigies or man-shaped green figures goes back to before the Roman invasion.

In Lewes, Sussex, 17 Protestant martyrs were burned at the stake, an inflammatory act that continues to unite the town in annual protest. Each November 5, Lewes burns the Pope, in fact, several Popes as the town has six bonfire societies, each with its own huge firework display.

Diminutive dynamite (November 11)
Fenny Poppers are set off today at Fenny Stratford, Bucks. These unusual small cannons – six in all – commemorate the founding of the local church by Dr B Willis and are set off at 8am, noon, 2pm and 6pm.

SATURDAY	1	All Saints' Day
SUNDAY	2	
MONDAY	3	
TUESDAY	4	
WEDNESDAY	5	Guy Fawkes' Night
THURSDAY	6	
FRIDAY	7	
SATURDAY	8	
SUNDAY	9	Remembrance Sunday
MONDAY	10	
TUESDAY	11	YOURS Christmas Special on sale
WEDNESDAY	12	
THURSDAY	13	
FRIDAY	14	
SATURDAY	15	
SUNDAY	16	
MONDAY	17	
TUESDAY	18	

Wednesday	19
Thursday	20
Friday	21
Saturday	22
Sunday	23
Monday	24
Tuesday	25
Wednesday	26
Thursday	27
Friday	28 December YOURS on sale
Saturday	29
Sunday	30 First Sunday of Advent, St Andrew's Day

This month don't forget to...

- [ ] Have your car checked over for the winter months to come.
- [ ] Put out nuts and bread for the birds – and a bowl of water for them too.
- [ ] Buy your poppy.
- [ ] Buy or make your marzipan for your Christmas cake.

Royal wedding

PIC: HULTON ARCHIVE

It happened in November...

November 5, 1921: Howard Carter discovered the tomb of King Tutankhamun in Egypt.

November 20, 1947: Princess Elizabeth married Prince Philip, the son of Prince Andrew of Greece, in a ceremony at Westminster Abbey.

November 14, 1952: Charts for pop single records were published for the first time in the New Musical Express.

November 19, 1959: The Archbishop of Canterbury said adultery should be made a criminal offence.

November 3-9

"You must be joking"

"I've just seen 40 men under one umbrella and not one of them has got wet."

"It must have been a very large umbrella."

"No. It wasn't raining."

PERFECT PUDDINGS

Sussex Pond Pudding

Serves 6

- 8 oz/225 g self-raising flour
- 4 oz/100 g suet
- 2 oz/50 g fresh white breadcrumbs
- Pinch salt
- Milk and water to mix
- 1 lemon
- 4 oz/100 g brown sugar
- 4 oz/100 g butter

1 Grease a 2 pint pudding basin.

2 Mix together the flour, suet, breadcrumbs and salt, using milk and water to form a soft dough. Reserve one third of the dough for the lid. Roll out the remainder into a circle and line pudding basin, leaving some pastry overlapping the edge.

3 Wash the lemon and prick it with a clean knitting needle, smear the lemon with butter and roll in the sugar. Place in the basin, together with any remaining sugar and butter.

4 Roll out the remaining pastry into a circle for the lid and place over the basin, sealing with water.

5 Cover with buttered greaseproof paper and seal with kitchen foil. Steam for about 3 hours and serve from the basin.

PIC: CANTERBURY CITY COUNCIL

CANTERBURY, KENT

Canterbury is where Christianity was first introduced to England by St Augustine, who came here from Rome in 597AD and founded his abbey in 598. Henry VIII destroyed the abbey in 1538, during the dissolution of the monasteries, but its foundations still remain.

Canterbury's famous cathedral has evolved over many years and became the most important pilgrimage site in northern Europe, after Thomas à Becket was murdered here in 1170 by knights loyal to Henry II. The cathedral also contains the tomb of the Black Prince (Edward, Prince of Wales), who was an admirer of Thomas à Becket and was buried here in 1376. His effigy on top of the tomb shows him in full armour – although his sword is said to have been stolen by Oliver Cromwell.

Chaucer, in The Canterbury Tales (written in 1380), described the journey of a group of pilgrims to the city in a series of stories that provide many insights into medieval England.

Well, fancy that!

No word in the English language rhymes with month, orange or purple.

TIP TIME

Now that the winter weather is approaching, make a few simple preparations in case your car breaks down. In your boot, keep a blanket, some gloves, a heavy jacket, hats, warm shoes, oil, anti-freeze, a bottle of water and some snacks.

Letter of my life

My husband died five years ago. He was a gentle man and an excellent father. After his death I found this letter, headed I Remember (40-plus years). He knew I would find it sooner or later and I read it over and over again. He has left me a wonderful gift and it brings me tremendous comfort…

'I remember when we first met, our first kiss and fell in love
Our first holiday and engagement, our wedding and honeymoon.
I remember our first-born – Stephen – and the snow.
Rusty our rescue dog and our sadness when he had to go.
I remember our second born – Adrian – when Stephen had a fall and had to go into hospital.
Our move to Meopham and our many happy years there.
I remember our holidays abroad after moving to Ash and the building of our swimming pool.
Trudie our rescue dog and Oz in the snow after our skiing holiday.
Blue our third and Teddy our fourth rescue dog, God bless them.
I remember Skipper our cat and Oz still expecting to see him when he visits us.
I well remember Larna, my retirement present, a very small unexpected arrival (another dog – the fifth).
I remember only the happiness in our lives after 40 years-plus together.
With all my love, more than you can imagine.'

Val Croxford, Ash,
near Sevenoaks, Kent

HEALTHY LIVING

Move more

Make it a daily challenge to find ways to move your body. Anything that moves your limbs is not only a fitness tool but a stress buster. Exercise does not have to be an hour in the gym

- ❑ Climb stairs if given a choice between that and the lift or escalator.
- ❑ Walk your dog or why not offer to walk someone else's.
- ❑ Dancing at any tempo – even in your lounge.

I WISH I'D SAID THAT...

"He who has health has hope, and he who has hope has everything. – Arabian proverb"

Pause for thought

Mrs P M McInerney from Milford Haven, Pembrokeshire, sent in one of her favourite poems:

Forever Faithful

by Dennis Lovell

We've been together many years, no man can break the tie.
Though she's never said she loves me, I just know those eyes can't lie.
She's always ever faithful, and she's always ever true,
If we were ever parted, I just don't know what I'd do.

She is always there to help me, at my every beck and call,
And always understanding when it's backs up to the wall.
She always seems so tireless, and forever stands the pace
For me, I know, no other will ever take her place.

The only thing she asks for is the odd occasional fuss,
But when I come to think of it, so do all of us!
She is a little jealous though, and can't stand competition,
But who can blame her just for this, when I'm her life-long mission?

We're growing old together now, and both a little grey,
But we muddle on together in our own sweet sort of way.
I know she'll never leave me, and there'll be no other man,
For she's my ever-faithful collie, she's my shepherd dog called Jan.

TREASURED PHOTO

Mr T Hook of Wantage sent us this lovely picture of his granddaughter Jennie. It was taken when she was very young and Mr Hook writes: 'It's not a shot one would be able to catch very often.'

November 10-16

Treasured Photo

Miss B L Higginson of Kettering won first prize when she wore this costume in a fancy dress competition. She writes: 'The photo was taken after the 1930 Metropolitan Hospital Carnival. As my father was disabled as a result of the First World War, my mother became a very competent dressmaker and made this costume for me. Note the lace-edged pantaloons.'

Healthy Living

Tips to avoid over eating

- ❑ Slow down, chew with purpose. Take at least 20 minutes to consume a meal.
- ❑ Eat only while sitting down. Extra food is consumed on the run.
- ❑ Drink a glass of water before eating. It will help you feel less hungry.
- ❑ Wait ten minutes before snacking – you may realise you aren't hungry after all.
- ❑ Keep healthy foods readily to hand in the front of your refrigerator shelves.
- ❑ Eat off smaller plates.

Pause for thought

The Picture I Could Not Keep

Her first picture
Clearly no scribble
Discernible head with arms
Legs, eyes, no nose
But a mouth grinning out at me.
Proudly presented
To a doze-shaken mother
Sitting up, rubbing sleep away.
My daughter, all too quickly,
Scrubbing out the picture
From the window
Inked with condensation.

Clare Gaen, Radyr, Cardiff

Tip Time

Use petroleum jelly to get rid of lipstick marks on clothing. Rub in and then launder garment as usual.

"You must be joking"

Exam howlers

- Johann Bach wrote a great many musical compositions and had a large number of children. In between he practised on an old spinster which he kept up in the attic.
- Madman Curie discovered radio and Charles Darwin was a naturalist who wrote the Organ of the Species.

Tea-Time Treats

Crumpets

- 8 oz/225 g flour
- 1 dessertspoon sugar
- ¼ teaspoon tartaric acid
- ¾ teaspoon bicarbonate of soda
- ½ pt/275 ml pint sour milk

1. Heat a frying pan.
2. Mix ingredients together and beat until quite smooth. Drop spoonfuls into a hot frying pan. Cook a few minutes on each side.
3. Serve warm with butter and jam.

Letter of my life

After 53 years of happy marriage I lost my husband and although my children and their families were very supportive and good to me, I was still lonely. After 12 months I wrote the letter that was to change my whole life!

I had been thinking of my teenage sweetheart, Royston, and wondered if he had been happy after we parted (we had been sweethearts for seven years and everyone assumed we would marry). But when war came he joined the Army, I went into the Land Army. We drifted apart and eventually both married – Royston to Marjorie.

I had been wondering if he and Marjorie were happy but had no idea where they lived, so I wrote the letter to 'Missing and Found' in the Daily Mail and they sent me an address in Shrewsbury. After two days I plucked up courage to phone, only to discover Marjorie had died four months previously. We chatted and half an hour later Royston rang me back to ask if I would be in that afternoon. He drove the 50 miles to see me and, as we chatted the years between seemed not to have happened. We were still on the same wavelength – the same sense of humour – and he was still the boy I had loved 57 years before! We started meeting for lunch, then short holidays together.

He gave up his home and came to live with me in August 2001, when he proposed and I accepted (on my birthday). We married in November of that year, with all our children and grandchildren present, and honeymooned on the Costa del Sol.

Mabel Haigh-Brown,
Rednal, Birmingham

Well, fancy that!
Despite accounting for just 1/50th of our body weight, the brain burns 1/5th of our calorie intake.

I WISH I'D SAID THAT...

"To die completely, a person must not only forget but be forgotten, and he who is not forgotten is not dead." – Samuel Butler, English author, painter and musician

PIC: VALE OF WHITE HORSE DISTRICT COUNCIL

WHITE HORSE COUNTRY, OXFORDSHIRE

Lying between the Ridgeway and the River Thames, White Horse Country stretches from the edge of Oxford to the threshold of the Cotswolds and is home to the oldest chalk figure in Britain, the White Horse of Uffington.

Legend has it that the horse was cut from the hillside by the Saxons in 871AD to celebrate King Alfred's victory over the Danes in battle. There is evidence, however, to indicate that the horse is actually far older that that, and may date back 2,000 years or more. There is an iron-age fort, known as Uffington Castle, at the top of the hill and it is thought that the horse might have been created by the people who lived there. It is said that if you stand in the horse's eye and turn around three times, your wish will be granted.

From the top of the hill, there are views across the Vale of the White Horse. There is also a hollow, known as the Horse's Manger, by a flat-topped hill called Dragon's Hill. The legend is that this is where St George slayed the dragon, and bare patches of chalk are said to be the places where the dragon's blood spilled.

Uffington village is also known as the birthplace of Thomas Hughes, author of Tom Brown's Schooldays, and whose home is now a museum.

November 17-23

Healthy Living

Sweet dreams

A good night's sleep is vital for maintaining health. Here are a few bed buying hints:

❑ Make sure the bed is 6in (15cm) longer than you or the taller partner if you share a bed.

❑ Don't buy a bed or mattress without lying down on it to see if it's comfortable.

❑ Buy the largest bed your room can take and the best your purse can afford.

"You must be joking"

"That's a very expensive coat for a struggling typist."

"Yes, I decided to give up struggling."

Tea-Time Treats

Almond Biscuits

Makes 12-15

- 3 oz/75 g butter
- 3 oz/75 g caster sugar
- 2 oz/50 g plain flour
- Pinch of salt
- 3 oz/75 g shredded almonds

1 Grease baking trays. Set oven to 190°C/375°F/Gas Mark 5.
2 Soften butter. Add sugar and beat well.
3 Sift flour and salt and add to the mixture with the almonds.
4 Put in teaspoonfuls on to trays, allowing room to spread.
5 Bake for 6-8 minutes. Allow to cool for a few seconds, then remove from tray with a sharp knife. Curl around a rolling pin until set.

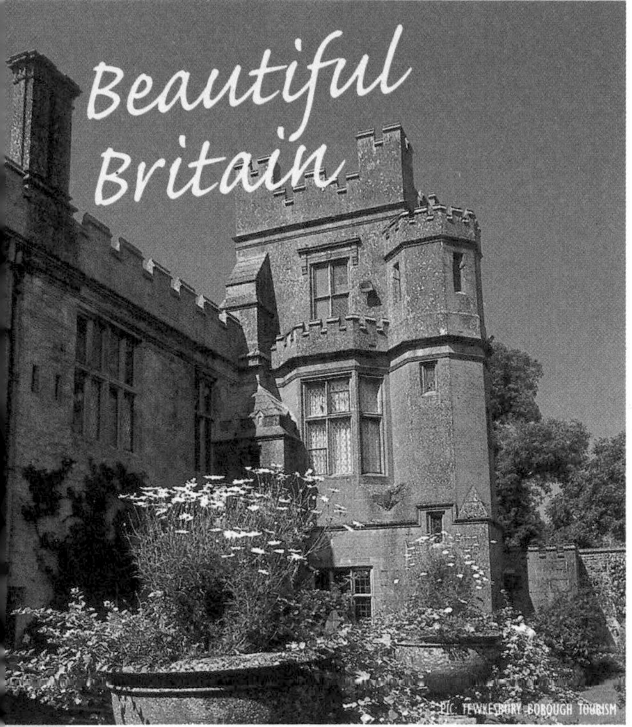
Beautiful Britain

PIC: TEWKESBURY BOROUGH TOURISM

Winchcombe, Gloucestershire

The Saxon town of Winchcombe was once a major pilgrimage centre, with many people coming to visit its Benedictine abbey. Its most famous building is Sudeley Castle, which was a refuge for Charles I during the Civil War and which was subsequently destroyed by Cromwell's victorious Parliamentarians – and some of the buildings in the town were constructed from materials taken from the demolished building.

The castle chapel contains the tomb of Catherine Parr, the sixth wife of Henry VIII, who outlived him and became mistress of the castle.

Two and a half miles from Winchcombe is Belas Knap, a 78ft long, 18 ft high burial chamber that is around 5,000 years old. It used to be believed that fairies lived inside these hills and people told stories of how those who were near them late at night could hear sounds of revelry inside. It was said that anyone who went inside and spent time with the fairies could stay only a day – but that when they emerged, they would find 100 years had passed.

Well, fancy that!

During an average lifetime, you will eat 600,000lb of food – roughly the equivalent to the weight of six elephants.

TIP TIME

Before climbing into the bath or shower, fill the hand basin with hot water and place your bottle of body lotion in it. When you get out of the shower or bath, your lotion will be lovely and warm.

TREASURED PHOTO

Mrs B G Humphries of North Petherton, Somerset, writes: 'Back in the 1940s I was working at The Odeon in Bridgwater. The photo shows some of the staff outside the cinema – I'm third from the right on the front row. The wages weren't much in those days and, as a cashier, I earned an extra 2/6d if I worked on a Saturday morning. It was lovely to hear the children sing along with the music and the words were shown on the screen as well...

Every Saturday morning, where do we go?
Getting into mischief? Oh dear no!
To the Mickey Mouse Club with our badges on,
Every Saturday morning, at The Odeon.'

I WISH I'D SAID THAT...

"If winter comes can spring be far behind?
– Percy Bysshe Shelley, English poet"

Letter of my life

In November 1942 I was in the Royal Engineers, stationed at Dingwall, Inverness. My fiancée was living with her parents at Gravesend, Kent.

I had arranged leave for our wedding, which was to be on Saturday, November 28. On Tuesday, November 17, I was notified of embarkation leave as from that night. Leaving Inverness that evening, I got off at Perth where my parents lived. On Wednesday morning I sent a telegram to Gravesend, 'Arriving tomorrow, wedding Friday'... that is, Friday the 20th, eight days earlier than the original date. You can imagine the panic at Gravesend! After the wedding we travelled back to Perth the same night. As it was our wedding night I splashed out and booked a sleeper on the train from Euston to Perth – only to find that LMS Railways had booked another lady to share the same compartment. No compensation in those days for loss of conjugal rights!

After four days I returned to my unit. I was away for 3½ years.

Jim Stewart,
Bexleyheath, Kent

Pause for thought

This was written by Vera Pheasant, of Derby, after suffering a bout of 'flu:

The 'Flu Blues

Here I am all sad and blue
In bed with this awful 'flu.
Isolated in a room, which used to be my son's
With posters staring from the wall
Complete with awful puns.

There's this magnificent MG
And Derbyshire's very best CC
Then dear old Snoopy strikes a pose
With that great ginormous nose
Telling me to 'think in style'
Which makes me rather want to smile.
For here I lie with stringy hair
And a smile with teeth so spare.

I'll have to get up pretty soon,
Kitchen sounds have spelled out doom.
To date a saucer, and a lid
And, cross my heart, I do not kid –
A metal fish slice bit the dust!
I really must reduce his protein
Or my home will be a has-been.

Up and down the stairs, of course,
I've christened him my Trojan Horse.
He says he's really more a male
Florence Nightingale!

November 24-30

Letter of my life

Mr D R Lowe, Southampton

While living in Devon, with my wife Joy and two young daughters Jane and Sally, I received a letter from my father in Lusaka, Zambia, to say that he had gone into hospital, but it was nothing serious. At that point my wife and children had never met him and I hadn't seen him for 15 years.

This was because I had joined the RAF at 15 and served until I was 30. Meanwhile my father had divorced my step-mother and emigrated to Zambia.

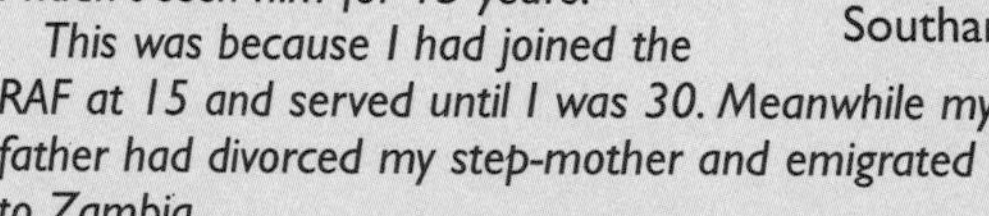

Things weren't going too well for us at the time. I had recently left the RAF and we had taken on a small country store, but it was extremely hard work with very little gain. So when we received my father's letter we, as a family, decided to sell up and go to South Africa as immigrants on an assisted passage.

We sold our home, the business and our van and sailed from Southampton on the Athlone Castle on November 28, 1962, bound for Capetown. It seemed like a big adventure for the ten days we were at sea. Then, when we were 24 hours from Capetown I was asked to report to the purser's office. That was when my world collapsed. Having been asked to take a seat I was then given a telegram to say that my father had passed away.

You can imagine my devastation: Not having seen my father for 15 years, knowing my wife and children had never met him, and after all the upheaval – and travelling 6,000 miles so far. Not knowing that his condition was serious was awful because, if we had known, maybe we could have borrowed the money to fly instead of the lengthy sea journey.

However, having travelled so far and with nothing to return home to, we decided to try and make a new life in South Africa. But this turned out to be extremely difficult. Zambia at that time was a very unstable area to take a young family to, so it was impossible to visit the place where my father had lived in his adopted country. We did manage to stick it out in Johannesburg for eight months and during that time I earned enough money to pay our passage home to England… where we had to start once more from the very bottom.

I WISH I'D SAID THAT…

"Advent. What was there to say 'bout it except that it went on forever and was nearly as bad as Lent?"
– Maeve Binchy, Irish novelist, from The Glass Lake

Beautiful Britain
PIC: PEAK PICTURES LIBRARY/RAY MANLEY

BAKEWELL, DERBYSHIRE

This is the largest town in the Peak District and has one of the oldest markets in the area, dating back to around 1300. The name comes from Badequella, its Domesday Book entry, which means 'bath-well' and relates to the warm springs found locally.

Bakewell's main claim to fame is probably its Bakewell tarts, although these were known as Bakewell puddings.

It is said they were first made by mistake in the kitchen of the Rutland Arms when a cook misread the recipe and spread egg mixture on top of the jam instead of stirring it into the pastry. Jane Austen stayed here in 1811 – and Bakewell features in her novel Pride & Prejudice.

There is evidence the countryside around Bakewell was inhabited in Neolithic times, but the town was built by the Saxons and there is a Saxon cross dating from around 800AD in the graveyard of All Saints Church.

"You must be joking"

Four tortoises were playing poker when they ran out of beer. They pooled their money and sent the smallest tortoise out for the beer.

Two days passed and there was no sign of the tortoise. "You know, Tommy's getting really slow these days," said one tortoise. A little voice from just inside the door said: "If you're going to talk about me like that, I won't go."

TREASURED PHOTOS

Walter King of Bath writes:
'These two photos are of my late sister Gertie who, when she retired, was an assistant matron. Gertie was a student nurse in 1926 – note the starched collar, cuffs and headdress. In the second photo, taken in 1966 – the year she retired – she is in her outdoor uniform, which she wore when off-duty.'

Well, fancy that!
Riddle: What is the one thing that all wise men, regardless of their politics or religion, believe is between heaven and earth?
Answer: And.

HEALTHY LIVING

Seasonal sniffles

Modern medicine has yet to find a cure for the common cold. Many of us rely on tried and trusted old-fashioned remedies. Garlic, onions, thyme, sage and vitamin C are said to be effective at preventing colds and chills.

And if a sniffle does strike, try a little Hot Buttered Rum: Put one teaspoon of brown sugar in a mug, sprinkle in some ground cloves and a dab of butter. Add a splash of rum and top with boiling water. Stir with a cinnamon stick and leave to cool slightly before drinking.

Pause for thought

What a way to start the day
Sifting through the ashes, grey.
First the paper, then the sticks
Then the coal and cinders mix.
Strike the match and light the paper
What an early morning caper.
Youngsters of today don't know
How we worked for fire to glow.
But instant heat
Is hard to beat
And central heating
Takes some beating!

Peter Stevens, Faversham, Kent

TIP TIME
A fast way to make breadcrumbs is to lightly toast the bread and then put in the blender.

PERFECT PUDDINGS

Jam Roly-Poly

If you don't want a steamy kitchen, this can be baked instead.

- 8 oz/225 g self-raising flour, sifted
- 2 teaspoons salt
- 4 oz/100 g vegetable suet
- 3 tablespoons fresh white breadcrumbs
- 1½ oz/40 g caster sugar, plus extra for dredging
- 5-6 fl oz/150-175 ml milk
- 4-6 tablespoons raspberry jam

1. Mix together flour, salt, suet and breadcrumbs. In a separate bowl, mix together caster sugar and milk, stirring well to dissolve sugar.
2. Stir enough sweetened milk into the flour mix to form a light dough. Turn dough out on to a floured surface and knead until smooth.
3. Roll out the dough to ¼ in/5 mm thickness to form a rectangle 9 x 11 in/23 x 28 cm. Spread the raspberry jam over the dough. Brush edges with milk and roll up like a Swiss roll.
4. Wrap in greaseproof and tie the ends with string. Steam for 30-40 mins, or until well-risen and cooked through. To bake, place seam down on a lightly greased baking tray. Bake for 30-40 minutes at 200C/400F/gas mark 6.

PIC: TATE & LYLE SUGARS

DO YOU REMEMBER...

...the liberty bodice?

TODAY the liberty bodice (liberty? It was anything but!) is remembered as a scratchy unlovely thing. A fitted vest of stiff cotton, it was unattractive and uncomfortable. We have corset manufacturers R & WH Symington of Market Harborough to thank for them!

The bodice was fastened down the front with rubber buttons and was practical, washable and gave the young lady a proper shape but without the restrictions of corsets, worn a generation before by their mothers.

Heavy seams gave a firm foundation but without the boning.

...Sandy Powell?

JUST like Arthur Askey (see March Do You Remember?), Sandy Powell had a famous catchphrase, 'Can you 'ear me, Mother?' that elevated him to a better spot on the bill.

Sandy was a wonderful visual comic and happily his two great routines – the dodgy ventriloquist and the even dodgier conjuror – are safe on film. His wonderful send-ups were not always seen for what they were and if he was working in clubs, people would tell him they could see his lips moving!

He was an astute businessman who had plumped for a royalty fee on each record he sold, rather than a flat fee. And he sold a great many records! Sandy died in 1982.

PIC: HULTON ARCHIVE

Sandy Powell

Brits for all seasons

A NATION OF ANIMAL LOVERS

AS a nation of animal lovers, we'll be at our wits' end this month. Guy Fawkes' Night (more like Fireworks Fortnight these days!) threatens to scare the most ferocious animal witless. Some dogs react so badly to the trauma of Bonfire Night that they have to be tranquillised for the duration of the fireworks season.

Outdoor animals, such as rabbits and guinea pigs, are particularly vulnerable to suffering heart attacks as a result of sudden loud noises, so a caring owner might find them a quiet corner indoors for the time being.

It's often said that British people think more of their pets than they do of other human beings. There's even a technical word for a cat lover – an ailurophile.

Animal Hospital is one of the most popular programmes on television, attracting between seven and eight million viewers per episode, and currently scheduled to run until the end of the year. Avid watchers are frequently to be heard in post office queues discussing the fate of some poor moggy or pup which has run into difficulties under Rolf Harris's watchful (and often teary) eye. The same degree of compassion and empathy is rarely aroused by human suffering.

These days, some pets are pampered more than ageing relatives: dogs have coats, rain-hats and even boots; cats have jewel-studded collars and slivers of fresh fish for tea; even budgies have more toys than they can possibly appreciate.

It's becoming more and more commonplace to learn of pet weddings and funerals, too: you can even buy a coffin for your pet on its sad demise. One pet cemetery provides silk-lined coffins with silver handles and engraved plates. There is even a Chapel of Rest where pets are laid out before a burial service takes place.

PIC: MIRROR

Rolf Harris

Solutions

Winter cryptic (Page 19)

D	I	S	C	O	N	T	E	N	T	■	S	N	O	W
E	■	K	■	A	■	■	■	I	■	D	■	A	■	I
C	R	I	C	K	E	T	■	G	R	E	C	I	A	N
K	■	■	■	L	■	I	■	H	■	C	■	L	■	T
■	H	I	B	E	R	N	A	T	I	O	N	■	■	E
F	■	C	■	A	■	G	■	S	■	D	■	N	■	R
R	A	I	N	F	A	L	L	■	S	E	T	O	F	F
O	■	C	■	■	■	E	■	H	■	■	■	T	■	E
S	A	L	U	T	E	■	S	O	L	S	T	I	C	E
T	■	E	■	W	■	S	■	A	■	P	■	C	■	D
I	■	■	W	I	N	T	E	R	G	R	E	E	N	■
N	■	Z	■	N	■	I	■	D	■	I	■	■	■	B
E	V	E	R	E	S	T	■	S	U	N	D	I	A	L
S	■	R	■	R	■	C	■	■	■	G	■	D	■	U
S	H	O	E	■	C	H	E	A	P	S	K	A	T	E

Word wise (Page 19)

Belt, Blue, Blur, Brut, Bury, Butt, Byre, Byte, Felt, Flue, Fret, Fuel, Furl, Fury, Left, Lure, Lute, Lyre, Rely, Ruby, Rule, True, Tube, Tuft, Turf, Yule, Beryl, Bluer, Bluey, Blurt, Brute, Burly, Butte, Butty, Butyl, Buyer, Flute, Flyer, Lefty, Rebut, Truly, Tuber, Tufty, Turfy, Utter, Belfry, Butler, Butter, Tetryl, Trebly, Tufter, Turtle, Buttery, Flutter, Utterly, Fluttery. The song title is: Butterfly (Andy Williams, 1957).

And the winner is… (Page 45)

■	C	■	E	■	F	■	G	■	■	■	G	■	C	■
G	L	A	D	I	A	T	O	R	■	D	A	V	I	S
■	A	■	E	■	R	■	N	■	B	■	R	■	M	■
L	I	O	N	■	G	R	E	G	O	R	Y	■	A	■
■	R	■	■	■	O	■	W	■	B	■	■	■	R	■
H	E	C	H	T	■	■	I	■	H	O	W	A	R	D
■	■	■	U	■	W	■	T	■	O	■	■	■	O	■
■	A	U	D	R	E	Y	H	E	P	B	U	R	N	■
■	L	■	■	■	E	■	T	■	E	■	M	■	■	■
S	P	A	C	E	K	■	H	■	■	M	A	R	T	Y
■	A	■	■	■	E	■	E	■	R	■	■	■	O	■
■	C	■	D	U	N	A	W	A	Y	■	F	A	M	E
■	I	■	E	■	D	■	I	■	D	■	O	■	A	■
O	N	E	A	L	■	A	N	N	E	F	R	A	N	K
■	O	■	D	■	■	■	D	■	R	■	D	■	D	■

Code-cracker (Page 59)

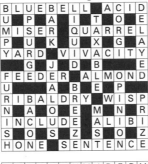

B	L	U	E	B	E	L	L	■	A	C	I	D
U	■	P	■	A	■	I	■	T	■	O	■	E
M	I	S	E	R	■	Q	U	A	R	R	E	L
P	■	U	■	K	■	U	■	X	■	G	■	A
Y	A	R	D	■	V	I	V	A	C	I	T	Y
■	■	G	■	J	■	D	■	B	■	■	■	E
F	E	E	D	E	R	■	A	L	M	O	N	D
U	■	■	■	A	■	B	■	E	■	P	■	■
R	I	B	A	L	D	R	Y	■	W	I	S	P
N	■	A	■	O	■	E	■	M	■	N	■	R
I	N	C	L	U	D	E	■	A	L	I	B	I
S	■	O	■	S	■	Z	■	S	■	O	■	Z
H	O	N	E	■	S	E	N	T	E	N	C	E

G	U	A	O	H	W	N	M	J	D	F	P	V
R	I	T	S	Q	X	Z	L	Y	E	K	B	C

The flower is: Bluebell.

Logic problem (Page 59)

Jimmy, Clocks forward, Brother, Sent to his room.
Molly, Bowl of water, Father, Washing-up.
Tommy, Salt in the sugar bowl, Mother, Pocket-money.

Skeleton (Page 75)

T	O	P	I	C	■	V	I	S	I	T
I	■	E	V	A	S	I	O	N	■	A
B	E	R	Y	L	■	E	N	A	C	T
I	L	K	■	F	E	W	■	R	U	T
A	L	S	O	■	L	■	R	E	L	Y
■	I	■	A	M	A	Z	E	■	I	■
S	P	A	R	■	N	■	D	A	U	B
A	S	S	■	A	D	O	■	O	R	E
M	E	T	E	R	■	B	O	R	E	S
B	■	E	V	I	D	E	N	T	■	E
A	I	R	E	D	■	Y	E	A	S	T

Lost for words (Page 75)

'I have played three presidents, three saints and two geniuses. If that doesn't create an ego problem, nothing does.'

Jigsnip (Page 103)

S	U	S	P	E	C	T	E	D
U	■	E	■	■	■	O	■	U
N	E	A	R	■	R	U	I	N
G	■	S	■	D	■	R	■	E
L	■	I	B	E	R	I	A	■
A	■	D	■	C	■	S	■	S
S	P	E	C	K	■	T	E	A
S	■	■	■	C	■	■	■	N
E	A	T	■	H	O	L	E	D
S	■	I	■	A	■	U	■	C
■	A	C	T	I	N	G	■	A
T	■	K	■	R	■	G	■	S
I	B	E	X	■	D	A	F	T
D	■	T	■	■	■	G	■	L
E	L	S	E	W	H	E	R	E

Pathfinder (Page 103)

Blackpool, Torquay, Skegness, Great Yarmouth, Porthcawl, Margate, Eastbourne, Bridlington, Bude, Troon, Portrush, Tenby, Cromer, Brighton, Bognor Regis.

Missing links (Page 129)

R	E	C	O	R	D	■	H	A	L	F
I	■	A	■	I	■	T	■	S	■	O
G	A	P	■	F	E	A	T	H	E	R
H	■	I	■	L	■	L	■	■	■	C
T	I	T	L	E	■	L	O	D	G	E
■	■	A	■	■	■	■	■	A	■	■
A	T	L	A	S	■	P	A	N	I	C
P	■	■	■	P	■	O	■	C	■	L
P	A	T	R	I	C	K	■	I	C	E
L	■	I	■	N	■	E	■	N	■	A
E	V	E	N	■	D	R	A	G	O	N

Cryptograms (Page 129)

1 'I never go out unless I look like Joan Crawford the movie star. If you want to see the girl next door, go next door.'

2 'The most important thing a woman can have, next to her talent, of course, is her hairdresser.' (Joan Crawford)

Letter set (Page 145)

H	O	G	■	M	U	S	T	Y
U	N	I	T	Y	■	O	R	F
G	E	L	■	S	■	A	I	L
E	■	L	A	T	E	R	A	L
■	T	■	D	I	M	■	L	■
H	A	N	D	F	U	L	■	P
A	L	E	■	I	■	O	A	R
R	O	E	■	E	L	O	P	E
E	N	D	E	D	■	K	E	Y

Hallowe'en quiz (Page 145)

1 The Jabberwock in *Through the Looking-Glass*, 2 Donald Pleasence, 3 Edgar Allan Poe, 4 Max Schreck, 5 Second sight, 6 Christopher Lee, 7 *Night on the Bare Mountain*, 8 Bob Hope, 9 Beowulf, 10 Godzilla, 11 The Minotaur, 12 *Frankenstein*, 13 The Chimera, 14 King Kong, 15 Abbott and Costello, 16 Salem, Massachusetts, in 1692, 17 Whitby, 18 Boris Karloff, 19 Robert Louis Stevenson, 20 An ogre.

Short story

SPELLING MISTAKES

By Susan Wright

Harrassed young mum Natalie tries to help Zak prepare for school tests but things don't go according to plan

"How do you spell 'how'?" Natalie asked her seven-year-old son.

Zak didn't reply, looking down and biting his lip. Natalie moved Ewan to her other breast and waited impatiently for Zak's answer.

"Well?" she prompted.

"Wuh?" Zak tried.

"No!" Natalie yelled. "For goodness sake, Zak, not 'wuh, *huh*'! How is 'huh, oh, wuh'. How many times do I have to tell you?"

Natalie saw the pain in Zak's eyes before he ran from the room.

Tears stung her own eyes. Why had she been so cruel? Shouting at poor Zak would only make matters worse. He found spelling so difficult and it wasn't his fault that she was exhausted and irritable and couldn't cope.

The doorbell made Natalie and Ewan jump.

"Coo-ee!" a voice called through the letterbox. "It's only me." That was all she needed, a visit from her mother-in-law.

"Stop that," she snapped at Callum, who was rattling the bars of his playpen as if he was locked in on death row. "I'll get you out in a minute."

She made herself respectable and headed for the front door, burping the baby as she went. She really didn't have time to make tea and polite conversation. She had to go and say sorry to Zak.

"Hello, dear," Val said. "How are you?"

"Fine," Natalie mumbled.

"Good. I've brought you a nice home-made chocolate cake. I thought it would make a bit of a change from shop-bought cakes."

As Val walked briskly towards the kitchen, Natalie closed the door and sighed. Did Val have to point out her inadequacies the minute she walked into the house?

"What are you doing in there?" Val said to Callum. "Do you want to get out? Come and have a cuddle with Nana Val."

Val lifted him out of his prison. Val had told Natalie that she'd never had a playpen for Mark, as if it was a form of child abuse.

"Heard from Mark lately?" Val asked.

Natalie nodded. "He phoned yesterday. They should be in Rotterdam now."

"Oh right. It won't be long now before he comes home."

Natalie didn't reply. It was roughly three weeks before Mark would pay off the ship, a lifetime away. Besides, when Mark was home he wasn't much help. He spent most of his three-month leave in bed or watching television.

Tears of self pity threatened as Natalie wished she could have a break, even for a few hours.

"Val," she said, "could you look after Callum while I go upstairs and check on Zak? I shouted at him. He's probably in bed, sobbing his heart out."

"I'm sorry," Natalie said, as she sat on Zak's bed. "I shouldn't have shouted at you, sweetheart." Zak didn't answer, just sniffed.

"Nana Val's downstairs," Natalie went on. "Are you coming to say hello?" Zak shook his head. He didn't want his grandmother to see that he'd been crying.

"Well, come down when you're ready. Nana Val wants to see you."

"Is Zak okay?" Val asked, her voice and face showing her concern. "Yes," Natalie lied. "He'll be down in a minute."

"I don't mean to be nosy, dear," Val said, "but what did Zak do wrong?"

"He didn't do anything wrong," Natalie admitted. "Zak's teacher asked me to help him with his spellings at home. Apparently, he got them all wrong in a test. But I can't seem to get through to him. We keep doing the same words. One day, I think he's learned them, the next he's totally forgotten them. I lost my rag because he couldn't spell 'how'."

"Oh dear," Val smiled. "He sounds like his dad."

"Mark?" Natalie frowned. "He can spell."

"He can now but he got the slipper at primary school after a spelling test because he got them all wrong. He came home crying. I decided to help him but it was hard work."

"I didn't know that Zak couldn't spell," Natalie blurted out. "I felt so guilty when the teacher spoke to me. She said he's way behind."

Natalie's voice rose with emotion as she went on.

"You see, Zak's class have their Standard Assessment Tasks this year. If Zak performs badly, it will reflect on his teacher. She said she hasn't got enough time to help him, but there aren't enough hours in my day either!"

"Coo-ee!" a voice called through the letterbox. That was all she needed, a visit from her mother-in-law

Natalie's words ended in a wail as the long threatened tears poured out. She couldn't pretend to be coping any more.

"I know you think I'm an awful mother. Zak can't spell, the house is a mess and I don't even make cakes!"

The last words came out with far more venom than she'd intended. Val didn't reply. Natalie looked at her through the blur of tears.

"I'm sorry," she whispered. "I shouldn't have said that."

"Oh, Natalie," Val replied, reaching out and taking her hand. "I wasn't criticising when I mentioned the cake. I thought it might help you. It must be so difficult with Mark away and your parents at the other end of the country. I'd happily help you with anything, Natalie, but I've always got the impression that you think I'm an interfering old bat."

Natalie didn't reply. Her silence confirmed Val's words.

"You can't go on like this, can you?" Val said. "You're exhausted. You're going to have a breakdown if you're not careful. Please let me help. I've got loads of time and I'd love to spend it with you and my grandchildren."

Natalie looked into Val's eyes. It was as if she were seeing her mother-in-law for the first time. Now she saw such kindness in Val's face, it made her start crying again.

"I don't deserve your help," she sobbed.

"Nonsense," Val replied. "Now, what are the children having for tea?" Natalie shrugged.

"I don't suppose it'll hurt, just this once," Val said, "if we all have sandwiches and chocolate cake. You sit there. I'll get it. Afterwards, I'll help you bath the children and get the little ones to bed. Then, you can have a long soak in the bath while I help Zak with his spelling. Does that sound okay?"

Natalie nodded and smiled. It sounded wonderful.

"Thank you," Natalie said. "You don't know how much this all means to me. I'm sorry for, you know, the past."

"So am I," Val said, "but let's think about the future now."

Later, relaxing in the bath, Natalie closed her eyes in pleasure. She couldn't wait to tell Mark that she and his mother had become friends. She'd tease him too, now she knew about the spelling test and the slipper! Smiling, she switched her attention to the voices in Zak's room.

She'd heard Val ask him to find his blackboard and chalk. Now, they were playing schools. Zak was the teacher, Val was the pupil.

"How do you spell 'how'?" Natalie heard Zak ask.

"Wuh?" Val suggested.

"No, Nana Val," Zak said in disgust. Then, obviously pointing at words Val had written on his blackboard, he told his grandmother,

"Look – it begins with 'huh'! It's 'huh, oh, wuh' – as in HOW NOW BROWN COW!"

December 2003

HIGH DAYS AND HOLIDAYS...

St Nicholas Day (December 6)

St Nicholas as patron saint of children gave rise to the tradition of boy bishops. The boy, in full regalia, ruled until Holy Innocents on December 28, officiating in all of a bishop's duties, except Mass. If a boy died in office he was given all the ceremony due to an adult bishop.

PIC: HULTON ARCHIVE

St Thomas the Apostle's Day (December 21)

Today is the Winter Solstice, 'St Thomas gray, St Thomas gray, The longest night and the shortest day'. A frosty St Thomas' means a bad winter ahead. Others say that today is ideal for weddings – it being the shortest day, there's less time to repent!

The commonest St Thomas tradition was mumping. A woman or child was entitled to knock on doors and ask for largesse – corn and milk made into Christmas loaves or frumenty.

New Year's Eve or Hogmanay (December 31)

Fire customs, ritually burning out the old year, have survived in a few places. At Stonehaven in Grampian, fireballs are whirled on wire strings around the participants' heads. At the beach, the blazing balls are hurled into the sea.

Fire is meant to drive out evil and purify the air for the coming New Year and must be kept burning tonight to ensure the survival of the household for the coming year.

MONDAY	1
TUESDAY	2
WEDNESDAY	3
THURSDAY	4
FRIDAY	5
SATURDAY	6
SUNDAY	7
MONDAY	8
TUESDAY	9
WEDNESDAY	10
THURSDAY	11
FRIDAY	12
SATURDAY	13
SUNDAY	14
MONDAY	15
TUESDAY	16
WEDNESDAY	17
THURSDAY	18

FRIDAY	19
SATURDAY	20
SUNDAY	21
MONDAY	22
TUESDAY	23
WEDNESDAY	24
THURSDAY	25 Christmas Day (Bank Holiday)
FRIDAY	26 Boxing Day (Bank Holiday)
SATURDAY	27
SUNDAY	28
MONDAY	29 January YOURS on sale
TUESDAY	30
WEDNESDAY	31

This month don't forget to...

- Visit your local Christmas market for those last-minute presents.
- Send your Christmas cards in good time.
- Plan your garden for next year – pore over those seed catalogues and dream away!
- Cheer a neighbour up and invite them in for a mince-pie and a cup of coffee.
- Enjoy the festive season!

PIC: MIRROR

December 31, 1900: At Stonehenge, Stone 22 and its lintel fell down.

It happened in December...

December 31, 1960: This was the last day for call-up to National Service. Compulsory service in the armed forces was abolished after this day.

December 13, 1973: A three-day working week was ordered by the Government, because of the coal-miners' work-to-rule and the Arab nations' oil embargo.

December 1, 1990: Breakthrough as the two sides of the Channel Tunnel were joined and people were able to walk through for the first time.

December 1-7

Treasured Photos

Peggy Norton, who sent us the picture, writes:
'On a promotional tour back in the '50s, Tommy Cooper visited Stretford, Greater Manchester. Tommy wasn't quite as well known then as he was later to become. My husband (*on the right in the photo*) was working as a TV service engineer at one of the firms on Tommy's itinerary. Apparently he made a great impression – hitting the place like a whirlwind – and was a naturally very funny man. The girl in the white beret was Tommy's personal assistant.

Healthy Living

Keeping cool can keep you slim
Scientists think that getting out into the cold increases your metabolic rate to keep the body warm, and therefore burns more calories. But don't take this as your cue to dash off into sub-zero temperatures wearing just a flimsy jacket for protection! The advice is to avoid sitting indoors throughout the winter, but to wrap up warm and take a brisk walk.

Letter of my life

Shirley Mitchell, London SE9

I wrote a letter to YOURS magazine some three years ago, about being a widow and how widows are poorly treated by society. My letter was printed as the 'star letter'.

As a result of that letter, many readers wrote to me and now I write to ten ladies, all widows, on a regular basis. I have even met up with four of them and we all get on very well.

We know about each other's families, our hobbies, likes and dislikes. We share our ups and downs, laughter and tears and cheer each other up when we're down.

If I hadn't written to YOURS I would never have known the lovely ladies I write to. They have all become good friends. Although losing my husband was devastating, some good has come out of it – all thanks to YOURS.

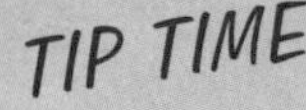

TIP TIME

If you don't keep your car in a garage in winter, peel and halve an onion and rub it over your windscreen. It doesn't smear and keeps ice from forming.

Tea-Time Treats

Pineapple and Cherry Cake

This makes a wonderfully moist cake and never fails to please, writes Joyce Pretty from Poole:

- 4 oz/100 g butter or margarine
- 7 oz/200 g tin pineapple, roughly crushed
- 6 oz/175 g soft brown sugar
- 1 lb/450 g dried mixed fruit
- 8 oz/225 g glacé cherries, cut up
- 2 eggs, beaten
- 8 oz/225 g self-raising flour
- 1 level teaspoon baking powder

1. Preheat the oven to 170°C/325°F/Gas Mark 3. Line a 8-9 in/20-23 cm tin with baking parchment.
2. Put butter, pineapple (and its juice), sugar, dried fruit, cherries into a saucepan. Heat until boiling. Remove from heat and allow to cool, then add eggs, flour and baking powder. Mix well.
3. Spoon mixture into tin. Wrap the tin with 2 or 3 sheets of brown paper and stand on 4 sheets of brown paper. Bake on middle shelf for 2-2½ hours.

STRATFORD-UPON-AVON

This old-world market town is in a beautiful setting on the River Avon and is best known as the place where William Shakespeare was born. His birthplace can be visited, furnished in Elizabethan style, much as it would have been when he was born here.

Despite his fame as the greatest playwright of all time, very little is actually known about William Shakespeare, Stratford-upon-Avon's most famous resident. There is much speculation about his personal life, but it is only his official records (which include the will in which he left his wife, Anne Hathaway, his 'second-best bed'!) that provide any actual facts about him. The home of Shakespeare's mother is now home to the Shakespeare Countryside Museum, which traces country life over the past 400 years. As well as various exhibits, there is a collection of rare farm animals. Close by is Anne Hathaway's cottage in Shottery, where she lived before she was married.

If all things Shakespearean threaten to overwhelm visitors there is respite at the Stratford Butterfly Farm, home to hundreds of moths and butterflies that fly freely among exotic plants, trees and flowers in a hothouse.

Well, fancy that!

Riddle: Where is the only place that yesterday always follows today? In a dictionary.

I WISH I'D SAID THAT...

"All shod with steel
We hissed along the polished ice,
in games confederate. – William Wordsworth, English poet"

Pause for thought

80 Not Out

Today dear Lord I'm 80
And there's much I haven't done.
I hope, dear Lord, you'll let me live
Until I'm 81.
But then, if I haven't finished all I want to do,
Would you let me stay awhile until I'm 82?
So many places I want to go,
so very much to see,
Do you think that you could manage to
make it 83?
The world is changing very fast
There is so much in store,
I'd like it very much to live
Until I'm 84.
And if by then I'm still alive
I'd like to stay 'til 85.
More planes will be up in the air
So I'd really like to stick
And see what happens to the world
When I'm 86.
I know dear Lord it's much to ask
(and it must be nice in heaven)
But I would really like to stay
Until I'm 87.
I know by then I won't be fast
And sometimes will be late
But it would be so pleasant to be
Around at 88.
I will have seen so many things
And had a wonderful time,
So I'm sure that I'll be willing
To leave at 89....
Maybe!

Lilian Bell, from Bradford, was sent this on her 80th

"You must be joking"

Two Eskimos sitting in a kayak were chilly, but when they lit a fire in the craft, it sank. It goes to show that you can't have your kayak and heat it.

December 8-14

Treasured Photo

Mrs G Williams of Wallasey, Cheshire, writes:
'This photo is of me in my uniform when I was a clippie on the Birkenhead buses during the Second World War. We all had to do our share while our men were at war. My boyfriend was in the RAF (Bomber Command) and received the DFC. We married later but he has now passed away. I will always be very proud of him.'

I wish I'd said that...

"A little preparation saves a lot of frustration. – Anon"

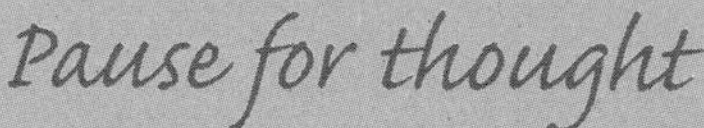

'I think A Year with YOURS is a brilliant idea!' writes Truda de Lyons-Pike, from Canterbury, Kent. 'You've included absolutely everything anyone could wish for. Here's one of my favourite sayings – although I don't know the source.'

Snowflakes are one of Nature's most fragile things, but look what they can do when they stick together!

Tip Time

If you have lots of Christmas tree ornaments that are missing hooks or caps, place them all in a bowl and use as a festive table centrepiece.

Well, fancy that!

Traffic lights were used before the advent of the motorcar. In 1868, a lantern with red and green signals was used at a London intersection to control the flow of horse buggies and pedestrians.

Healthy Living

Memory games

Memory training is superb exercise for the brain. Try these techniques for remembering names:

- ❑ During conversation, try to use the name.
- ❑ Link the name to an image – ones that rhyme are particularly easy to remember, for example, Neil, holding a wheel.
- ❑ If you can't find a rhyme, link the person with someone famous who shares the same name.

Perfect Puddings

Marmalade and Treacle Tart

Serves 6

- 8 oz/225 g shortcrust pastry
- 8 oz/225 g white breadcrumbs
- 8 oz/225 g golden syrup
- 4 oz/100 g marmalade
- 2 tablespoons lemon juice

1. Preheat oven to 180°C/350°F/Gas Mark 4.
2. Roll out pastry on lightly floured surface and line an 8 in/20 cm flan dish. Trim the edges and reserve the leftover pastry. Sprinkle the breadcrumbs evenly over pastry base.
3. Warm the syrup and marmalade gently in a saucepan over a low heat. Stir in lemon juice. Pour mixture over breadcrumbs.
4. Cut the extra pastry into strips to make a lattice pattern. Cook for 25-30 minutes until golden brown.

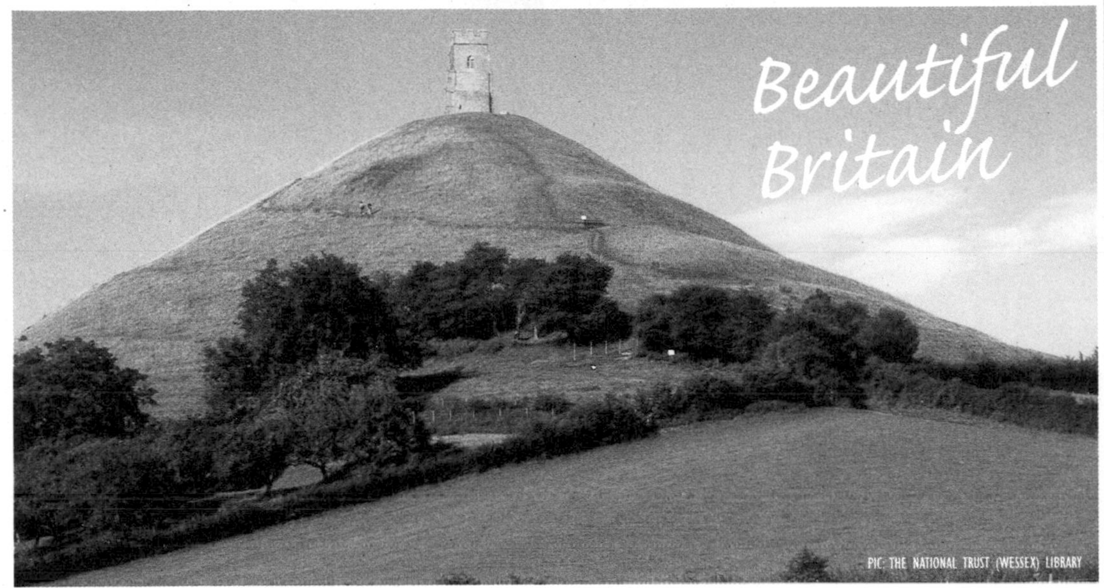

PIC: THE NATIONAL TRUST (WESSEX) LIBRARY

GLASTONBURY, SOMERSET

Legend has it that Glastonbury Tor (a tall, grassy hill topped by the remains of a medieval church) may be a gateway to the underworld – and Glastonbury Abbey is also thought by some to be the burial place of King Arthur and Queen Guinevere. Bursting with myths and legends, this market town attracts many new age visitors who are keen to have their futures read or stock up on candles, crystals and tarot cards.

Tucked away in the abbey grounds is a thorn tree that flowers in spring and at Christmas. It was supposedly grown from the tree that sprouted when Joseph of Arimathea, said to have come here after Jesus was crucified, put his staff into the ground.

Glastonbury Abbey was destroyed by Henry VIII during the Dissolution of the Monasteries in the 16th century – and the last abbot was hanged, drawn and quartered on Glastonbury Tor.

Letter of my life

Mrs G Long, Sompting, West Sussex

My husband and I had been trying for nine years to have a child. I had attended hospital and seen so many doctors and was always told there was no reason why I shouldn't conceive.

Eventually a doctor said if we were so keen to be parents why not try to adopt a baby. So we did.

We had to attend several meetings and interviews and were told that, if we were successful, we would hear within a few weeks.

I will never forget the day I received our 'special' letter, informing us that we had been accepted as suitable adoptive parents. I read it over and over again and then contacted my husband at work. He was also elated and couldn't wait to get home to celebrate. Later that day I received a dozen red roses from him, which I thought was lovely.

We eventually adopted twins, a boy and a girl. They have always been such a joy and are now 36 years old. We now have nine wonderful grandchildren and are so very happy.

That letter from the adoption society certainly changed our lives, as we were never lucky enough to conceive a baby.

"You must be joking"

Visitors were looking round the Chamber of Horrors. An attendant approached one of them and pointed to a woman who was standing motionless, staring at one of the gruesome exhibits.

"Excuse me, sir, is that lady anything to do with you?"

"Yes," said the man. "She's the mother-in-law."

"Well, please keep her moving. We're stock taking."

December 15-21

Pause for thought

Mrs J E Oliver from Tadworth, Surrey, tells an inspirational story:

Nine years ago, my seven-year-old granddaughter, Lucy, complained of pains in her legs. By the next morning the pain had spread to her hip. After numerous hospital tests she was diagnosed with rheumatoid arthritis of the hip. She was allowed home a week later, provided she remained in a wheelchair and didn't put any pressure on her hip. She spent the next 13 weeks in her wheelchair.

At the beginning of December Lucy's teacher rang to ask if she could attend school again. On the Friday of that week the teacher suggested that instead of writing the usual Christmas letters to Santa, the children should each write a prayer. Just three days later, on the Monday morning, Lucy woke up, free from pain and – to her mother's disbelief – walked down the stairs and then shortly after walked into her classroom.

There was uproar among the children when they saw her and the headmistress looked in to see what the commotion was about. Then, on reading the prayers that the children had written, discovered that most of them had said they wished Lucy could walk again.

Lucy is now fine and well, and nearly 17, with no repercussions of what happened years ago.

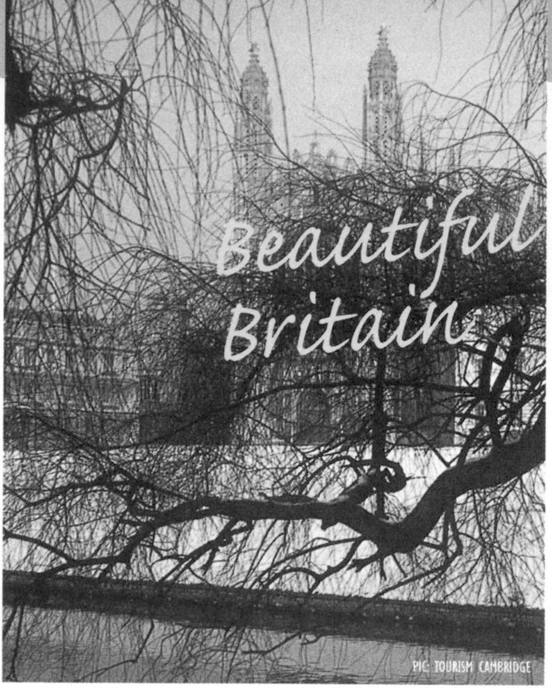

PIC: TOURISM CAMBRIDGE

Cambridge

This university town is famous for its cobbled streets, its academic distinction, its cyclists, its beautiful setting on the River Cam and much more besides.

However, there was a settlement here 1,000 years before the first college of the university was founded in 1284 – a Roman fort, close to the River Cam. Later came a Saxon castle and market town, followed in 1066 by the Normans. The Domesday Book records that in 1086 there were 400 full citizens in Cambridge.

Cambridge University now comprises 31 colleges. Conditions for students now are very different to those of hundreds of years ago when no women were allowed to study here, students had to get up and pray at 4.45am and go to bed at 8pm having had only one hour of free time during the day.

Cambridge's choir and chapel at King's College are world-famous and one of the high points of this season is the King's College Christmas Eve carol service.

Tip Time

To prevent Christmas wrapping paper from unrolling and getting crumpled, cut an empty toilet roll holder down one side. Slide this around the tube of wrapping paper. The paper won't unroll and you just slide off the cardboard 'cuff' when you want to use the wrapping paper.

Healthy Living

Stay warm and toasty

- ❑ Reduce draughts. Old newspapers laid under carpets will stop cold seeping through.
- ❑ Several layers of light clothing keep the body warmer than one or two thick items.
- ❑ Warm the bed before getting into it, and a dressing gown placed close to hand to be put on immediately on rising.

TREASURED PHOTO

Emily Turton of Widnes treasures this picture, taken more than 50 years ago, at Gretna Green:

'Looking at it recaptures for me the magic and wonder of our first holiday after the war. On my 40th birthday we celebrated my brother-in-law's homecoming from mine-sweeping in the Navy, and my husband had just recovered from cancer. What a wonderful holiday it was and my first visit to beautiful Scotland. On our way home we called at Gretna Green, where we had a mock marriage over the anvil – first my husband and me, then my sister and her husband. The pretend-blacksmith loaned us the wreath, veil, top hat and flowers. It was so romantic. In the photo, I am the bride.'

I WISH I'D SAID THAT...

"Those who warn of a population explosion picture a world with too many people and not enough food – like the average cocktail party. – Bill Vaughan"

"You must be joking"

A little boy got lost at a football match. A policeman noticed him crying and went over to him. "What's the matter, sonny?" asked the policeman.

"I've lost my dad."

"What's he like?" ask the policeman.

"Beer and staying in bed," said the boy.

Well, fancy that!

Eskimos have 15 words for the English word, 'snow'.

Letter of my life

Mrs D Longbottom, Halifax

My husband sailed away in December 1941 to an unknown destination. I wrote to him every week for two years. I didn't know where he was or whether he was dead or alive. Finally, I received this typed letter from him… 'I am now in a Japanese prisoner of war camp in Java. I am constantly thinking of you. It will be wonderful when we meet again. The Japanese treat us well, so don't worry about me and never feel uneasy. Dear Dora, I hope you received the last letter and are all in good health and spirits as I am. Yours until we meet again, Bill xxx'

It was a very traumatic time because of all the news we were reading about the way the Japanese treated their prisoners, and this was the only communication I had from him in four years.

Bill never received any of my letters and after the war I got them all back!

TEA-TIME TREATS

Truffles

Makes 30-35

- 4 oz/100 g cake crumbs
- 4 oz/100 g caster sugar
- 4 oz/100 g ground almonds
- 6-8 tablespoons apricot jam, warmed and sieved
- 1 tablespoon rum, to taste
- Icing sugar

1 Crumble the cake crumbs finely and add the sugar, ground almonds and 5 tablespoons apricot jam to bind it and give a fairly sticky mixture. Add rum to taste.

2 Shape into small balls and roll in icing sugar.

December 22-31

TEA-TIME TREATS

Nutty Chocolate Christmas Tree

- 1 lb 2 oz/500 g plain or milk chocolate chips
- 8 oz/225 g roughly chopped nuts, eg hazelnuts, almonds, walnuts
- 4 oz/100 g mini marshmallows
- 3 tablespoons golden syrup
- Silver/gold balls/small sweets
- 8 oz/225 g coloured marzipan or sugarpaste icing
- Royal icing
- Icing sugar, to dust

1 Cover 2 or 3 baking sheets with non-stick parchment and draw 6 six-point stars on them, measuring 8 in/20 cm, 7 in/18 cm, 6 in/15 cm, 5 in/13 cm, 4 in/10 cm, and 3 in/7.5cm in diameter.

2 Put chocolate chips in bowl and microwave on defrost for about 7 or 8 minutes until melted. Add the nuts, marshmallows and golden syrup and stir until mixed.

3 Evenly spoon the chocolate mixture on to the baking sheets to cover the stars. Sprinkle over silver/gold balls and small sweets to decorate. Leave to set. Peel the stars off the parchment.

4 Shape the marzipan or sugarpaste into a 'tub' for the tree and place on a board. Spread a little royal icing on the tub and place the largest chocolate star on top. Leave to set. Spread royal icing in the centre of the star and place the next largest star on top. Leave to set, then build up the tree using the stars in decreasing order of size, allowing to set between each layer.

5 Dust the finished tree with icing sugar and place a paper star on top.

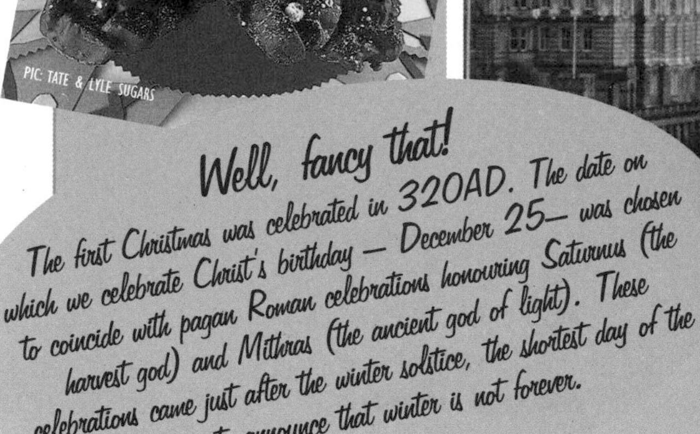

PIC: TATE & LYLE SUGARS

Well, fancy that!

The first Christmas was celebrated in 320AD. The date on which we celebrate Christ's birthday – December 25– was chosen to coincide with pagan Roman celebrations honouring Saturnus (the harvest god) and Mithras (the ancient god of light). These celebrations came just after the winter solstice, the shortest day of the year, to announce that winter is not forever.

I WISH I'D SAID THAT...

"A journey of a thousand miles begins with one step. – Ancient Chinese proverb"

Letter of my life

This letter isn't in the category of 'life saver' but I've treasured it for a long time. It was written by my 13-year-old daughter in December 1960. My husband and I had left her doing her homework because we had to go out to tell relatives that her sister had died of a brain tumour. Of course, we were very late home and were surprised to find the letter. It was even written on a sweet paper bag. We realised that she would also be grieving for Anne, her sister, and the letter brought us back to earth:

'Mum, I am annoyed with you, because I have not had my hair washed as it is difficult doing it by kettles. My hair will not be nice for tomorrow. Please iron my gym vest. Good job I did not leave the washing-up. Have gone to bed. The back door is not locked. Janet'.

Mrs V L Holloway, London

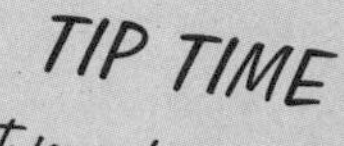

TIP TIME

Put some dried herbs or seasonings such as cinnamon in your fireplace to scent your home at Christmas.

Beautiful Britain

EDINBURGH

Home to the biggest Hogmanay celebrations in Scotland, Edinburgh holds massive street parties and events all over the city on December 31. Edinburgh also lists the largest arts festival in the world, as well as a major international film festival, among the world-class events it hosts. The Scottish capital is dominated by Edinburgh Castle – a symbol of Scottish power and independence – and steeped in history. This bustling metropolis has masses to see and do.

But Edinburgh is also a city with a haunting past and beneath its lively, vibrant streets there is evidence of an underground city that dates back hundreds of years. Part of this underworld, now providing the foundations for the City Chambers, is Mary King's Close, one of many medieval passages in the city. It is possible to visit Mary King's Close and see the shops, taverns and houses – but beware! The Black Death claimed many lives here in the 17th century and the ghosts of those who died are said to haunt the street to this day.

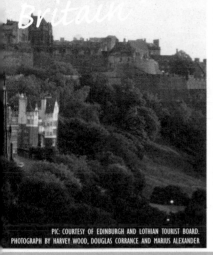

PIC: COURTESY OF EDINBURGH AND LOTHIAN TOURIST BOARD. PHOTOGRAPH BY HARVEY WOOD, DOUGLAS CORRANCE AND MARIUS ALEXANDER

TREASURED PHOTO

Dawn Prestwich has treasured memories of the time she met Sir Norman Wisdom:

'About four years ago, I was asked to hold a reception for a number of local children and young people who had been making up parcels for the Norman Wisdom Romanian appeal, and I readily agreed. To my surprise, the day before the occasion I received a telephone call to ask if it would be all right if Norman came along. Was it all right! I was thrilled to bits as I had seen nearly all his films and never thought I would meet him. It proved a lovely afternoon. Norman was so good with the young ones and charmed everyone there. It will always stay in my memory.'

Pause for thought

A Christmas carol

(to the tune of 'As with Gladness Men of Old')

Can we believe when we are told
Christ was born in a stable cold?
Many long years have passed since when
That message willed God's peace to men.
But the earth's still torn in strife,
While men have no respect for life.

Only His way can show us how
The world can solve its problems now.
He is the Way, the Truth, the Life,
Our only means of real relief.
Open our eyes that we might see
Amazing grace that sets us free.

Once He came, He'll come again,
Mankind must accept His reign.
At this season of the year
Are we ready should He appear?
For we all His will must do
If we would be His subjects too.

T H Hook, Wantage, Oxfordshire

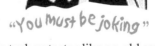

"You must be joking"

"This turkey tastes like an old settee."

"Well, you kept asking for something with plenty of stuffing."

HEALTHY LIVING

Too much festive spirit?

If you have over-indulged try these simple steps to reduce heartburn, indigestion and relieve that bloated or gassy feeling.

- ❑ Add a squeeze of lemon to a glass of water and drink with your meal.
- ❑ Chew on a little fennel or parsley.
- ❑ Eat some live yoghurt.

DO YOU REMEMBER...

PIC: HULTON ARCHIVE

...Christmas past?

From A Child's Christmas in Wales by Dylan Thomas (1914-1953):
After lunch, the uncles sat in front of the fire, loosened all buttons, put their large moist hands over their watch chains, groaned a little and slept.

Mother, aunts and sisters scuttled to and fro, bearing tureens. Aunt Bessie, who had already been frightened twice, by a clockwork mouse, whimpered at the sideboard and had some elderberry wine. The dog was sick.

Auntie Dosie had to have three aspirins, but Auntie Hannah, who liked port, stood in the middle of the snowbound back yard, singing like a big-bosomed thrush.

I would blow up balloons to see how big they would blow up to; and, when they burst, which they all did, the uncles jumped and rumbled.

In the rich and heavy afternoon, the uncles breathing like dolphins and the snow descending, I would sit among festoons and Chinese lanterns and nibble dates and try to make a model man o' war, following the Instructions for Little Engineers and produce what might be mistaken for a sea-going tramcar.

...trying to stay awake for Santa?

If you stayed overnight at Auntie and Uncle's house, you'd worry Santa wouldn't find you. Mum would suggest writing him a note and sending it up the chimney. After pleading to stay up 'just five minutes more', you'd hang a stocking over the fireplace – or if you were lucky, put a pillowcase at the end of your bed before sneaking a look outside to see if just one snowflake had fallen.

Waking up early you'd feel the bottom of the bed with your foot and hear a rustling noise. Santa hadn't forgotten you! Racing downstairs you'd spy a half-eaten carrot in the fireplace, a few forlorn mincepie crumbs and an empty sherry glass.

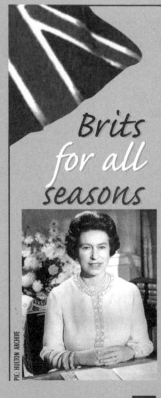

Brits for all seasons

PIC: HULTON ARCHIVE

GOD SAVE THE QUEEN

CHRISTMAS is a time of tradition: Finding a lucky coin in the Christmas pud; dressing the tree, exchanging cards and presents; pulling crackers and reading out the awful jokes; wearing party hats and humming to carols as you peel chestnuts for the stuffing.

There is one British tradition, however, that dominates Christmas Day in many households – the Queen's speech. For royalists and republicans alike, this annual address to the nation is essential viewing, whether it evokes warm sentiment for Her Majesty or provokes a blazing row over the future of the monarchy. Many families plan their Christmas meal around the speech, followed by a snooze in front of The Great Escape.

The idea for a Christmas speech by the sovereign was first put forward by John Reith, the founder of the BBC, to King George V in 1932, and the first address was delivered by 'wireless' live that Christmas to the Empire Service (now the BBC World Service). The time of 3pm was chosen as the best moment to reach most countries in the Empire.

The first televised address was also transmitted live in 1957. Today, modern technology has made it possible to watch and hear the broadcast on the Internet, although the programme is actually recorded before Christmas.

Memorably, Her Majesty labelled 1992 her 'annus horribilis'. It was the year which marked the end of three royal marriages: Those of the Duke and Duchess of York, Princess Anne and Captain Mark Phillips and finally, Charles and Diana, as well as the fire at Windsor Castle.

Love it or hate it, the tradition of the Queen's speech is one of the annual landmarks that define us as a nation. Happy Christmas!

THE CHRISTMAS CAKE

Shirley Boyens sent in this poignant letter written by her cousin to his three daughters...

Then and now – Peter Farrow, the boy in the story, shown as a four-year-old and today

My darling girls, I'd like to tell you a story...

The winter of 1945 was a cold one in London and a few days before Christmas it snowed. The white blanket brightened the drab streets but had failed to mask the terrible bomb damage.

An icy wind began to blow and the small boy lowered his head as he walked into it. He was dressed in short pants, an open-necked shirt and a short jacket. His long socks rested around his ankles. In those days, children didn't have summer and winter clothes, they only had clothes they wore all year round, and these were his. The wind grew stronger, so he did what he always did when he was cold – he started to run.

He was on his way to buy bread for his granny, with whom he lived. As he ran he thought about how his life might soon change. The war had just ended but he didn't know if that was a good thing or not. The council had repaired his school and he would soon be expected to attend. He was nine and a child of the war. He knew about the enemy too – the Germans – and he hated them. He'd never actually seen them, but he knew they were different from us.

But there were more important things to think about just now. It would be Christmas in a few days. There were never many presents but there was something of far greater value sitting on a shelf in the pantry – Grandma's Christmas cake.

His grandmother always seemed to find the ingredients to create her masterpiece, despite the restrictions of ration books and shortages. She'd mix the butter, eggs, raisins, nuts, cherries and spices into a stiff mixture that would emerge from the oven to be the golden centrepiece of Christmas. He watched in awe every step of the cake's creation and when the icing was applied he was allowed to scrape the bowl. He wasn't allowed any cake until Christmas Day, and then he always ate it slowly, to make the pleasure last longer, and to savour the divine taste.

Still running, he rounded the corner and stopped in his tracks. There, on the corner, GERMANS... four of them! The boy had heard grown-ups talking about wounded German prisoners of war being treated at the local military hospital. There they stood, obviously lost. They wore blue uniforms with POW written in yellow on their backs. The boy looked them over and thought how like the English they appeared. They were shivering too.

He sprinted home and when he told his grandmother she didn't seem surprised or worried Germans were invading her neighbourhood. She just shook her head and looked sad. "They must be freezing and they're only boys." Then she went to the cupboard and took out her Christmas cake. Taking a knife, she cut off a third and sliced it into four. She then put each piece in kitchen paper.

The boy watched in silence. 'What's she doing?' he thought. 'It isn't Christmas Day, and I couldn't eat all that in one go!' His grandmother put the pieces in a bag and said: "Take this to the German soldiers – and hurry before they leave."

The boy couldn't believe his ears – how could she waste her precious cake on Germans? But he did as he was told and took the cake back to where he'd seen the four men.

He approached the shivering men cautiously. He held out the cake and said: "This is for you." One German took it from the boy and unwrapped the cake. He said something to the others in a strange language then the tallest man asked: "Who sent this?" The boy replied: "My grandmother." They spoke again in their strange tongue then the tall man said: "Please thank her for us," and that was it.

This is a true story. The little boy was me and that wonderful grandmother was Ellen Sofia McDermott, your great grandmother. Not long before this happened, she'd been told that her youngest son had been killed serving in India. The year before, her son-in-law, had been killed in action in Anzio, Italy. He was my father and your grandfather. Her grief was deep, but it never tainted her loving heart. Where others saw the enemy, she saw cold young boys.

Every Christmas I remember this example of Christian charity and this year I thought I'd share it with you. Much love,

Merry Christmas, Dad.

RESERVED
FOR
TOMMY COOPER
AMBASSADOR
It's one of the family now